Immigration in America's Future

Foundations of Social Inquiry
Scott McNall and Charles Tilly
Series Editors

Criminological Controversies: A Methodological Primer
John Hagan, A. R. Gillis, and David Brownfield

Immigration in America's Future
David M. Heer

What Does Your Wife Do? Gender and the Transformation of Family Life
Leonard Beeghley

FORTHCOMING IN 1996

Social Change
Thomas D. Hall, Darrell La Lone, and Stephen K. Sanderson

Sexual Politics
Sheila Tobias

Contact Westview Press for information about additional upcoming titles.

Immigration in America's Future

Social Science Findings and the Policy Debate

David M. Heer
University of Southern California

WestviewPress
A Division of HarperCollins*Publishers*

Foundations of Social Inquiry

Copyright © 1996 by Westview Press, Inc., A Division of HarperCollins Publishers, Inc.

Published in 1996 in the United States of America by Westview Press, Inc., 5500 Central Avenue, Boulder, Colorado 80301-2877, and in the United Kingdom by Westview Press, 12 Hid's Copse Road, Cumnor Hill, Oxford OX2 9JJ

Library of Congress Cataloging-in-Publication Data
Heer, David M.
    Immigration in America's future : social science findings and the policy debate / David M. Heer.
        p.   cm. — (Foundations of social inquiry)
    Includes bibliographical references and index.
    ISBN 0-8133-8739-6 (hc). — ISBN 0-8133-8740-X (pbk.)
    1. United States—Emigration and immigration—Government policy.
2. United States—Emigration and immigration—History.   I. Title.
II. Series: Foundations of social inquiry (Boulder, Colo.)
JV6483.H395   1996
325.73—dc20   95-52167
                                                                              CIP

The paper used in this publication meets the requirements of the American National Standard for Permanence of Paper for Printed Library Materials Z39.48-1984.

10   9   8   7   6   5   4   3   2   1

Contents

List of Illustrations   *vii*
Acknowledgments   *xi*

1 Overview   1

**2 The Volume and Character of Future Immigration:
The Values at Stake**   7

Standard of Living, 8
Equity, 10
Preservation or Modification of Existing American Culture, 11
Ethnic and Class Conflict, 13
The Power of the United States in International Affairs, 14
Notes, 15

3 The Influence of Social Science Findings   17

The Relationship Between Social Science Findings
   and Value Judgments, 17
The Validation of Social Science Findings, 20
Drawing Policy Conclusions, 24
Notes, 25

4 The History of U.S. Immigration Law   27

Unrestricted Entry: 1789 to 1874, 27
Initial Restriction: 1875 to 1917, 37
Maximum Restriction: April 1917 to December 1941, 42
Liberalization: December 1941 to April 1980, 50
Concern with Illegal Immigration: April 1980 to the Present, 58
Conclusion, 70
Notes, 71

5 Patterns of Immigration to and from the United States   77

The Inflow of Legal Immigrants, 80
Undocumented Immigrants, 88
The Foreign-Born Population of the United States in 1990, 101
Sojourners and Settlers: Emigration from the United States, 109
The Net Contribution of Immigration of the
   Foreign-Born to Population Change, 116

The Context of Reception: Legal Rights Dependent on
  Immigration Status, 120
Becoming a U.S. Citizen, 124
Residential Segregation of the Foreign-Born Within
  Metropolitan Areas, 129
Notes, 133

6 Determinants of Immigration   137

UN Forecasts of Future World Population, 137
A Conceptual Scheme for Determining Individual
  Propensities to Migrate, 145
Structural Determinants of Propensities to Immigrate, 150
Summary and Conclusions, 158
Notes, 159

7 Enforcement of Immigration Law   161

The Activities of the Bureau of Consular Affairs, 161
The Activities of the INS, 164
Immigration-Law Enforcement: Effectiveness
  and Side Effects, 171
How Prior Illegal Immigration Facilitates Legal Immigration, 177
How Extending Rights to Undocumented Residents May
  Encourage Illegal Immigration, 179
Notes, 179

8 The Impact of Immigration   183

Standard of Living, 183
Equity, 194
Preservation or Modification of Existing American Culture, 196
Ethnic and Class Conflict, 201
The Power of the United States in International Affairs, 202
Notes, 206

9 Proposals for Change in U.S. Immigration Law   209

Current Public Opinion Concerning Immigration, 209
Suggestions for Revisions to Immigration Policy, 210
Reaching Your Own Policy Conclusions, 222
Notes, 222

Bibliography   225
About the Book and Author   237
Index   238

Illustrations

Tables

4.1   Foreign-born and total population of the United States, 1790–1990   28

4.2   Number of permanent legal immigrants to the United States by decade, 1821–1830 to 1981–1990, as a percentage of the U.S. population at middecade   29

4.3   Percentage distribution of permanent legal immigration to the United States by region of last residence, 1821–1830 to 1981–1990   30

4.4   Ethnic composition of the U.S. population, 1790   31

5.1   Immigrants by major category of admission, fiscal years 1992 and 1991   81

5.2   Immigration limits for fiscal year 1992   82

5.3   Comparison of top nation and all nations by major category of admission and percentage of total immigrant admissions per category, fiscal year 1992   85

5.4   Number and percentage distribution of immigrants by region and country of birth for the top twenty countries of birth, fiscal year 1992   86

5.5   Distribution by age and sex of immigrants in fiscal year 1992 compared to total U.S. population on July 1, 1992   88

5.6   Estimates of undocumented aliens in the United States by country of birth and legalization applicants by type and country of birth   95

5.7   Percentage distribution by age and sex of undocumented aliens and legalization applicants   97

5.8   Legal status of mothers and fathers of Mexican origin, Los Angeles County, 1980–1981   98

5.9   Characteristics of the total legalized population and the legalized population born in Mexico resident in the United States since 1982   102

5.10 Demographic characteristics of the native population and foreign-born population by year of arrival and country of birth, 1990   104

5.11 Social characteristics of the native population and
         foreign-born population by year of arrival and country
         of birth, 1990   105

5.12 Labor force characteristics of the native population and
         foreign-born population by year of arrival and country
         of birth, 1990   107

5.13 Income characteristics of the native population and
         foreign-born population by year of arrival and country
         of birth, 1990   108

5.14 Estimates for the United States of legal immigration and
         noncitizen legal resident emigration by area of origin or
         destination, 1970–1980   114

5.15 Net contribution of immigration to the future size of the
         U.S. population, 1995–2050   118

5.16 Possible effects of net immigration on U.S. population size,
         age composition, and dependency ratios   119

5.17 Percentage naturalized by end of fiscal 1991 for the
         immigration cohort aged sixteen years old and over
         in 1977 by country of birth   126

5.18 Naturalized citizens among the foreign-born population
         of the United States by country of birth, 1990   127

5.19 Indices of dissimilarity with respect to residence for
         ethnic groups, Los Angeles County, 1980   132

6.1   UN medium-series projection of world population
         for 1995–2030   141

6.2   UN medium-series projection of absolute population
         change by quinquennium from 1990 population base
         to 2030   143

6.3   UN medium-series projection of average annual rate
         of population change by quinquennium from 1990
         population base to 2030   144

6.4   1992 emigration rates for nations with the most
         immigrants to the United States and possible
         structural determinants of variation in these rates   152

7.1   Deportable aliens located, 1925–1992   168

8.1   Percentage distributions by mother tongue and ability to
         speak English for mothers and fathers of Mexican
         origin, Los Angeles County, 1980–1981   197

8.2   Percentage distribution by language spoken at home
         for persons of Mexican origin, 1989–1990   198

8.3   Percentage distribution of responses to question whether
      U.S. citizens and residents should learn English for
      persons of Mexican origin, 1989–1990   199
8.4   Percentage distribution of responses to question whether
      English should be the official language of the United
      States for persons of Mexican origin and non-Hispanic
      whites, 1989–1990   199
8.5   Percentage distribution of responses to question
      on attitude toward bilingual education for persons
      of Mexican origin who are U.S. citizens, 1989–1990   200
8.6   Percentage distribution of responses to question on
      objectives of bilingual education for persons
      of Mexican origin who are U.S. citizens, 1989–1990   201

Figures

5.1   Density of Mexican persons born outside the United States
      per square mile in 1986 by census tract of residence
      in Los Angeles County   131

8.1   Relationships among population size, standard of living,
      and military power   205

Photographs

Koreatown, Los Angeles, California   78
Little India, Artesia, Los Angeles County, California   78
Trinidadian barber shop, Boston, Massachusetts   138
Vietnamese family, Oakland, California   139
Men about to cross the U.S. border, Tijuana, Mexico, 1988   162
Border crossers, Tijuana, Mexico, 1988   163
Israeli and Iranian garment manufacturers and Japanese
    garment exporter, garment district, Los Angeles, California   184
Soviet Jewish girls at Chabad Day Camp, West Hollywood,
    California, 1994   185

Acknowledgments

Much of this book was written in the fall of 1993 when I was on sabbatical at El Colegio de la Frontera Norte (COLEF) in Tijuana, Mexico. I wish to thank Jorge Bustamante, president of that institution, for providing me with an office there. An important part of Chapter 4 could not have been written without access to the library at COLEF. Moreover, contact with the faculty and the ongoing research at that institution considerably broadened my intellectual horizon.

I am also indebted to Amentha Dymally, administrative assistant of the Population Research Laboratory at the University of Southern California, for her many actions that facilitated the writing of this book. Thanks are also due to Professor Maurice D. Van Arsdol, Jr., who was director of the Population Research Laboratory during most of the time in which this book was being prepared.

At Westview Press, I wish to thank senior editor Mr. Dean Birkenkamp, assistant editor Jill Rothenberg, editorial assistant Annemarie Preonas, associate project editor Laurie Milford, and my copy editor, Alice Colwell. All of these persons helped immeasurably to improve this book.

I wish to express my appreciation to Professor Charles Tilly of the New School for Social Research, who, as editor of the Foundations of Social Inquiry Series of Westview Press, made cogent comments on the entire manuscript. Thanks are also due to two anonymous reviewers who also helped me improve the manuscript.

I also wish to thank Professor Steven J. Gold, of the Department of Sociology, Michigan State University, for allowing me to use his very fine photographs for this work.

Finally, I wish to thank my wife, Kaye, for her willingness to endure my often unpleasant moods for the entire period in which the writing of this book took place.

David M. Heer

1 Overview

One of the most contentious issues facing the United States today is immigration policy. Two basic questions have emerged: What should be the number and characteristics of the immigrants to be admitted legally to the United States every year? And what should be done about illegal immigration to the United States? The two questions are obviously related. Suppose, in answer to the first, we decided to allow entry to anyone who wished to come to the United States as a permanent legal resident. In adopting this policy, we would also eliminate undocumented immigrants (i.e., persons whose arrival had been outside the law)—and so we would also have adopted a policy with respect to the second question. Conversely, if we decided to impose very tight restrictions on legal immigration and therefore decreed that most persons who wanted to immigrate to the United States would not be allowed a legal slot, we would magnify the problem of illegal immigration.

Why has immigration policy become such an important issue? A major reason is the tremendous increase in the volume of immigration. During the decade ending on September 30, 1992, the total number of persons granted the status of permanent legal immigrant was almost 9 million. During the previous decade the number had been less than 5 million, and in 1963–1972 it had been only around 3.5 million. Moreover, of the nearly 9 million persons who became permanent legal immigrants between 1983 and 1992, more than 2.7 million received that status only because the Immigration Reform and Control Act of 1986 converted them from their status as undocumented immigrants.[1]

Nevertheless, the 1990 census showed that only 7.9 percent of the total population of the United States was foreign-born (some 20 million persons out of a total of about 249 million).[2] Although this was the highest proportion of foreign-born since 1940, the number fell far short of the record: 14.8 percent in 1930.[3]

Perhaps another reason the salience of immigration policy has increased is the changing nationality composition of America's immigrants. As recently as 1951–1960, more than half of all immigrants to the United States were from Europe and only 6 percent from Asia. By 1981–1990 only 10 percent of all immigrants came from Europe and 37 percent from Asia. Moreover, there was an even greater shift in the composition of immigration from the two nations bordering the United States—Mexico and Canada. From 1951 to 1960 there were substantially more immigrants from Canada than from Mexico, but from 1981 to 1990 the number of immigrants from Mexico (including those legalized by the 1986 Immigration Reform and Control Act) was more than ten times the number of immigrants from Canada.

The purpose of this book is to help readers consider our future national immigration legislation. The book will demonstrate how social science findings—together with a conscious recognition of the values that we esteem most highly—are necessary in this regard. The next chapter, "The Volume and Character of Future Immigration: The Values at Stake," is a necessary prerequisite to the rest of the book. In this chapter we examine five classes of values that may be affected by immigration policy: (1) the standard of living in the United States, (2) equity, (3) the preservation or modification of existing American culture, (4) ethnic and class conflict, and (5) the power of the United States in international affairs. A key point in Chapter 2 is that a policy that maximizes one value may work to the detriment of another. For example, an immigration policy that increases the power of the United States in international affairs may adversely affect the nation's standard of living.

In Chapter 3 we examine how the findings of social science influence the immigration debate. This chapter emphasizes that social science cannot resolve the immigration debate because different groups with different values within the society benefit differentially from any given immigration policy. Nevertheless, the teachings of social science may allow each interest group to find a policy most conducive to its values. An immigration policy adopted after consideration of certain studies may then be an intelligent compromise negotiated by the several differing interest groups, allowing each group to preserve the maximum amount of its own values.

My argument for the importance of social science findings, however, assumes that such findings are valid. Accordingly, we need to examine the meaning and validity of such data. In Chapter 3 we consider two types of findings, inductive and deductive, and review the famous essay by the leading German social scientist, Max Weber, advocating a value-free social science. We then look at a well-known essay by Alvin Gouldner that attacks the concept of a value-free sociology. Finally, we review the ideas of the famous Swedish sociologist Gunnar Myrdal on the relationship between facts and valuations in social science. In Chapter 3 I emphasize that whereas social scientists cannot be free from values, the findings of social science may indeed be value-free, as scholars with disparate values can accept the same set of findings. Obviously, some criteria are needed to determine which findings should be accepted and which should not. These criteria are the canons of the scientific method.

Many so-called findings may not meet these criteria and accordingly may not be accepted by all parties to a value or policy dispute. In such cases a particular interest group will seize upon "evidence" that makes its own policy position more attractive to outsiders and rejects contradictory findings. Opposing interest groups will denounce as mere myth the data that diminish their credibility but proclaim the veracity of other findings whose validity is equally in doubt.

Chapter 4 looks at the history of U.S. immigration and immigration law. In each section we pay close attention to the role that presumed proof from social science played in the policy debates important during each historical period. The first part of the chapter considers the long interval from 1789 to 1875 when the United States experienced a large flow of immigrants but in which there were no federal laws of any sort restricting the volume or characteristics of immigrants (with the arguable exception of the abolition of the slave trade in 1808). The policy of unrestricted immigration was not without its severe critics, and we examine that criticism, especially that of the Know-Nothing movement of the 1850s. The second period covered in Chapter 4 begins in 1875 and ends in April 1917, when the United States entered World War I. During this time the volume of immigration to the United States was unprecedented, and the government took its first steps to restrict the flow, particularly from Asia. The third period, from the beginning of U.S. participation in World War I to the beginning of its participation in World War II, was marked by the most restrictive immigration laws in American history and by very low levels of immigration. The fourth period, from 1941 through 1980, involved more liberal immigration policy and consequently a much higher level of immigration. During this war and subsequent cold war, the impact of U.S. immigration policy on the standing of the United States in the international arena assumed great prominence. This led to the end of policy favoring immigration from northwest Europe at the expense of southeast Europe and Asia; it also led to the salience of refugee immigration. At the end of this period, the problem of illegal immigration, predominantly from Mexico, had become an exceedingly controversial issue. In the final period, after 1980, the Immigration Reform and Control Act of 1986 wrought major change with respect to undocumented immigrants, and the Immigration Act of 1990 created the most liberal set of immigration regulations in the United States since before 1921.

Chapter 5 is concerned with the patterns of immigration to and from the United States. The first section examines the current patterns of legal immigration, including data on immigration by main category of admission, country of birth, intended metropolitan area of residence, and age and sex distribution. The second section discusses the available data concerning the number, country of origin, geographic distribution, and other characteristics of undocumented immigrants. The third section contains a description from 1990 census data of the characteristics of foreign-born persons from each major nation of origin as compared to all foreign-born persons and U.S. natives. The fourth section concerns sojourners and permanent settlers, examining data on emigration from the United States to other nations, with a particular focus on the phenomenon of return migration among foreign-born persons who have immigrated to the United States. The fifth section looks at the extent to which the immigration of the foreign-born population contributes to current and future population change in the United States. The sixth section concerns the different receptions given to refugees, regular legal immigrants, and undocumented immigrants and describes the legal privileges and handicaps of these three types of immigrants. The seventh section looks at naturalization: how many immigrants become naturalized citizens and the characteristics of naturalized citizens versus immigrants who have not become naturalized citizens. The final section of the chapter treats the phenomenon of ethnic enclaves, sections of a city where most of the inhabitants are immigrants from a particular area of the world. This phenomenon is important because it is debatable whether enclaves hasten or retard the assimilation of immigrants.

Chapter 6 examines the determinants of immigration to and from the United States. The first part of the chapter introduces a conceptual scheme used to analyze the individual decision to migrate. The second part examines the structural determinants of immigration patterns from a macroperspective. The final section explores the place of the United States within the world immigration market, focusing on why immigrants choose to immigrate to the United States rather than to other immigrant-receiving nations such as Canada and Australia.

Chapter 7 concentrates on immigration-law enforcement. The first section discusses the work of the Bureau of Consular Affairs of the U.S. Department of State in issuing visas for permanent and temporary residence in the United States. The second section looks at the activities of the Immigration and Naturalization Service, including its border patrol. The third section treats the effectiveness of immigration-law enforcement as well as the side effects resulting from that enforcement. In the fourth section we examine how under current circumstances undocumented immigration is an aid to eventual legal immigration, and in the final section we consider to what extent granting certain rights to undocumented immigrants may encourage illegal immigration.

Chapter 8 attempts to summarize social science findings concerning the impact of immigration on American values. The first section deals with the standard of living in the United States, the second with equity, the third the preservation or modification of existing American culture, the fourth ethnic and class conflict, and the fifth the power of the United States in world affairs.

The final chapter considers proposals for change in U.S. immigration law. The first section provides data on the attitude of the American population toward immigration as revealed in recent public opinion polls. The second section presents a nutshell summary of my own proposals for change in immigration law. In the final sections I discuss in more detail my own and alternative proposals concerning the proper volume of immigration and the status of legal entrant; ways of dealing with undocumented immigrants, refugees, and asylees; and the criteria by which nonrefugee immigrants and legal entrants should be admitted.

Notes

1. U.S. Department of Justice, Immigration and Naturalization Service, *Statistical Yearbook of the Immigration and Naturalization Service, 1992* (Washington, D.C.: Government Printing Office, 1993), pp. 30–32.

2. U.S. Bureau of the Census, "One in Four of Nation's Foreign Born Arrived Since 1985," *Census and You*, Vol. 28, No. 2 (February 1993), p. 1.

3. John Higham, *Send These to Me: Immigrants in Urban America*, rev. ed. (Baltimore: Johns Hopkins University Press, 1984), p. 15.

2 The Volume and Character of Future Immigration: The Values at Stake

As the dawn of the twenty-first century approaches, the problems of international immigration have assumed greater salience for most high-income nations of the world, including the United States, Australia, Canada, Hong Kong, Israel, Japan, New Zealand, Singapore, and most West European states. The population of these nations forms only a small proportion of the world's total, about 15 percent, whereas around 85 percent of the world's population lives in one of the economically less developed nations. The contrast in per capita income between the high-income and less-developed nations is staggering. In China and India, the nations with the largest populations, per capita income is less than 10 percent of that in the United States, Germany, or Japan.[1] The large income differences between the high-income and the economically less developed nations, coupled with the much larger populations in the latter, create strong pressure for migration into the former nations from the latter. Augmenting this pressure are revolutions in transportation and communication. The revolution in transportation has greatly reduced the cost of international travel, whereas the revolution in communications, particularly the advent of television, has brought the great wealth of the rich nations into the consciousness of the poor ones. Adding fuel to this fire is the civil unrest in so many of the less-developed nations, which frequently erupts into bloody conflict between differing ethnic groups or simply between haves and have-nots. This civic conflict in turn creates a flood of people seeking status as refugees or asylees, who may flee to a neighboring nation but then often seek entry into whichever high-income nation may be willing to accept them. Others use the airlines to reach one of these nations and there make claim for political asylum. In summary, the pressure for immigration from the poor nations to the rich has reached an unprecedented level—and this pressure is exerted upon all rich nations of the world, not just the United States.

Nevertheless, among even the economically developed nations, the United States is particularly favored. It has the world's highest gross domestic product (GDP) and the highest standard of living.[2] It is therefore not surprising that at present many more people desire to immigrate to the United States than legislation legally allows.

Currently, there is sharp debate in the United States with respect to immigration policy. Opinions vary dramatically concerning what legal limits should be set on the number and characteristics of immigrants to the United States and what should be done to discourage illegal immigration. In a democracy such as that of the United States, citizens can influence affairs by advocating policies that are enacted into legislation. The purpose of this chapter is to list and briefly discuss the values many or all American citizens hold dear that may be affected either positively or negatively by policies intended to control the volume and character of immigration to the United States.

Policies are mechanisms designed to ensure that a value or series of values is achieved given constraints inherent in a real situation. It is relatively easy to formulate policy when there is only one value or even more than one value, provided that all values are mutually compatible. Dilemmas occur when we wish to uphold several values that cannot simultaneously be maximized. In such a case policy must be designed to advance the sum of all values as much as possible, or at least as much as is necessary to achieve majority support among legislators. In most instances policy succeeds in advancing some values only at the expense of other values. For that reason, it is important to begin any discussion of immigration policy by discussing the values that are at stake.

Standard of Living

Perhaps the most important value at stake with respect to U.S. immigration policy is how the policy will affect the standard of living of the existing American population. Yet no one is just an "average" American; everyone is a member of a particular group. Because immigration policies that will improve the standard of living of one group may have negative impacts on the standard of living of other groups, we have to know how a changed number of immigrants of a particular type would affect the living standards of *each* group within American society.

In much of the economic literature concerning immigration, economists distinguish three groups: unskilled workers, skilled workers, and owners of land and capital. In understanding the relationships among unskilled workers, skilled workers, and owners of land and capital, economists make use of two key concepts: substitutes and complements in the production process. Substitutes may be defined as persons with a set of skills identical to those of a given class of workers. Complements possess a set of skills different from a given class of workers but necessary for the production process to occur. The addition by immigration of a new worker into the American labor market causes the marginal productivity of substitutes to fall and that of complements to rise.

Let us assume that a newly arrived immigrant worker is unskilled. Then the consequence of that worker's arrival should be to reduce the marginal productivity of other unskilled workers who are substitutes for the immigrant and to raise the marginal productivity of the complements to unskilled labor, namely, skilled workers and land and capital. In any given local labor market, one may expect substitutes to a newly arrived immigrant worker to experience a fall in wages, a rise in the rate of unemployment, or an increased rate of migration out of the local labor market. Complementary workers in the local labor market may experience an increase in wages and a lower unemployment rate; furthermore, there should be an increased rate of migration of complementary workers into the local labor market. Finally, owners of land and capital in the local area should likewise benefit through higher returns on their assets and consequently a higher price should they decide to sell these assets. Conversely, a decline in the number of unskilled immigrants would cause benefits to substitutes but harm to complements. Consequently, unskilled workers would be expected to gain, but both skilled workers and owners of land and capital might suffer.

Up to now we have discussed the consequences of immigration only for the groups constituting the components of production. What are the results of increased immigration for consumers? A larger volume of immigrants allows employers more choice in whom they employ. The workers they choose are thus likely to produce more per dollar paid out in wages than would be the case with a smaller volume of immigration. That is to say that either employers may pay less for the same level of productivity from each worker or, alternatively, each worker they hire at the previously prevailing wage will be of higher quality and produce more than previously. Because of competition among employers, some or most of this increased productivity would lead to lower prices and therefore savings for consumers. But consumers would have to pay more for the costs of land and capital. For example, a higher volume of immigration may lead to higher prices for housing, increasing rents and the prices of owner-occupied homes.

The picture of the impact of immigration we have drawn so far excludes the effects of taxation and the distribution of benefits from government-sponsored entitlement programs. In fiscal 1989, federal, state, and local governmental outlays for social welfare expenditures—for example, social security, Medicare, Medicaid, veterans' benefits, Aid to Families with Dependent Children (AFDC) and education—cost $956 billion and represented 18.6 percent of total gross national product

(GNP).[3] Thus an important issue concerning any particular immigrant is whether government benefits extended to that immigrant exceed the taxes he or she pays. Since entitlement programs redistribute income from the rich to the poor and from economically active age groups to children and the elderly, the greatest short-term economic benefit to other taxpayers will come from the arrival of well-to-do immigrants who are economically active.

We have up to now also ignored long-term effects of immigration. One economist-demographer, Julian Simon, believes that any increase in population brings a higher standard of living because more population means more creative minds, and more creative minds bring a higher rate of technological progress.[4] But Simon's opinion is hotly contested. In 1972 President Richard Nixon's Commission on Population Growth and the American Future declared that "no substantial benefits would result from continued growth of the nation's population," and "recognizing that our population cannot grow indefinitely and appreciating the advantages of moving now toward the stabilization of population," the commission recommended that "the nation welcome and plan for population stabilization."[5] To the extent that future immigration could cause an undue increase in population, it would adversely affect the standard of living of future generations. In contrast, if below-replacement fertility means that the United States is in danger of population decline, the situation regarding immigration would be quite different. If the U.S. population begins to decline in the future, a very high proportion of the population will be beyond the age of retirement. In that case a continuous influx of working-age immigrants who paid social security tax and bore lots of children might serve to stabilize U.S. population size, balance its age distribution, and preserve the financial soundness of the social security system.

Changes in the volume of immigration, then, are likely to create gains in standard of living for some sectors of the preexisting population of the United States and losses for other sectors. As a result, no immigration policy will meet with universal approval from the American people. Nevertheless, there is no doubt that the standard of living of all Americans will be affected adversely by the admission of immigrants who are disabled or already retired, because such immigrants would receive the customary benefits from government entitlement programs but would not contribute much by way of taxes to pay for those entitlements.

Equity

Libertarians and egalitarians have different notions of equity. Libertarians believe that equity is achieved when each individual is rewarded in proportion to his or her economic contribution to society within a free market. Egalitarians believe that equity is achieved only when the gap between rich and poor is small. Thus, within a nation, egalitarians favor a policy of substantial income transfer from the rich to the poor by means of progressive taxation and means-tested entitlement programs, whereas libertarians tend to favor a lower rate of taxation and lesser volume of transfers. A logical consequence of the libertarian definition of equity is that there ought to be a free international labor market and all persons throughout the world should have the right to migrate to any nation of their choice.

However, believers in the egalitarian notion of equity have a dilemma in deciding the desirable level of immigration to the United States. They must decide whether equity is best conceived in terms of a context strictly within the United States or within a context that includes the whole world. In other words, is equity achieved by a policy that raises the status of the nation's existing poor at the expense of denying an opportunity to the much poorer potential immigrant from outside the United States or by a policy that does the opposite? For example, legislation that would successfully reduce the number of undocumented, mostly unskilled immigrants from Mexico to the United States might raise the wages of unskilled workers born in the United States but deprive many unskilled workers in Mexico of the opportunity substantially to improve their meager standard of living.

Our notions of equity compel many of us to react strongly against actions by governments abroad that persecute individuals for their religion, ethnicity, or political persuasion. Accordingly, we may believe that such persons should be allowed to immigrate to a safe haven and if necessary be admitted for permanent residence in the United States. But those ideas that make us sympathetic to the plight of the politically persecuted may conflict with other values we hold dear, such as the concern for our standard of living, mentioned in the previous section, and the preservation or modification of existing American culture, which we turn to in the following section.

Preservation or Modification of Existing American Culture

The history of conflicts over immigration policy in the United States shows the importance of the perceived effect of immigration on the preservation of existing American culture. At various points in American history, unrestricted immigration has been seen as threatening the prevalence of the English language, the Protestant religion, and the very existence of civil liberties and democracy.

In a brilliant essay on why population growth was so much faster in the British North American colonies than in Europe, Benjamin Franklin in 1755 expressed a negative opinion of German settlers in Pennsylvania. At that time German immigrants and their descendants represented about one-third of the total population of the colony. "Why," Franklin asked, "should the Palatine boors be suffered to swarm into our settlements and by herding together establish their language and manners to the exclusion of ours? Why should *Pennsylvania*, founded by the *English*, become a colony of aliens, who will shortly be so numerous as to germanize us instead of our anglifying them?"[6] Today few Americans share Franklin's sentiments toward Americans of German descent. But the reason may lie precisely in that the Germans are no longer new immigrants but have been fully assimilated.

A more recent illustration of Americans' long-standing concern over immigration relates to an experience my wife had in Los Angeles. She was on her way home from an appointment west of downtown and was on a street that provided a passage between two heavily traveled boulevards. The neighborhood was inhabited almost entirely by Hispanics from El Salvador, Guatemala, and Mexico. As she was passing through the intersection, her car was hit by a car coming from her left. The driver had ignored a stop sign. My wife was not injured, but the back of her car was badly damaged. She left her car to confront the occupants of the other car and was dismayed to find out that none of them spoke English (she did not speak Spanish). She guessed that the driver did not have automobile insurance because he did not show her any insurance card; she did take down the license plate number. Later she complained bitterly about how exasperating the incident had been. My wife's complaint was essentially the same as that of Franklin. Both of them expected that in a society of interacting individuals everyone should be able to communicate with everyone else in the same language.

Still, not all Americans see the existing American culture as ideal. A strong intellectual current insists that the diversity of cultures in the United States has been one of its strongest assets. A prominent spokesperson for this viewpoint was the famous nineteenth-century philosopher Ralph Waldo Emerson. He wrote, "The energy of the Irish, Germans, Swedes, Poles, and Cossacks, and all the European tribes . . . will construct a new race, a new religion, a new state, a new literature, which will be as vigorous as the new Europe which came out of the smelting-pot of the Dark Ages."[7] Believers in cultural diversity have obviously been much more in favor of higher and less restricted levels of immigration than those who place a high value on preserving American culture as it is.

It is significant that the United States remains an English-speaking nation even though only 39 percent of all Americans claim full or partial ancestry from an English-speaking country.[8] And there is no doubt that Protestants, who once were the overwhelming majority of the total population, are now decreasingly prevalent. The massive immigration of Roman Catholics to the United States from Ireland in the middle of the nineteenth century evoked widespread opposition from those who saw them as a threat to the ascendancy of Protestantism in the United States. Moreover, among recent immigrants to the United States, Protestants make up only a small proportion, and a substantial number are not even Christian but adherents of Islam, Buddhism, Judaism, Hinduism, and other religions.

Some have argued that the preservation of a democratic republican form of government in the United States depends on keeping out immigrants from nations without a comparable political tradition. Thomas Jefferson, the most notable proponent of this view, believed that immigrants from such nations would adhere to the political principles of the state from which they came or would believe in "unbounded licentiousness."[9] In contrast, Annelise Anderson, a contemporary scholar, contends that excessive efforts to eliminate undocumented immigrants from the United States by introducing a compulsory national identification card might end up destroying our civil liberties by creating the capability for totalitarian control of all private citizens.[10]

Ethnic and Class Conflict

Immigration in the United States has traditionally been associated with ethnic conflict, as members of newly arrived immigrant groups have clashed with those of other ethnic groups who arrived earlier. The conflicts are often related to (1) the desires of the older ethnic groups to preserve their culture and to reduce economic competition from the members of the newer groups and (2) the desires of the newer immigrant groups to preserve their culture and to avoid discrimination based on ethnic or immigrant status. Many scholars therefore infer that high levels of immigration—particularly from groups that differ in culture, race, religion, and language from the majority of persons already in the United States—are undesirable in that they serve to promote ethnic conflict.

Furthermore, high levels of immigration of unskilled workers may reduce the existing ratio of the average wage among unskilled workers to the average wage among skilled workers. This increase in income inequality might in turn intensify the level of class conflict within American society. Conversely, an influx of highly skilled immigrants might reduce the level of income inequality in the United States and hence serve to reduce the level of class conflict.

The Power of the United States
in International Affairs

Most Americans take pride in the United States' power in international affairs. They also wish the nation to maintain its present degree of power. The volume and character of immigration may affect U.S. influence in five different ways.

Military Power

The first of these is linked to the way in which the volume and age composition of immigration may affect the total population size and age composition of the United States and how these in turn may affect the country's military power. Age and sex composition is obviously important since members of the armed forces are predominantly young adult males. The size of the total population is also significant: French economist-demographer Alfred Sauvy contends that the population size that will maximize a nation's military might is larger than the population size that will maximize per capita income.[11] Sauvy assumes that military power reaches a height when the total GNP minus that necessary for population subsistence is maximized. The population size that will maximize this amount, however, is always larger than that which will maximize the average per capita income. Thus, according to Sauvy, one must choose between maximizing the standard of living and maximizing military power. Thus even though an increased flow of immigrants might reduce the average standard of living, it might also augment the power of the United States in global conflict.

Foreign Relations with Particular Nations

The second way immigration influences the international standing of the United States relates to how the volume of immigration from a specific nation colors that nation's attitude toward the United States. For example, if U.S. law is highly restrictive of immigration from a particular nation, the government of that nation may become resentful and may ally itself with other powers that are antagonistic to the United States. Perhaps the best example of this was Japanese resentment at the total exclusion of Japanese immigration into the United States beginning in 1924. No doubt this animosity helped lead to the Japanese alliance with Germany and Italy and to the attack on Pearl Harbor on December 7, 1941.[12]

Immigrants as Foreign-Policy Pressure Groups

The admission of immigrants of certain nationalities may also weaken U.S. influence in world affairs because the presence of such immigrants precludes the United States from developing alliances with countries that might otherwise wish to be friendlier with the United States. For example, Greeks' and Armenians' antipathy to Turkey made it difficult for the United States, which had sizable populations of both groups, to have an effective alliance with Turkey during the cold war, when the United States avidly sought allies against the Soviet Union.

Immigrants as a "Fifth Column"

Fourth, certain classes of potential immigrants to the United States might constitute a "fifth column," dedicated to destroying the United States. As a result of concern over this issue, the Internal Security Act of 1950 made past or present membership in the Communist Party or any of its affiliates (and also the Fascist Party or any of its affiliates) specific grounds for exclusion from the United States.

Immigration Policy and Competitive Moral Standing

Finally, nations who might ally themselves either with the United States or with the enemies of the United States come to have perceptions of the general character of U.S. immigration policy. One can plausibly argue that from 1945 through 1991, in which the United States was engaged in a cold war with the Soviet Union, U.S. refugee policy was designed mainly to increase the standing of the United States versus the Soviet Union in world affairs. The United States could not afford to ignore people who wanted to leave the Soviet Union or any of its allied nations (such as Hungary, Cuba, or Vietnam) because the United States wanted to advertise how poorly such nations treated their own citizens. Furthermore, their wish to come to the United States showed that the U.S. system was better than any Communist system. As a consequence, the United States opened its doors to anyone able to escape from a Communist nation. Moreover, the United States felt a special obligation to those who had supported it during the lengthy war in Indochina and who might face special persecution after the victory of the Communists in 1975. Consequently, the U.S. government admitted several hundred thousand refugees from Vietnam, Laos, and Kampuchea, most of whom had held high positions in the former anti-Communist government or army or who had been directly associated with U.S. armed forces fighting there. If the United States had not admitted into this country immigrants from Indochina following the U.S. withdrawal, many Americans believed the United States would not succeed in recruiting allies to fight against the Soviet Union in other parts of the world.

Notes

1. World Bank, *World Development Report 1993* (New York: Oxford University Press, 1993), pp. 238–239, 296–297.

2. Ibid.

3. U.S. Bureau of the Census, *Statistical Abstract of the United States, 1992* (Washington, D.C.: Government Printing Office, 1992), p. 356.

4. Julian L. Simon, *The Ultimate Resource* (Princeton, N.J.: Princeton University Press, 1981), pp. 196–215.

5. Commission on Population Growth and the American Future, *Population and the American Future* (Washington, D.C.: Government Printing Office, 1972), pp. 12, 120.

6. Glen Weaver, "Benjamin Franklin and the Pennsylvania Germans," *William and Mary Quarterly*, Vol. 14 (1957), pp. 536–559. The quotation appears on p. 549.

7. Maldwyn Allen Jones, *American Immigration*, 2d ed. (Chicago: University of Chicago Press, 1992), pp. 137–138.

8. U.S. Bureau of the Census, "German, Irish, English, Afro-American Top '90 Ancestry Lists," *Census and You*, Vol. 28, No. 2 (February 1993), p. 6. In making this calculation I have summed the following ancestries: Irish, English, American, Scotch-Irish, Scottish, and Welsh.

9. "Thomas Jefferson on Population," *Population and Development Review*, Vol. 19, No. 1 (March 1993), p. 178. The cited material was originally published in 1787 in his *Notes on the State of Virginia*.

10. Annelise Anderson, *Illegal Aliens and Employer Sanctions: Solving the Wrong Problem* (Stanford, Calif.: Hoover Institution Press, 1986).

11. Alfred Sauvy, *General Theory of Population* (New York: Basic Books, 1969), pp. 51–64.

12. Robert A. Divine, *American Immigration Policy, 1924–1952* (New Haven: Yale University Press, 1957), p. 23.

3 The Influence of Social Science Findings

In this chapter we examine how social science findings can influence the immigration policy debate. For purposes of our discussion, we take a broad view of social science findings, defining them to include deductive and inductive conclusions and conclusions that combine both deductive and inductive reasoning. We begin by examining the relationship between social science findings and value judgments.

The Relationship Between Social Science Findings and Value Judgments

In a well-known essay published in 1917, German social scientist Max Weber discussed value judgments in the social sciences.[1] His main point was that scientific statements must be completely separate from value judgments, that is, "evaluations of a phenomenon . . . as worthy of either condemnation or approval."[2] The social sciences, in other words, must be value-free.

What precisely could be the contribution of social science to questions of policy? Weber wrote:

> It seems to me to be possible to establish without a shadow of a doubt that, in the area of practical political value-judgments (especially in the fields of economics and social policy), as soon as guidance for a valued course of action is to be sought, all that an empirical discipline with the means at its disposal can show is (i) the unavoidable means; (ii) the unavoidable side effects; (iii) the resulting conflict of several possible value-judgments with each other in their practical consequences.[3]

Weber declared that the scope of academic teaching could include both social science and value judgments only if the instructor "imposes on himself the unconditional obligation of rigorously making clear to his audience, and above all to himself, in each individual case (even at the expense of making his lectures boring) which of his statements on that occasion is an assertion of fact, either logically demonstrable or empirically observable, and which a practical value-judgment."[4] But Weber also emphasized another point:

Among those scholars who did not believe they ought to renounce the making of practical value-judgments in their empirical discussions, it was precisely the most passionate . . . who were the most tolerable. For precisely because of the force of passion in their words, the hearer was at least put in a
position to allow, for his own part, for the way in which the subjectivity of the
teacher's value-judgment introduced a possible element of distortion into
his statements and so to do for himself what the teacher, because of his emo-
tions, remained incapable of doing. In this way, the influence exercised on
the minds of young students would continue to retain the genuine depth of
feeling which, I assume, those who support the making of value-judgments
in academic teaching would want to ensure without the audience's being led
by misguided teaching into confusing the different domains with each other,
as is bound to happen when the statement of empirical facts and the chal-
lenge to take up a practical position on the great problems of life are both
submerged in the same sea of cool dispassionate analysis.[5]

I am in complete agreement with Weber on two points: Social science
ought to be value-free, and if professors wish to include in their writings
both social science and advocacy of policy positions, they should always
clearly distinguish between the two.

What is often considered to be the most devastating critique of
Weber's position was set forth by sociologist Alvin Gouldner in 1962.[6] A
close reading of Gouldner's essay, however, demonstrates that he was
less critical of what Weber actually wrote than of certain misinterpreta-
tions of Weber's words. Gouldner made three major points in his essay.
First, he argued that under contemporary conditions in the United
States sociology professors should set forth their value positions. In support of this view, Gouldner pointed out that Weber himself had used a
very pragmatic argument in urging professors to abstain from setting
forth their value preferences to their students. Weber had argued that if
professors espoused political positions that the German government
did not favor, the government could retaliate by destroying the auton-
omy of the universities. Gouldner believed that contemporary American
universities were in no such danger. Moreover, he believed that "professors are, like all others, entitled and perhaps obligated to express their
values."[7] Second, he condemned those sociologists who espoused a
value-free sociology "to justify the sale of one's talents to the highest
bidder."[8] In particular, he condemned sociologists who "had no hesita-
tion about doing market research designed to sell more cigarettes, although well aware of the implications of recent cancer research."[9] Third,
Gouldner argued that sociologists' acceptance of the premise of a value-
free sociology would lead them to forget that sociology can exist only because society provides it with support. According to Gouldner:

Social science can never be fully accepted in a society, or by a part of it,
without paying its way; this means it must manifest both its relevance and

its concern for the contemporary human predicament. Unless the value relevance of sociological inquiry is made plainly evident, unless there are at
least some bridges between it and larger human hopes and purposes, it
must inevitably be scorned by laymen as pretentious wordmongering.[10]

In my opinion Gouldner's third point is extremely important. In writing
this book, I have tried my best to observe Gouldner's prescription of creating bridges between social science findings and human hopes and
purposes.

In violation of chronological but not pedagological order, let us now
look at the conclusions of Swedish sociologist Gunnar Myrdal, best
known for his monumental 1944 work, *An American Dilemma: The
Negro Problem and Modern Democracy.*[11] In this book he included a
lengthy appendix titled "A Methodological Note on Facts and Valuations
in Social Science." His main concern was a subject to which Weber had
earlier alluded: the extent to which social scientists' own value judgments might affect their acceptance or rejection of so-called scientific
statements. Myrdal began his appendix as follows:

> The biases in popular beliefs about social reality and the deeper conflicts of
> valuations rationalized by these popular theories can be made apparent
> through comparison with "objective" truth as this is revealed by scientific
> research. But the scientist himself is not necessarily immune to biases. In
> the light of the history of scientific writings on the American Negro prob-
> lem, the biased notions held in previous times and the opportunistic ten-
> dencies steering them stand out in high relief against the better controlled
> scientific views of today. Our steadily increasing stock of observations and
> inferences is not merely subjected to continuous cross-checking and criti-
> cal discussion but is deliberately scrutinized to discover and correct hidden
> preconceptions and biases. Full objectivity, however, is an ideal toward
> which we are constantly striving, but which we can never reach. The social
> scientist, too, is part of the culture in which he lives, and he never succeeds
> in freeing himself entirely from dependence on the dominant preconcep-
> tions and biases of his environment.[12]

What was Myrdal's solution to the problem of bias in social science?
Myrdal wrote,

> Biases in social science cannot be erased simply by "keeping to the facts"
> and by refined methods of statistical treatment of the data. Facts, and the
> handling of data, sometimes show themselves even more pervious to ten-
> dencies toward bias than does "pure thought." . . . Neither can biases be
> avoided by the scientists' stopping short of drawing practical conclusions.
> Science becomes no better protected against biases by the entirely negative
> device of refusing to arrange its result for practical and political utilization.
> As we shall point out, there are, rather, reasons why the opposite is true. . . .
> Biases in research are much deeper seated than in the formulation of
> avowedly practical conclusions. They are not valuations attached to research

but rather they permeate research. They are the unfortunate results of con-
cealed valuations that insinuate themselves into research in all stages, from
its planning to its final presentation.

The valuations will, when driven underground, hinder observation and
inference from becoming truly objective. This can be avoided only by making the valuations explicit. There is no other device for excluding biases in
social sciences than to face the valuations and to introduce them as explic-
itly stated, specific, and sufficiently concretized value premises.[13]

I agree with Myrdal that the best way to minimize bias in the social
sciences is for all social scientists to be frank about their own value
premises. Only a minority of social science findings are close to being
certainly true, whereas many findings presumed true are at least to
some degree tenuous. With respect to tenuous findings, it is important
to know the biases of those social scientists who assert the findings to be
true. What criteria can be used to differentiate more certain findings
from more tenuous ones? We explore this question at some length in the
next section.

The Validation of Social Science Findings

At the beginning of this chapter, I stated that I would assume social science findings to include deductive conclusions, inductive conclusions,
and conclusions that combined elements of both forms of reasoning. I
think all social science methodologists would agree that the most valid
conclusions are those that are consistent with commonly accepted theory (deductively valid) and are supported by empirical findings (induc-
tively valid). Nevertheless, many presumed findings are derived only
from deduction and cannot be validated by empirical studies. These deductive findings may even be universally accepted by social scientists,
but only if the particular theory has been very well tested under similar
circumstances and found invariably to be correct. Economists are fond
of deductive reasoning to predict the behavior that can be expected
given that markets are free and individuals act to maximize their monetary incomes. These models are valuable precisely because much empirical behavior has been shown to be consistent with the behavior that
such models predict. Still, there is no doubt that the models are applied
to situations where it is doubtful that a free market exists or even that individuals are attempting to maximize their monetary incomes.

The criteria for the validation of empirical findings are complex. First,
operational definitions of the concepts in the theory have to be devised
and then tested for validity and reliability. Assuming reliable and valid
operational definitions have been devised, methodologists agree that

the best way to test a theory is through an experiment in which a treatment is applied to randomly selected subjects and withheld from other subjects also randomly selected. In general in the social sciences, however, experiments are not possible, leaving sociologists to resort to statistical analysis in which other variables that might affect the result are controlled. But the statistical analyst may not control all relevant variables, and most statistical analysis is conducted on samples rather than on whole populations. Accordingly, the conclusions may be marred by sampling error and high rates of nonresponse.

Moreover, many so-called empirical findings are not really completely empirical. Instead, they are based on particular models. The model may assume that the several independent variables are linearly related to the dependent variable when in fact the relationship between the dependent variable and the independent variables may be multiplicative. Sometimes examination of the data can determine whether a particular model is more appropriate than another model. Often, however, two or more models may fit the data equally well.

There may of course be problems if more than one model fits the data. Let us look, for example, at some research conducted by Robert Warren and Jeffrey Passel, work in which I also had a small input.[14] This illustration is prolonged and difficult to understand; however, I use it because it involves an area in which I have considerable expertise, and it neatly illustrates the point I wish to make.

Warren and Passel were intent on estimating the number of undocumented immigrants who were counted in the 1980 census. Their basic idea was to make use of two data sets. The first data set was a count of legal aliens in the United States as of January 1, 1980. At that time all legal aliens in the United States were required by law to register their place of residence with the Immigration and Naturalization Service (INS) each January. The second data set was the count of foreign-born persons who were not naturalized citizens in the 1980 census, counted as of April 1. Warren and Passel assumed that by subtracting the adjusted number of legal aliens from the adjusted number of foreign-born nonnaturalized citizens, they could obtain the number of undocumented persons counted in the 1980 census.

As a first step, Warren and Passel adjusted the number of registered legal aliens to estimate the number on April 1, 1980, rather than January 1. They also adjusted the number of legal aliens for underregistration (I omit the details of this last adjustment since it was so complicated). Turning their attention to the accuracy of the census count of the number of foreign-born persons who were not naturalized citizens, Warren and Passel compared the number of foreign-born persons in the 1980 census who said they were naturalized citizens with the number of foreign-born persons who had actually been naturalized according to the records of the INS. They then reduced the number of naturalized citizens in the 1980 census from the reported 7.107 million to 6.118 million, a difference of 989,000. The adjustment for persons born in Mexico was especially high: The number of naturalized citizens born in Mexico as reported from the 1980 census was 580,000; the number that Warren and Passel believed to be true was only 205,000, a difference of 375,000.

I had made arrangements to collaborate with Jeffrey Passel on an article comparing my estimation of the number of undocumented Mexicans in Los Angeles County, based on my survey of recent Mexican-born mothers living in the county, to the estimates he and Warren were making.[15] I read his preliminary paper, delivered in 1983, in which he described his adjustment for misreporting of the number of naturalized citizens in the 1980 census. If naturalized citizenship was misreported, I wondered, shouldn't we expect some misreporting of whether individuals were born in the United States?

I examined the figures for people of Mexican descent born in the United States in various years and tallied in the 1970 census and compared each of these with the numbers in the same birth cohort in the 1980 census. A birth cohort is defined as all persons who were born during a certain period; the members of a particular cohort can be traced from an earlier census to a census taken a decade later, for example, by comparing the number of persons in the earlier census of a given age group with the number of persons in the later census who are ten years older than the age group first considered. That is, persons aged ten to fourteen years in the 1980 census and twenty to twenty-four years old in the 1990 census would be members of the same birth cohort.

Even after I had adjusted the figures for mortality, the 1980 count showed too many persons of Mexican origin born in the United States for each birth cohort compared to the 1970 number in that same cohort. I therefore concluded that some individuals who stated in the 1980 census that they were of Mexican origin but were born in the United States were not telling the truth and were in fact born in Mexico. I mentioned my investigation and my conclusion to Passel. He reminded me that in order to make a valid inference in this matter, one must also control for differential undercount and overcount of persons of Mexican descent in both the 1970 and 1980 census. He did think it was probable that there was some misreporting of nativity among persons of Mexican descent in the 1980 census and promised to investigate the matter thoroughly and adjust his estimates of undocumented Mexicans to take this into account.

Passel completed his work and concluded that the proper adjustment for false reporting of nativity was 205,000 persons, a figure equal to 8.8

percent of the originally reported number of persons of Mexican descent born outside the United States in 1980. This adjustment automatically increased the estimated number of undocumented Mexicans counted in the 1980 census by 205,000. Warren and Passel's final estimate of the number of undocumented Mexicans counted in the 1980 census was 1,131,000; this number would have been only 926,000 without the correction for misreporting of nativity.

Because the adjustment was originally my idea, I have worried about it ever since. I suggest two alternatives produced by new deductive assumptions. The first would produce a larger estimate of the number of undocumented Mexican immigrants than that prepared by Warren and Passel; the second would produce a smaller number. Consider first the alternative that would produce a larger estimate. Warren and Passel assumed that in the 1980 census some 205,000 persons who were really undocumented Mexican immigrants reported that they were born in the United States, whereas they assumed that in the 1970 census everyone of Mexican descent reported nativity truthfully. This assumption might be correct if only undocumented Mexican immigrants reported nativity incorrectly and there were no undocumented immigrants counted in the 1970 census. But if we suppose that some undocumented persons of Mexican descent did misreport nativity in the 1970 census, it then follows that almost as many as the exact number who misreported nativity in the 1970 census should be added to the number of undocumented Mexican immigrants in the 1980 census. So the true number of undocumented Mexicans counted in the 1980 census could be substantially higher than Warren and Passel estimated.

In contrast, consider an assumption that would reduce the estimated number of undocumented Mexicans counted in the 1980 census. Warren and Passel assumed that everyone of Mexican descent who was born in the United States never left the United States. But it is often alleged that many Mexican mothers give birth in the United States so that their children will be native-born American citizens, immediately returning to Mexico with their newborn infants. If this were true, many of the young adults counted in the 1980 census as born in the United States of Mexican descent might have been born in the United States in the late 1950s or early 1960s but had been living in Mexico at the time of the 1970 census and had only returned to the United States in the late 1970s. Accordingly, Warren and Passel would have exaggerated the number of undocumented Mexicans in the United States in 1980. To the credit of their estimate, it should be said that if both alternative assumptions were true, each would tend to cancel out the effect of the other, and the resulting estimate might be quite close to that which Warren and Passel actually made.

My main point is that Warren and Passel's estimate of undocumented immigrants in the United States depended not only on empirical data but on deductive assumptions. These deductive assumptions are debatable. Moreover, in the debate over what to do about undocumented immigration, those who favor stricter control are likely to believe that the true number of undocumented immigrants in the United States is high, whereas those who oppose tighter control are likely to proclaim the true number to be low.

To proceed from the particular to the general, my illustration shows that the value judgments of social scientists may bias the deductive assumptions they make in order to produce their findings. Yet we are likely to arrive at the truth more quickly if social scientists are divided in their value judgments than if there is unanimity among them. If there is a division of opinion, the veracity of dubious assumptions will be challenged and further research may determine which deductive assumptions are correct and which are not.

Drawing Policy Conclusions

Each of us can draw personal policy conclusions concerning proper immigration policy. The first step is to examine all of the values at stake and to decide how significant each is to us. The next step is to integrate social science findings into the thought process. Weber suggested that social science findings could be important in three different ways: (1) in describing the inevitable means to achieve a given value, (2) in outlining the unavoidable side effects of achieving that value, and (3) in showing how the means used to achieve a given value might react negatively or positively on the achievement of other values. In deciding what particular policies we wish to approve, then, we attempt to look at the consequences of a particular policy for all the values we want to uphold and choose the policy that best sustains the weighted sum of these values. This task would be easier if social science findings were always of the highest validity. Unfortunately, this is not the case. In order to develop your personal preferred policy, you will have to pick the findings you are prepared to accept; once you have done this, you will be able to decide which policy you favor. Of course, if you believe only a small minority of others will approve of the policy that appears to best fit your own values, you may decide to advocate in public a policy that is more likely to meet with general acceptance. And as social science accumulates more valid findings concerning a given phenomenon, you must be prepared to change your previous policy conclusions to take into account the revised findings.

Notes

1. Max Weber, "Value-judgments in Social Science," pp. 69–98 in W. G. Runciman, ed., *Max Weber: Selections in Translation* (Cambridge: Cambridge University Press, 1978).

2. Ibid., p. 69.

3. Ibid., p. 85.

4. Ibid., p. 70.

5. Ibid.

6. Alvin W. Gouldner, "Anti-Minotaur: The Myth of a Value-free Sociology," in William Feigelman, ed., *Sociology Full Circle: Contemporary Readings on Society* (New York: Praeger, 1976), pp. 14–22. Originally published in *Social Problems*, Vol. 9, No. 3 (Winter 1962).

7. Ibid., p. 18.

8. Ibid., p. 20.

9. Ibid.

10. Ibid., p. 21.

11. Gunnar Myrdal, *An American Dilemma: The Negro Problem and Modern Democracy* (New York: Harper & Brothers, 1944).

12. Ibid., p. 1035.

13. Ibid., pp. 1041–1043.

14. Robert Warren and Jeffrey S. Passel, "A Count of the Uncountable: Estimates of Undocumented Aliens Counted in the 1980 United States Census," *Demography*, Vol. 24, No. 3 (August 1987), pp. 375–393.

15. David M. Heer and Jeffrey S. Passel, "Comparison of Two Methods for Estimating the Number of Undocumented Mexican Adults in Los Angeles County," *International Migration Review*, Vol. 21 (Winter 1987), pp. 1446–1473.

4 The History of U.S. Immigration Law

In this chapter I focus on the history of the legislation that has shaped immigration to the United States. To place this legislative past into context, I also review the history of the volume and characteristics of the immigrant flow into the nation. I attempt to explain why U.S. immigration law evolved as it did, focusing on the history of the policy disputes behind the laws. In this review I carefully examine the values purported to be at stake with respect to immigrant flows and the validity of the social science findings supporters and opponents of certain immigration policies utilized to back their views.

To guide the reader into an understanding of the chronological relationship between the volume and type of immigration and immigration policy, I present three tables. The first, Table 4.1, relates the foreign-born population of the United States at each census date to the total population. The second, Table 4.2, relates the number of legal immigrants during a particular decade to the estimated population of the United States at the middle of that decade. The third, Table 4.3, provides the percentage distribution by area of origin of the legal immigrants during each decade.

Unrestricted Entry: 1789 to 1874

From 1789 to 1874—for close to ninety years—the federal government had no laws directly restricting immigration. Nevertheless, during this period laws were placed into effect that directly or indirectly served to reduce the immigrant flow into the United States. The Constitution, ratified in 1789, did allow Congress to prohibit the importation of slaves beginning in 1808; moreover, in 1807 Congress enacted legislation that made the slave trade illegal as of 1808. The prohibition of the importation of slaves did not prohibit immigration per se; it simply restricted the legal status of immigrants to that of free persons. No doubt the 1808 law did indirectly and drastically reduce the volume of immigration to the United States from Africa. Moreover, even though no direct restrictions on immigration were enacted into federal law during this period, some state governments did restrict the immigration of paupers. Finally,

TABLE 4.1   Foreign-Born and Total Population of the United States, 1790–1990 (in thousands)

	Population		
	Total	*Foreign-born*	*Percent Foreign-born*
1790	3,929	500	12.8
1800	5,308	600	11.3
1810	7,240	800	11.1
1820	9,638	1,000	10.4
1830	12,866	1,200	9.3
1840	17,069	1,400	8.2
1850	23,192	2,245	9.7
1860	31,443	4,139	13.2
1870	39,818	5,567	14.0
1880	50,156	6,680	13.3
1890	62,948	9,250	14.7
1900	75,995	10,445	13.6
1910	91,972	13,630	14.7
1920	105,711	14,020	13.7
1930	122,775	14,283	11.6
1940	131,669	11,657	8.8
1950	151,326	10,431	6.9
1960	179,323	9,738	5.4
1970	203,302	9,619	4.7
1980	226,546	14,080	6.2
1990	248,710	19,767	7.9

SOURCES: Population data is from U.S. Bureau of the Census, *Statistical Abstract of the United States, 1992* (Washington, D.C.: Government Printing Office, 1992), p. 8. The numbers of foreign-born persons from 1790 through 1840 are estimates from Ernest Rubin, "Immigration and the Economic Growth of the U.S.: 1790–1914," *RGEMP [Research Group for European Migration Problems] Bulletin,* Vol. 7 (October–December 1959), pp. 87–95. The numbers of foreign-born persons from 1850 through 1990 are taken from the various decennial censuses.

it is important to mention that within this period some groups did favor federal legislation to control immigration either directly or indirectly. Before we determine the values that the opponents and proponents of free immigration held, let us discuss briefly the origins of the nation's population at the time of its first census in 1790.

According to the census of 1790, the total population of the United States was slightly more than 5 million. Of these about one-half million were American Indians; the remainder were either immigrants from Europe or Africa or the descendants of such immigrants. As shown in Table

TABLE 4.2   Number of Permanent Legal Immigrants to the United States by Decade, 1821–1830 to 1981–1990, as a Percentage of the U.S. Population at Middecade (in thousands)

	Number of Immigrants	Middecade Population[a]	Immigrants as Percent of Population[b]
1821–1830	143	11,252	1.3
1831–1840	599	14,968	4.0
1841–1850	1,713	20,131	8.5
1851–1860	2,598	27,318	9.5
1861–1870	2,315	35,631	6.5
1871–1880	2,812	44,987	6.3
1881–1890	5,247	56,552	9.3
1891–1900	3,688	69,471	5.3
1901–1910	8,795	83,983	10.5
1911–1920	5,736	98,841	5.8
1921–1930	4,107	114,243	3.6
1931–1940	528	127,222	0.4
1941–1950	1,035	141,498	0.7
1951–1960	2,515	165,324	1.5
1961–1970	3,322	191,313	1.7
1971–1980	4,493	214,924	2.1
1981–1990	7,338	237,628	3.1

[a] The middecade population is computed as the arithmetic average of population between the two consecutive decennial census dates.

[b] No data on immigrants from Mexico from 1886 through 1893 are available. Complete records on the number of immigrants arriving by land from Mexico and Canada were not kept until 1908. Prior to 1934, migrants from the Philippines were not recorded as immigrants.

SOURCE: U.S. Department of Justice, Immigration and Naturalization Service, *Statistical Yearbook of the Immigration and Naturalization Service, 1990* (Washington, D.C.: Government Printing Office, 1991), pp. 48–51.

4.4, of the total population that was not of American Indian descent, persons of African descent constituted 19.3 percent. Almost all of these were slaves, who made up 17.8 percent of the total. Of the population of European descent, the majority came from England or Wales; the rest came from other northwest European nations. Prominent among these were Germany, Scotland, Ireland, and the Netherlands.[1]

The population composition of the United States in 1790 resulted from the immigration policies in effect among the thirteen original British colonies that had transformed themselves into the United States of America. In contrast to the laissez-faire nature of immigration policy

TABLE 4.3   Percentage Distribution of Permanent Legal Immigration to the United States by Region of Last Residence, 1821–1830 to 1981–1990

	Total	Northwest Europe[a]	Southeast Europe	Asia[b]	Other Eastern Hemisphere	Canada[c]	Mexico[d]	Other Western Hemisphere
1821–1830	100.0	86.6	2.8	0.0	0.0	2.1	4.4	4.0
1831–1840	100.0	92.5	1.1	0.0	0.0	2.6	1.2	2.5
1841–1850	100.0	95.9	0.3	0.0	0.0	2.5	0.2	1.1
1851–1860	100.0	94.6	0.8	1.6	0.0	2.3	0.1	0.5
1861–1870	100.0	88.8	1.1	2.8	0.0	6.7	0.1	0.5
1871–1880	100.0	75.9	4.9	4.4	0.4	13.6	0.2	0.5
1881–1890	100.0	76.3	13.9	1.3	0.3	7.5	0.0	0.6
1891–1900	100.0	55.9	40.8	2.0	0.1	0.1	0.0	0.9
1900–1910	100.0	37.4	54.6	3.7	0.2	2.0	0.6	1.5
1911–1920	100.0	25.3	50.1	4.3	0.4	12.9	3.8	3.2
1921–1930	100.0	32.0	27.9	2.7	0.4	22.5	11.2	3.2
1931–1940	100.0	38.1	27.6	3.1	0.8	20.5	4.2	5.5
1941–1950	100.0	49.6	10.4	3.6	2.1	16.6	5.9	11.8
1951–1960	100.0	39.6	13.4	6.1	1.1	15.1	12.0	12.8
1961–1970	100.0	18.2	15.7	12.9	1.6	12.4	13.7	25.6
1971–1980	100.0	6.6	11.2	35.3	2.7	3.8	14.2	26.1
1981–1990	100.0	5.2	5.2	37.3	3.0	2.1	22.6	24.6

[a] Northwest Europe includes Austria (and Austria-Hungary when Hungary was not specified), Belgium, Denmark, France, Germany, Ireland, the Netherlands, Norway, Sweden, Switzerland, and the United Kingdom. All other European nations are considered part of southeast Europe. Turkey is included in Asia.

[b] Prior to 1934, migrants from the Philippines were not recorded as immigrants.

[c] From 1820 to 1898, figures for Canada include all of British North America. Complete records on the number of immigrants arriving by land from Canada were not kept until 1908.

[d] No data on immigrants from Mexico from 1886 through 1893 are available. Complete records on the number of immigrants arriving by land from Mexico were not kept until 1908.

SOURCE: U.S. Department of Justice, Immigration and Naturalization Service, *Statistical Yearbook of the Immigration and Naturalization Service, 1990* (Washington, D.C.: Government Printing Office, 1991), pp. 48–51.

during the early decades of the United States, the policies of the British colonies had often been quite restrictive with respect to the type of persons desired, though a high volume of immigration from proper sources was generally considered desirable.[2] Immigration was fostered by what was known as the headright system. For example, in the Virginia Colony planters who agreed to pay for the Atlantic passage of an indentured servant were not only granted that person's servitude during a four- to seven-year indentureship but were also given 50 acres of land.[3]

TABLE 4.4   Ethnic Composition of the U.S. Population, 1790

Group	Percentage of Total
English and Welsh	49.2
Scots	6.6
Ulster Irish	4.8
Other Irish	2.9
Germans	7.0
Dutch	2.5
French	1.4
Swedish	0.5
Free black	1.5
Slave black	17.8
Unassigned	5.6

SOURCE: American Council of Learned Societies, 1932, as cited in David Ward, "Immigration: Settlement Patterns and Spatial Distribution," in Stephan Thernstrom, ed., *Harvard Encyclopedia of American Ethnic Groups* (Cambridge: Harvard University Press, 1980), p. 503.

As a result of these colonial policies, almost all the non-Indian population was Protestant. Although the first Irish Catholics came to the Virginia Colony in the 1620s, only Lord Baltimore, the founder of the Maryland Colony, had encouraged immigration of Catholics, and this encouragement ended by 1699.[4] The first Jewish settlers (only twenty-three in number) came to the Dutch colony of New Amsterdam (later the British colony of New York) in 1654; other Jewish settlements soon appeared in Newport, Rhode Island; Savannah, Georgia; Charleston, South Carolina; and Philadelphia, Pennsylvania. All these original Jewish settlements were composed of Sephardic Jews (i.e., descendants of the Jews expelled from Spain in 1492). Only in 1740 did the British Parliament allow Jews in the colonies to be granted citizenship after seven years of residence and exempt them from taking the oath of citizenship "upon the true faith of a Christian."[5]

By 1790 there were pronounced regional differences in the ethnic composition of the U.S. population. In New England the English and Welsh were overrepresented and all other ethnic groups underrepresented. In the Middle Atlantic states (New York, New Jersey, and Pennsylvania), the English and Welsh were slightly underrepresented and various other European origins, including Ulster Irish (i.e., Presbyterian Scotch-Irish from northern Island), Germans, Dutch, and French, were very much overrepresented. In the southern states, blacks were greatly overrepresented and the various European groups were for the most part slightly underrepresented.[6]

There are no official data on the number of immigrants in the United States until the year 1820. Scholars agree, however, that the volume of immigration to the United States was very slight from its founding in 1789 until 1815, the year the Napoleonic Wars in Europe ended. There were two principal reasons for this small immigrant volume. The first was the policy of the British government in discouraging immigration. Specifically, in 1788 the British Parliament passed a statute extending to Ireland a long-standing ban with respect to the emigration of skilled artisans previously in force only in the remainder of the United Kingdom. Another act of Parliament, in 1803, reduced the number of passengers British ships could carry. As a consequence, ship owners could not make a profit transporting indentured servants to America. These two acts of Parliament resulted in a major reduction in the large volume of immigration from Ireland to the United States that had occurred during the last few decades of the colonial period. The second reason was the large-scale war between the French and other European nations. Because of the conflict, the substantial migration from Germany to America also practically ceased.[7]

Despite events that limited the flow of immigrants, the administration of George Washington warmly encouraged immigration. Secretary of the Treasury Alexander Hamilton, in his *Report on Manufactures,* recommended that efforts be made to attract skilled immigrant artisans. President Washington was himself temporarily involved in a scheme to import artisans but finally decided it would be inappropriate for the president of the United States to entice the subjects of another nation into violation of domestic laws. A major force in shaping pro-immigration attitudes during the Washington presidency came from land speculators who had obtained sizable tracts of land west of the Appalachian Mountains. They believed that a large flow of immigrants would provoke westward migration and lead to a rise in the price of their land.[8]

I have emphasized that until 1882 the United States had no laws directly restricting immigration. This is correct in itself. But laws with respect to naturalization or the deportation of undesirable aliens might indirectly affect the volume of potential immigrants. In fact, naturalization, that is, citizenship for immigrants, was an issue the First Congress of the United States debated in 1790. The resulting Naturalization Act of 1790 decreed that free white immigrants must be resident for only two years in the United States before being granted citizenship. In opposing the bill, however, several members of Congress urged for a much longer period of residence before citizenship could be granted.[9] Opponents of the 1790 law were therefore pleased when Congress in 1795 enacted legislation requiring a minimum period of five years of residence prior to naturalization.[10]

The revolution in France soon made the issue of naturalization salient in American politics. The ruling Federalist Party was antagonistic to the ideals of the French Revolution. The Republican Party, led by Thomas Jefferson, was sympathetic. The turmoil of the revolution in France caused many people to seek refuge in the United States. The refugees included not only French royalists but British radicals sympathetic to the revolutionary regime in France and Irish who, encouraged by the revolution, conspired to overthrow British rule. The Alien and Sedition Acts of 1798 represented an attempt by the Federalist Party under President John Adams to control the political power of what they considered to be undesirable radical elements among the immigrant population. The two Alien Acts increased the required years of residence prior to naturalization from two to fourteen years; moreover, the president was given the power to seize and expel resident aliens suspected of subversive activities. The Sedition Act applied to everyone, but in practice it was foreign-born radical journalists who were most subject to prosecution and imprisonment. The Federalist rule was, however, short-lived. In 1801 Thomas Jefferson became president, and in 1802 Congress passed a law reducing the years of residence prior to naturalization to five. Jefferson personally proposed allowing immigrants to apply for citizenship immediately upon arrival.[11]

In the Overview I mentioned that Chapter 6 contains a detailed discussion of the position of the United States in the world immigration market. But it is appropriate to bring the concept of the world immigration market into the present chapter because of its relevance for the flow of immigrants into the United States during the first part of the nineteenth century. The basic idea is that if several nations desire to attract immigrants, immigrants will come to the nation that offers them the best deal. Accordingly, a government may increase the flow of immigrants to its own nation by providing subsidies. It is significant that in the early nineteenth century several governments were offering substantial subsidies to immigrants. Among the most important of these was Russia. In the reign of Czar Alexander I, many Germans were enticed to migrate into the Caucacus, a region the Russian government wished to settle because of its fear that the area would otherwise be invaded by foreign powers. Many of the Germans died on the way, and the effort was soon abandoned. A few years later the Russian government provided similar subsidies for Germans to settle in Poland, at that time under Russian rule. This campaign proved to be remarkably successful: From 1818 to 1828 some 250,000 Germans arrived in Poland under these special auspices. During the same period the number of Germans who came to the United States was less than 10,000.[12]

A second competitor of the United States in the world immigration market was Brazil. In 1818, when Brazil was still a Portuguese colony, the Portuguese government began a campaign to attract Swiss settlers to Brazil by offering bounties and special privileges. The Swiss who went to Brazil did not find the place to their liking, and many returned to their homeland. Shortly afterward Brazil declared its independence. In 1822, undaunted by the earlier failure to attract Swiss immigrants, officials of the newly independent nation entered into negotiations to recruit German immigrants. From 1822 to about 1827, approximately 4,000 to 5,000 Germans immigrated to Brazil. Although not a large number, it was of the same magnitude as the number of Germans who arrived in the United States during the same period.[13]

A third player in the world immigration market was Canada, still under British rule. I mentioned earlier that the British Parliament in 1788 had banned the emigration of skilled artisans from Ireland. In 1823 the British Colonial Office, in a further attempt to reduce the flow of Irish settlers to the United States yet attend to the difficult economic situation in Ireland, began a program of assisted migration of Irish to Canada. The British government paid the costs of the Atlantic passage first for a group of 500 Irish and then for a second group of 2,000. Unfortunately for the goals of the British government, a significant number of these Irish soon crossed the border and settled in the United States.[14]

Would the U.S. government compete with Russia, Brazil, and Canada in the world immigration market by giving financial subsidies to settlers? The question became salient when a representative of the German confederation, Baron von Fürstenwater, came to Washington in 1818 with a proposal that the United States provide financial assistance to German settlers in the United States by giving them easier terms in acquiring land than those available to American natives. President John Quincy Adams rejected the proposal. He declared that the United States would invite none to come but would not keep out any who wished to come on their own. With respect to the purchase of western lands, natives and foreigners would be treated alike.[15]

Table 4.2 indicates that there was an exponential increase in the number of immigrants to the United States each decade from 1820 to 1860. One reason for this increase was a new development in British emigration policy. In 1825 the British government repealed its laws prohibiting the emigration of skilled artisans from either Great Britain or Ireland. A major reason for this change was the fear that if Irish emigrants were not allowed to sail to foreign lands, they would instead migrate to Great Britain and lower the state of the British peasantry to that of the Irish.[16]

A second and major reason for this jump was a reduction in the cost and hardship involved in the Atlantic passage. Although steamships had not yet appeared, sailing ships were better designed. The new longer and narrower ships were speedier than their predecessors. Moreover, navigational devices were improved, more lighthouses were built, and ocean maps became more accurate.[17] Reduced costs of transport increased trade between Europe and America. Because the goods going from America to Europe (such as cotton, tobacco, and lumber) were bulky, whereas the manufactured goods coming from Europe were not, shipping lines eager to fill their ships on the passage from Europe offered cheap fares to steerage passengers bound for the New World.[18] The French port of Le Havre, which specialized in importing cotton, was used by many immigrants from southwest Germany who sailed to New Orleans and then up the Mississippi River to St. Louis, Cincinnati, and other parts of the Midwest. Other immigrants from Germany used the port of Bremen, which specialized in tobacco imports, to sail for Baltimore. The linen trade in Ulster (northern Ireland) was dependent upon the importation of flaxseed from Pennsylvania; Presbyterians of Ulster thus secured cheap passage from Belfast to Philadelphia.

But the most important bulk import into Ireland was lumber from Canada, either from Quebec, Halifax in Nova Scotia, or St. John, New Brunswick. By the early 1830s the cost of passage from Ireland to Quebec was only half the cost of transport from Ireland to New York. Transport costs to Halifax and St. John were even lower. All three of these Canadian ports were close to New England. Consequently, the emerging migration of Catholic Irish into Puritan New England, which began in the 1820s, was in large part accomplished in two stages: a transatlantic voyage to Canada and then travel to New England.

Another major channel of trade between North America and the British Isles was between Liverpool and New York. Packets between these two cities were frequent, and a large proportion of immigrants from Great Britain and Ireland to North America employed this route despite the greater cost than the voyage to Canada. What was important was the reduction over time in the cost: In 1816–1819 passage from British ports to New York cost £10 to £12. By 1832 passage could be obtained for £6 in a packet and £4 on freight vessels.[19]

Perhaps largely because of the tremendous decline in the cost of transport, the mix of Irish immigrating to America rapidly changed: The initial waves were Scotch-Irish Presbyterian from Ulster, later immigrants were predominantly Irish Catholic. The economic position of the Scotch-Irish had always been substantially higher than that of the Catholics, and it had been easier for them to finance the voyage when fares were higher.[20] By the mid-1830s Catholics had become the majority of immigrants from Ireland, and by 1840 only about 10 percent of those immigrating to the United States from Ireland were Protestant.[21]

Cheaper transport was not the only reason for the rise in Irish immigration to the United States. The great famine in Ireland, occasioned by the blight of the potato crop beginning in 1845, created a massive out-migration. Between 1846 and 1851 over 1 million persons sailed from Ireland, most of them for the United States. U.S. immigration data indicate that almost 800,000 persons arrived in the United States from Ireland during 1841–1850 and more than 900,000 during 1851–1860.[22]

The tremendous influx of Irish Catholics into the United States following the potato famine created a whiplash of resentment, particularly in New England, which previously had been ethnically and religiously homogeneous. In 1850 a secret organization emerged with the name of the Order of the Star-Spangled Banner; its motto was "America for Americans." The organization promoted establishment of laws excluding paupers and criminals from entry to the United States, restriction of office-holding to native-born Americans, and extension of the required period for naturalization from five to twenty-one years.[23] These policies would preserve the political dominance of the Protestant faith and reduce the tax burden of the native population. Because the Order of the Star-Spangled Banner was a secret organization, members were ordered to respond to inquiries with the words, "I know nothing about it." Their movement was thus termed the Know-Nothing movement.

In 1854 the Know-Nothings gained control of the Massachusetts legislature.[24] In that state they succeeded in passing a law disbanding foreign militia units and an amendment to the state constitution prohibiting immigrants from voting until they had been naturalized for two years. By 1855 the Know-Nothings had elected six governors, dominated several state legislatures, and sent a sizable delegation to Congress. In 1856 the movement, metamorphosized into the American Party, nominated former president Millard Fillmore as its presidential candidate. His resounding defeat ended the political power of the Know-Nothings.

The collapse of the movement was in large part because the issue of the extension of slavery into the western territories had come to dominate American politics. The American Party was split into two wings with diametrically opposed views on the issue. In the northern states members of the American Party saw the Catholic Irish as opponents of their negative views on the extension of slavery. Southern members of the American Party opposed immigration, most of which was directed to the north, because they saw it as simply increasing the wealth and power of the North over the South. The southerners greatly feared that the growth of northern representation in Congress would mean losing the battle over the preservation of slavery.[25]

From 1851 to 1860 the flow of immigrants came predominantly from three nations. The largest number, 952,000, came from Germany; almost as many, 914,000, came from Ireland; and there were 424,000 from Great Britain.[26] The discovery of gold in California in 1848 initiated a new flow of immigration into the United States, that of Chinese. About 41,000 Chinese came to the United States during the 1850s and more than 64,000 during the 1860s, many of them employed to construct the transcontinental railroad that was completed in 1869. The opposition to the presence of these Chinese immigrants in California was intense.[27] An initial result of the anti-Chinese sentiment was a reaffirmation that Chinese could not become naturalized citizens. This was achieved indirectly: A law passed in 1870 to amend the existing legislation that only free whites could be naturalized extended the privilege of naturalization to aliens of African nativity and to persons of African descent—and no one else.[28]

Initial Restriction: 1875 to 1917

The period between 1875 and 1917 saw the largest decadal flow of immigrants to the United States in its entire history. In 1890 and 1910 the foreign-born population as a percentage of the total population reached peaks that have never been equaled. Another feature of immigration during this period was its shift from origins predominantly in northwest Europe to southern and eastern Europe. A major reason for the flood of immigrants into the United States was the reduced cost and much greater speed of transportation. Steamship passage across the Atlantic had been initiated in the early 1850s. Whereas the transatlantic voyage by sail had taken from one to three months, a voyage by steam took only ten days. By 1875 almost all transatlantic passengers traveled by steam rather than sail.[29]

In 1875 the U.S. government passed its first law directly restricting immigration: Legislation prohibited the entrance of convicts and prostitutes into the United States. A major reason for the law's passage was alarm at the large number of Chinese prostitutes who were being imported into the nation, presumably to service the Chinese men who were simultaneously being brought in to help build the railroads in California. Nevertheless, it was feared that they would corrupt the morals of all young men in the area.[30] For the first time in its history, the United States had created a new category of persons—illegal aliens.

Also in 1875 the U.S. Supreme Court issued a ruling that paved the way for further federal legislation concerning immigration. Previously, individual states had exercised powers to prohibit the entrance of paupers into their ports. The Supreme Court ruled that laws in California, Louisiana, and New York that restricted immigration were unconstitutional since only the federal government had the right to regulate foreign commerce.[31] The Court's ruling greatly increased the pressure for a federal law to control who should be allowed to immigrate to the United States.

Meanwhile the clamor against the Chinese immigrants in California intensified. In 1868 the federal government had concluded a treaty with China guaranteeing the Chinese free entry into the United States. In 1878 Senator Aaron Sargent, a Republican from California, introduced into the U.S. Congress a joint resolution to undo this treaty. He declared:

> Whereas it appears that the great majority of Chinese immigrants are unwilling to conform to our institutions, to become permanent citizens of our country, and to accept the rights and assume the responsibilities of citizenship; and
>
> Whereas they have indicated no capacity to assimilate with our people, Therefore
>
> Resolved, etc., That the President of the United States be requested to open correspondence immediately with the governments of China and Great Britain with a view of securing a change or abrogation of all stipulations in existing treaties which permit the unlimited immigration of Chinese to the United States.[32]

An 1879 referendum among voters in California revealed that more than 150,000 voters opposed Chinese immigration and less than 1,000 favored it. Responding to the agitation against Chinese immigration, President Rutherford B. Hayes negotiated another treaty with the Chinese government in 1880. According to the terms of the new agreement, China recognized the right of the United States to "regulate, limit, or suspend such coming or residence, but may not absolutely prohibit it."[33] In conformity with what the new treaty with China allowed, the Chinese Exclusion Act of 1882 suspended the immigration of Chinese into the United States for ten years but did not ban it indefinitely.[34]

A second immigration law enacted in 1882 contained other important innovations. In response to the Supreme Court decision that the states were not allowed to regulate immigration, the new law levied a head tax of 50 cents on each immigrant arriving by vessel at a U.S. port. Furthermore, it declared that "any convict, lunatic, idiot, or any person unable to take care of himself or herself without becoming a public charge" would be forbidden to land and returned at the expense of the owner of the vessel that had brought the immigrant to the United States. Significantly, Congress in 1882 voted down a more stringent proviso that would have excluded all persons *likely* to become public charges, not just those deemed to be public charges on arrival.[35]

The Chinese Exclusion Act, although supposedly only temporary, was renewed for an additional ten-year period in 1892. In 1902 legislation was enacted extending the suspension of Chinese immigration until such time as a new treaty with China could be negotiated. In effect, Congress now intended that the ban on Chinese immigrants should be permanent.[36] Yet the three consecutive Chinese Exclusion Acts did not end the immigration of Asians to the West Coast; they merely shifted the origin of immigrants. The Meiji era, inaugurated in Japan in 1868, ended Japanese isolation, the Japanese government allowing its citizens to emigrate abroad. By 1900 there were over 85,000 Japanese in the United States: 61,000 in Hawaii and 24,000 on the mainland, mostly in California.[37]

Following the victory of Japan over Russia in the war of 1905, the power of the Japanese in world affairs could not be denied. In 1906 the Japanese government complained to the United States that Japanese students were legally segregated from other children in San Francisco schools. The Japanese demanded an end to this practice. President Theodore Roosevelt intervened in the dispute. In early 1907 he persuaded the San Francisco school board to rescind its segregation; in return he negotiated with the Japanese government the so-called gentlemen's agreement by which Japan voluntarily agreed to suspend the immigration of workers to the United States. The only Japanese who would be allowed to immigrate in the future would be nonworkers joining family members already in the United States. It was also understood that in consequence of this voluntary agreement the United States would not enact legislation formally excluding Japanese immigrants from the United States.[38]

Meanwhile, as a result of the Spanish-American War, the Philippines in 1899 had been transformed from a Spanish colony into a colony of the United States. With the elimination of immigrant workers from China and Japan, workers from the Philippines had no competition from other Asian laborers (Korea, a colony of Japan, was included in the 1907 gentlemen's agreement). Although a number of Filipinos went to Hawaii to work in the sugarcane mills and fields, the immigration was not large. By 1920 there were fewer than 6,000 Filipinos residing in the United States.[39]

No major measures with respect to the control of immigration were enacted from the time of the gentleman's agreement with Japan until February 1917. From 1875 to 1917, however, the volume and character of immigration became far more salient to the American public. Immigration from eastern and southern Europe reached high levels around 1900 and continued until the outbreak of World War I in 1914. From 1901 through 1910 almost 8.8 million immigrants were admitted to the United States. Only 1.7 million of these came from Great Britain, Ireland, Germany, or Scandinavia. Approximately 2.1 million came from Austria-Hungary, 1.6 million from Russia, and 2 million from Italy.[40] Of the immigrants from

Austria-Hungary, Russia, and Italy, practically none were Protestants; almost all were either Catholic or Jewish.

The growing strength of the Roman Catholic church in the United States provoked a reactive social movement among Protestants. The American Protective Association founded in Iowa in 1887 had as its purpose opposition to Catholic influence in politics and the defense of the public school system. The members of this organization, most living in the midwestern states, included not only native Protestants but also many Protestant immigrants, especially from Ulster, Canada, and Scandinavia. Because a large number of its members were immigrants, the American Protective Association, although it purported to favor immigration restriction, did not take an active role in attempting to alter immigration policy.[41]

The Immigration Restriction League instead became the leader in the fight for immigration restriction during the following quarter century. This organization was founded in 1894 by five graduates of Harvard College, all of whom came from distinguished Boston Brahmin families. The group had a single political goal: to induce Congress to pass legislation establishing a literacy test in which a passing score would be a necessary prerequisite for legal immigrant entrance to the United States. Senator Henry Cabot Lodge of Massachusetts, in collaboration with league members, introduced such a bill to Congress in late 1895.[42] The issue as defined by the Immigration Restriction League was whether America should "be peopled by British, German and Scandinavian stock, historically free, energetic, progressive, or by Slav, Latin and Asiatic races, historically downtrodden, atavistic, and stagnant."[43] The legislation designed to achieve this goal, the literacy test, was based on the further fact that the level of literacy among immigrants from eastern and southern Europe was much lower than that of immigrants from northwestern Europe. The bill sponsored by Senator Lodge provided for excluding any immigrant unable to read printed passages from the Constitution, five lines in length, in any language. The final legislation drafted by a conference committee of senators and members of the House of Representatives in 1897 passed the House by a vote of 217 to thirty-six, with 125 abstentions, and the Senate by a vote of thirty-four to thirty-one, with twenty-five abstentions. The bill was then vetoed in March 1897 by outgoing president Grover Cleveland, a Democrat.[44] Although many Americans sympathized with the views of the Immigration Restriction League, opinion was not unanimous. One important group fighting against restriction of immigration was the National Association of Manufacturers, whose interest lay in securing the highest-quality laborer at any given wage. Clearly, restriction of immigration impeded this objective. Additional interest groups opposing the literacy requirement were made up of immigrants from particular origins likely to be affected by the legislation.[45]

Proponents of the literacy test were heartened on March 4, 1897, when William McKinley, a Republican, became president. McKinley had supported the literacy requirement in his inaugural speech. Congress did not then pass legislation demanding a literacy test, perhaps because of its concern with the outbreak of war between the United States and Spain over the situation in Cuba and Puerto Rico. Upon the assassination of McKinley in 1901, Theodore Roosevelt became president. In his initial annual message to Congress, he, too, supported the literacy test.[46] But the economic depression that had pervaded the 1890s and may have fostered anti-immigrant sentiment had ended. In the new period of prosperity, public opinion was more likely to be swayed by arguments that America needed immigrants for its economic development. Beginning in 1904 and continuing through 1912, the Republican Party platform no longer contained a plank in favor of immigration restriction.[47] When Congress finally passed another bill instituting the literacy test, in 1913, Republican president William Taft vetoed it.[48]

A new interest group, organized labor, then joined in the fight over the literacy test. Beginning in 1906 the American Federation of Labor (AFL) took an active role in supporting the literacy test. Union leaders believed the large flow of immigrant workers, who could be used to break strikes, could imperil the union movement.[49] Social scientists also entered the debate over immigration restriction. Social science (other than history) was just establishing itself within American universities in the period from 1875 to 1917. Several leading social scientists took up the cause of immigration restriction; among the most prominent was economist Francis Walker, whose many accomplishments included serving as superintendent of the U.S. Census Bureau for the 1880 census, first president of the American Economic Association, and president of the Massachusetts Institute of Technology. In 1890 Walker declared the new immigrants to be "beaten men from beaten races: representing the worst failures in the struggle for existence. They have none of the ideas and aptitudes which . . . belong to those who are descended from the tribes that met under the oak trees of old Germany to make laws and choose chieftans." Walker also developed the argument that immigration had not caused an increase in the American population because—though it had directly increased population growth—it had a contrary indirect effect: The presence of numerous immigrants created competition for the native population; as a result, the native population reduced its fertility. The reduction of the fertility of the native population caused a decline in population growth equal to the increase induced by immigration. Immigration thus had no effect on the overall magnitude of population growth in the United States.[50] A second individual at the forefront of the battle for immigration restriction was Edward Ross, professor of sociology at Stanford University and an early president of the American Sociological Association. Ross argued that unchecked Asian immigration might lead to the extinction of the American people. In advancing his argument, Ross accepted Walker's contention that Asian immigration would cause competition between Asians and native citizens, leading to the reduction in fertility of the latter group. Ross used the flamboyant term "race suicide" to describe the result.[51]

Not all social scientists agreed with Walker and Ross. One who opposed their ideas was Franz Boas, professor of anthropology at Columbia University, born in Germany of Jewish descent. In his *Mind of Primitive Man*, published in 1911, Boas attacked the idea that certain races were biologically superior to others.[52]

In 1915 Congress again passed a bill prescribing a literacy test for immigrants. President Woodrow Wilson vetoed the bill. A second immigration bill went through the House and Senate in early 1917. Again, Wilson vetoed it. This time, however, there were sufficient votes to override his veto. Thus the Immigration Act of 1917 became law.[53] In addition to establishing a literacy test in English or any other language, the act created a new Asiatic barred zone. No person could be admitted as a legal immigrant to the United States who came from an area including India, Indochina, Afghanistan, Arabia, the East Indies, and other smaller Asian countries—but not China or Japan, which were covered by earlier legislation or agreements.

It soon became evident that the literacy test would prove of less utility in stemming immigration from southern and eastern Europe than its proponents had expected. Literacy among the young in southern and eastern Europe had increased substantially since the 1890s, when Cleveland had vetoed the first act instituting a literacy test.[54] Perhaps this was why the literacy test was finally enacted: Employers knew that the legislation would not hinder their interests.

Maximum Restriction: April 1917 to December 1941

Shortly after the Immigration Act of 1917 was passed over President Wilson's veto, the United States declared war on Germany. The U.S. entrance into World War I soon ensured the victory of the Allied powers, and an armistice was signed on November 11, 1918. The war in Europe had drastically limited immigration to the United States. Would peace bring another tide of immigrants to the United States? Not immediately;

in 1919 the number of immigrants (141,000) was barely greater than it had been in 1918. By 1921, however, the number of immigrants exceeded 800,000, about two-thirds the number that had come to the United States in 1914.[55] Moreover, and perhaps of more importance, the proportion of all immigrants whose origins were in eastern and southern Europe remained high.[56]

The year 1921 was marked by economic recession in the United States. The economic situation was extremely important in determining popular reaction to the large number of immigrants arriving in the United States at that time. American workers, fearing for their jobs, were in no mood to countenance job competition from foreigners. As a consequence, the American Federation of Labor gained a large following for its strong support of immigration restriction.[57]

What was known as the red scare of 1919–1920 also contributed to negative public feelings about east European Jewish immigrants. In November 1917 the Bolshevik Party came to power by means of a revolution in Russia. Some of the Russian Jewish immigrants who had come to America in the wave of the "new immigration" were supporters of the Bolshevik cause and were members of the newly formed American Communist Party. In 1919 and 1920 Attorney General A. Mitchell Palmer arrested thousands of alien radicals, and hundreds of them were deported, many of them to Russia in a ship often called "the Soviet ark."[58]

The original strategy of the Immigration Restriction League had been to stem the flow of eastern and southern European immigrants indirectly by means of the literacy test. Given the failure of the literacy test to accomplish this goal, those who saw immigration from eastern and southern Europe to be undesirable decided to accomplish their aim directly, by means of a quota. In the camp favoring restriction by quota were, as earlier, a number of social scientists, both amateur and professional. Perhaps the most prominent of the amateur social scientists was Madison Grant, a New York patrician and founder of the New York Zoological Society, whose book *The Passing of the Great Race,* first published in 1916, was reprinted in 1921. Grant argued for the importance of genetics over environment for explaining differences in the success of nations. He divided the races of Europe into three types: Nordic, Alpine, and Mediterranean. Of these three the Nordic was far superior to the other two; he deemed it the "great race." Grant also maintained that interbreeding between the races resulted in a product containing the characteristics only of the inferior race. Grant excluded Jews entirely from the European races. In accordance with his views on the effects of miscegenation, he declared, "The cross between any of the three European races and a Jew is a Jew."[59]

Among the professional social scientists in sympathy with Grant was Lothrop Stoddard, a Bostonian with a Ph.D. in history. In *The Rising Tide of Color,* published in 1920, Stoddard predicted the danger to the white race from the much higher population growth rates of the nonwhite races. Ellsworth Huntington, a respected professor of geography at Yale University, also provided ammunition for the restrictionist movement in his 1924 book *The Character of Races as Influenced by Physical Environment, Natural Selection and Historical Development.* Another scientist with similar ideas was Henry Fairfield Osborn, a leading biologist, eugenicist, and demographer who not only served as head of the American Museum of Natural History in New York but was also an early president of the Population Association of America, the organization of professional demographers. In order to strengthen his argument on racial differences, Osborn even claimed that Christopher Columbus was in fact of Nordic descent.[60]

Psychologists also provided ammunition for the restrictionist movement. The IQ test, developed in France prior to World War I, was purportedly a measure of genetic mental ability, uninfluenced by environmental factors. Robert Yerkes, president of the American Psychological Association, was in charge of testing military recruits for the U.S. Army during World War I. From his analysis of mental test scores of these recruits, he concluded that soldiers born in northern Europe scored almost as well as native whites, whereas soldiers born in southern or east European nations scored significantly lower. Psychologist Carl Brigham, in his *Study of American Intelligence,* concluded, "The intellectual superiority of our Nordic group over the Alpine, Mediterranean and negro groups has been demonstrated."[61] Brigham did not take into account the possibility that soldiers born abroad might have a less than perfect knowledge of the English language and might score lower than if English were their native tongue. Nor did he take into account any other environmental factors that might have affected the scores.

Republican Warren Harding was inaugurated as president of the United States in March 1921. In contrast to Wilson, Harding favored the movement to restrict immigration. The way was now clear for a drastic alteration in America's immigration law. The Immigration Act of 1921 became law on May 19. Congressional support for the new law had been overwhelming: In the Senate the vote in favor of the bill had been seventy-eight to one, with seventeen abstentions. The basic intent of the law was to set a low quota on immigration, with separate quotas assigned to each nation equal to 3 percent of the number of foreign-born persons of that national origin enumerated in the 1910 census of the United States. The only exceptions to this rule were that (1) no immigration would be permitted from the nations constituting the Asiatic barred zone according to the law of 1917 and (2) immigration by persons who had resided continuously at least one year in a Western Hemisphere country would remain unrestricted. The act was to continue in force for only one year.[62] The result of the act was to establish a ceiling of 358,000 immigrants from the Eastern Hemisphere. Of these, 200,000 were allotted to northwest European nations, 155,000 to nations in southern and eastern Europe, and 3,000 to other Eastern Hemisphere nations outside the Asiatic barred zone. The following year the temporary law was extended for an additional two years, though many members of Congress were interested in still further restriction.[63]

The result of the demand for more restrictions was the Immigration Act of 1924, which, unlike the 1921 act, was designed to be permanent. The new law made two significant changes. First, the act abrogated the gentleman's agreement with Japan and prohibited all immigration from that nation by the indirect means of barring immigration from all nations whose subjects were not legally eligible to become U.S. citizens. Second, quotas for immigration from other Eastern Hemisphere nations were reduced, with the reduction greatest for the nations of eastern and southern Europe.

The demand for the legal prohibition of all Japanese immigrants came mainly from Californians. Discrimination against Japanese immigrants in California had been widespread. In 1913 California had passed a law barring all persons ineligible for naturalization (including the Japanese) from acquiring real estate. In 1923 the California Joint Immigration Committee was formed in order to press Congress to bar further immigration of Japanese. The organization joined representatives of the American Federation of Labor, the American Legion, and the National Grange. Responding to a warning from the Japanese government, the U.S. secretary of state, Charles E. Hughes, argued that Japan should receive a token quota of about 150 immigrants per year. The Japanese ambassador to the United States in turn wrote Secretary Hughes that "grave consequences" would follow if Congress passed legislation to exclude all Japanese immigrants. The message proved counterproductive. Senator Henry Cabot Lodge referred to it as a "veiled threat," and the Senate passed the Japanese exclusion provision by a vote of seventy-one to four.[64] In signing the Immigration Act of 1924, President Calvin Coolidge indicated his personal opposition to the Japanese exclusion provision but said he would not veto the act simply because of it. The Japanese were offended by the act, declaring a national day of mourning.[65] The resentment did not die down and became one of several incitements leading to Japan's attack on Pearl Harbor in 1941.

The Immigration Act of 1924 determined the volume of immigration from the Eastern Hemisphere, setting up a new system of quotas on a temporary basis, later to be replaced by a second, permanent system. Both systems were more restrictive than that established in the 1921 act. The new temporary system allocated immigration quotas on the basis of 2 percent of the foreign-born population of the United States as of the time of the 1890 census. This lowered the total Eastern Hemisphere quota to 164,000 per year. What is more important, the quotas for the eastern and southern European nations were reduced much more severely than the quotas for northwestern European nations. For example, the quota for Italy went from 42,000 to 4,000.[66]

The permanent quota system did not come into effect until 1929. It reduced slightly the total Eastern Hemisphere quota to 154,277. This quota applied only to the so-called principal immigrant in a family. Accompanying wives and children were allowed to enter outside the quota; the actual number of immigrants could thus be much higher than the quota.[67] The new permanent quota system was supposed to be based on the national origins of the total white population of the United States as of 1920, although there was no direct question concerning national origins for the total population in the 1920 census. The job of determining this figure was turned over to the Quota Board, a group of six statistical experts employed by the federal government and headed by Joseph Hill of the Census Bureau. The Quota Board was faced with a daunting task that could be accomplished only by making assumptions (about the national origins of the white population of the United States in 1790, about fertility, and about emigration) that could not be unanimously accepted as valid.[68]

The board's initial results also proved to be politically embarrassing. Compared to the temporary quota, the new quota for Great Britain approximately doubled, whereas the quotas for Germany, Norway, Sweden, and the Irish Free State were more than cut in half. President Coolidge was displeased with the results. So was Senator Albert Johnson of Washington State, the author of the 1924 Immigration Act. He wrote Coolidge that presidential opposition to the findings would save the Republican Party no fewer than twenty seats in the coming 1926 elections in states with large numbers of German, Scandinavian, and Irish voters. A study by a private organization, the American Council of Learned Societies (ACLS), got the Quota Board off the hook. The ACLS study, headed by a prominent genealogist and the distinguished immigration historian Marcus Hansen, determined that an earlier study the Quota Board had used to determine the national origins of the white population in 1790 from surnames in the 1790 census was biased. The ACLS concluded that only 60 percent of the white population in 1790 was of English origin, rather than 82 percent. In 1928 the Quota Board accepted the findings of the ACLS study and reduced somewhat the quota for

Great Britain while increasing it for Germany, the Irish Free State, Norway, and Sweden.[69]

Congress was divided over the issue of the new national origin quotas that would automatically go into effect on July 1, 1929, unless Congress moved to repeal them. In April 1929 the newly elected president, Herbert Hoover, called for repeal of the quotas, but the Senate Immigration Committee tabled a repeal bill. A motion to discharge the Immigration Committee from further consideration of the bill was narrowly defeated in the Senate. Senators from the southern states, where the white population was predominantly of British descent, were almost unanimously against this motion, which would help to decrease the immigration quota for Great Britain and increase the quota for other northwest European nations. Senators from the midwestern states, where there were large numbers of citizens of German, Scandinavian, and Irish stock, were almost unanimously in favor. Thus the ethnic backgrounds of each senator's constituents largely determined the vote to retain a new national origins quota system that disproportionately favored immigration from Great Britain alone.[70]

Not all social scientists supported the national origins quotas once they were enacted. Some preferred individual tests of fitness rather than what were in effect group tests of fitness. Among these was Joseph J. Spengler, a young economist and demographer who later would be elected president of both the American Economic Association and the Population Association of America.[71]

There had been considerable debate in Congress concerning restrictions on immigrants from the Western Hemisphere. A motion to include these nations under the quota system of the 1924 Immigration Act was defeated in the Senate by a vote of sixty to twelve. The debate on this amendment focused on immigration from Mexico; there was no opposition to immigration from Canada, and there was very little immigration from any other country in the Western Hemisphere. Opposition to quotas for Western Hemisphere nations was most intense among business interests in the southwestern states, who wanted to ensure access to Mexican immigrants as a source of cheap labor.[72] The strong interest of the business sector was no doubt the crucial factor in the decisive defeat of the motion.

But the issue of Mexican immigration did not die. In May 1924 Congress passed legislation authorizing the creation of the U.S. Border Patrol.[73] The purpose of the border patrol was to prevent unauthorized entry into the United States across either its northern border with Canada or its southern border with Mexico. At the time the patrol was established, Mexicans who wished to immigrate legally to the United States had to pass the literacy test, pay a $10 fee for a visa, and pay the $8 head tax.[74] Nevertheless, prior to the creation of the border patrol, many Mexicans had apparently crossed the border and worked in the United States without bothering to take the literacy test or to pay the necessary fees for legal entrance. The evidence appears in census figures: From 1900 to 1920 the number of persons in the United States born in Mexico increased by 383,000, whereas the number of legal immigrants from Mexico was only 269,000.[75]

Mexicans were not the only ones who crossed the border illegally. Chinese who wanted to enter the United States would often come to Mexico first, and many European immigrants would immigrate to Canada before illegally entering the United States. To deal with the number of long-term illegal immigrants already in the United States, Congress in 1929 passed legislation providing the first amnesty for undocumented persons; if they wished, illegal entrants who had been in the United States since June 30, 1921, were allowed to legalize their status.[76]

The stock market crash in autumn 1929 initiated America's Great Depression, which lasted more than ten years. Congress reacted in 1930 and almost passed legislation that would have further drastically reduced the number of immigrants. Following the adjournment of Congress in July 1930, President Hoover decided to take matters into his own hands. At the time legislation allowed the United States to reject any immigrant "likely to become a public charge." In September 1930 the State Department issued a press release announcing, "If the consular officer believes that the applicant may probably be a public charge at any time, even during a considerable period subsequent to his arrival, he must refuse the visa." The new policy represented a radical reinterpretation of what the public charge legislation in fact implied. The apparent success of the administrative change was indicated almost immediately; by February 1931 less than 10 percent of the available quota for Eastern Hemisphere immigrants was being used. After taking office in 1933, President Roosevelt retained Hoover's interpretation of the public charge provision.[77]

The national origins quota laws of 1921 and 1924, the reinterpretation of the public charge provision, and the scarcity of jobs during the Great Depression all contributed to the sharp drop in immigration to the United States during the 1930s as compared to the 1920s. From 1921 to 1930 the United States had admitted more than 4.1 million immigrants; from 1931 to 1940 the number barely exceeded 500,000.

Not only were there relatively few immigrants during the Great Depression, but many immigrants, as well as their American-born children, were forced to leave the United States. The great majority were Mexicans living in the southwestern states. Some were undocumented persons; others were legal immigrants who might otherwise have become public charges. The law allowed for the deportation of any legal immigrant who had become a public charge during his or her first five years of legal residence in the United States. Although relatively few legal immigrants were formally deported, many left when they were confronted by the threat that if they were officially deported as public charges they would not be able to reestablish legal status.[78]

The issue of Filipino immigration was also hotly debated during the early 1930s. Restrictionists wished to end the exclusion of the Philippines from the Asian barred zone. On the other side of the fence were the Hawaiian Sugar Planters Association and Filipino political leaders. The issue of immigration from the Philippines was eventually linked to the issue of independence for the islands. Independence was of course favored by Filipino political leaders and, of more importance, by American growers of sugarcane and sugar beets, who wanted to end competition from imports from the Philippines; Philippine independence would mean that a tariff on sugar from the Philippines could be instituted. The Philippines Independence Act of 1934 provided for independence of the islands after a ten-year period as a commonwealth, during which it was to be given a quota of fifty immigrants per year.[79]

The 1930s also witnessed the rise to power of Hitler in Germany. Beginning in 1933 and peaking in 1938, a large number of German Jews and other opponents of the Nazi regime sought to leave Germany. Those who reached the United States included an array of brilliant intellectuals, the most notable of whom was Albert Einstein.

Despite pressure from Jewish leaders and certain prominent Protestant and Catholic individuals, the U.S. government did not open the nation's doors to refugees from Nazi Germany beyond the numbers that could enter within the existing quotas. And public opinion overwhelmingly backed the government's policy: According to a survey conducted by *Fortune* magazine in 1939, 83 percent of the public was opposed to loosening restrictions for refugees. In order to aid refugees within the existing law, President Roosevelt had the State Department permit consuls outside of Germany to issue immigration visas under the German quota to persons who had already fled that nation. Another reform was instituted in early 1941 by negotiation with the Canadian government. This allowed refugees who were already in the United States on temporary visas to be prescreened for immigrant visas, cross into Canada, and then return to the United States as permanent legal immigrants. This procedure skirted the provision that an alien could not change from visitor to immigrant status without leaving the United States.[80]

The outbreak of World War II in Europe in September 1939 created new fears of alien subversion in the United States. In 1940 the United States passed legislation requiring that all aliens be fingerprinted on admission and that they register their residence on an annual basis.[81]

Liberalization: December 1941 to April 1980

Immediately following the conclusion of World War II, the United States became involved in its lengthy ideological battle with the Soviet Union. Throughout this period the goal of maximizing the power of the United States in international affairs helped determine immigration policy. It had an important effect in ending the United States' long-standing discrimination against Asian immigrants and the nation's acceptance of millions of refugees from nations under Communist rule. In part because of more liberal legislation, there was a tremendous rise in the volume of immigration to the United States during this period.

World War II strained the human resources of the United States. With immigration from Europe cut off by the war, the United States looked southward for immediate labor power. The result was an agreement with the government of Mexico for the initiation of the Mexican Labor Program (commonly called the *bracero* program). Participants in the program were not considered to be immigrants but were allowed entrance to the United States as temporary workers in agriculture and were afforded certain protections with respect to housing, transportation, food, medical needs, and wages.[82]

On December 7, 1941, the Japanese bombed Pearl Harbor. Following the U.S. declaration of war upon Japan, China, which had been at war with Japan since 1937, became an ally of the United States. It was immediately recognized that there was an incongruity between having China as an ally and prohibiting the immigration of Chinese into the United States. A visit to the United States in 1942–1943 by Madame Chiang Kai-shek, wife of the the Chinese president, catalyzed U.S. support for China. In May 1943 the Citizens' Committee to Repeal Chinese Exclusion was organized. In hearings before Congress, one witness declared, "If this is a war for world unity and world freedom, then the United States cannot practice double standards of international morality—one for the whites and the other for the Asiatics." Congressman Walter Judd of Minnesota opined that repeal of Chinese exclusion "would invigorate and galvanize" the Chinese "into more active effort and resistance, as no amount of pronouncements or Atlantic Charters or even of planes and guns can do." Despite the opposition of restrictionists, the bill to end Chinese exclusion passed both the Senate and the House in fall 1943. It provided a token quota of 105 immigrants per year for persons of the Chinese race, including those born not only in China but in any other part of the world. President Roosevelt signed the bill into law "with particular pride and pleasure."[83]

With the end of World War II and the start of the cold war, the United States tried to maximize its strength against that of the Soviet Union.

The newly independent nation of India became an early focus of attention in the battle for allies. Would India align itself with the Communist bloc or with the United States and its allies? In 1946 Congress passed legislation providing a token quota of 105 immigrants per year for persons of Asian Indian descent, whether born in India or elsewhere. The same legislation further allowed for token immigration from the Philippines, which finally became an independent nation on July 4, 1946.[84]

President Harry Truman also resolved to do something about the plight of European Jews who had survived the Holocaust and of other displaced persons, but he was constrained by U.S. immigration law. In a directive issued in December 1945, Truman authorized the use of unused visas from particular national quotas. Most of the available quotas were for German or Austrian nationals. Of some 40,000 persons admitted to the United States under this program from 1946 through 1948, 28,000 were Jewish survivors of the Holocaust.[85] But the potential number of refugees in Europe was far greater than the number that could be accommodated under existing law. In October 1946 President Truman announced that he would ask the next Congress for new legislation to deal with displaced persons. Jewish activists aligned themselves with groups seeking a larger flow of ethnic Germans displaced from their former homes in the Baltic states and elsewhere in Eastern Europe in order to escape rule by newly installed Communist governments.[86] The basic mechanism proposed was the borrowing of numbers from the future quotas of each nation together with the use of German or Austrian quota numbers for the use of ethnic Germans born in East European nations.[87] The resultant Displaced Persons Act of 1948 excluded the possibility of immigration for some 100,000 persons, mainly Jews, who had entered displaced persons camps after December 22, 1945. Truman signed the bill with reluctance, stating that the cutoff date "discriminates in callous fashion against displaced persons of the Jewish faith."[88] The debate over European refugees continued in Congress until 1950, when Truman signed into law a revision of the 1948 act with liberalized provisions both for Jews and for East European Germans.[89] Altogether some 410,000 persons were admitted to the United States under the 1948 act and its 1950 revision.[90]

Meanwhile the cold war had intensified. The fall of China to the Communists in 1949 fed the hysteria concerning the danger to the United States of domestic Communists. The Korean conflict, which began in summer 1950, pitted U.S. troops against Communist troops from North Korea and China. The Internal Security Act of September 1950 prohibited the legal immigration to the United States of any present or past member of the Communist or Fascist Party or their affiliates. This act revised existing law that had merely prohibited the immigration of persons advocating the violent overthrow of the government. Truman vetoed the bill after its passage by Congress, objecting in particular to the provision banning the immigration of past members of certain parties. Congress overrode his veto, and the bill became law.[91]

In the early 1950s pressure was placed upon Congress to modify the national origin quotas embedded in the 1924 Immigration Act. Jews and Italian Americans were particularly resentful of the act, and each of these two groups had more political power than they had had in the 1920s. Nevertheless, the majority of Congress was not yet ready for radical reform, and Senator Pat McCarran of Nevada, chairman of the Senate Judiciary Committee, which was in charge of legislation on immigration, was prepared to defend existing law. The reformers, most notably Senators Herbert Lehman of New York and Hubert Humphrey of Minnesota, introduced a bill that did not abolish the national origins quotas but did allow the use of unused quotas from northwestern European nations to be allotted without regard to national origin. In addition, their bill would have shifted the quotas to be based on the national origins of the U.S. population as of the 1950 census instead of the 1920 census. Senator McCarran's bill made few changes in existing law. One of the most important changes it did make was further to ease the restrictions on immigration from Asia. The McCarran bill allowed Asian immigrants to become naturalized citizens and allowed a quota of 100 persons for each Asian nationality regardless of actual country of birth. This feature of the bill was a sop to those who feared that additional Asian nations would fall under the Communist yoke unless their inhabitants perceived the United States to be more racially tolerant.[92]

Paradoxically, however, the bill made it more difficult for inhabitants of British, Dutch, and French colonies in the Caribbean to enter the United States. Under the preexisting law, inhabitants of these colonies could come to the United States under the quota of the respective home country. The quota for Great Britain was, of course, the most generous of all. Moreover, most of the colonial population in the Caribbean lived under British rule. The new bill gave a quota of only 100 persons to each colony or dependency of another nation.[93] Almost all the affected individuals from these colonies were blacks. Congress obviously believed it was still acceptable to discriminate against countries on racial grounds as long as there was no threat of a local Communist takeover.

Although black immigrants did not benefit from the 1952 bill, women did. The 1952 legislation not only allowed a male American citizen to bring a wife into the nation without quota but also permitted a female citizen to bring in a husband without quota and without reference to how long the two had been married.[94] Another innovation in the 1952 bill was the introduction of a preference system to distribute visas among citizens of a given nation. The highest preference was given to immigrants with levels of education, training, or abilities that were deemed to be of benefit to the United States.[95] The so-called Texas proviso was also a significant component of the bill. Included in the bill as the result of the efforts of two well-known Texans, Senator Lyndon B. Johnson and Sam Rayburn, Speaker of the House of Representatives, this proviso clearly stated that the act of employing an illegal alien was not to be considered an unlawful practice.[96]

President Truman did not sympathize with Senator McCarran and the other restrictionists; he vetoed the McCarran bill. Congress overrode his veto, and the bill emerged as the Immigration Act of 1952. Nevertheless, the debate between restrictionists and liberalizers had commenced, and the liberalizers would win a major victory in little more than a decade.

The Immigration Act of 1952 had not included any provisions for the admission of refugees. Meanwhile, the Displaced Persons Act of 1948 had expired at the close of 1951. In detailing reasons for his veto of the 1952 act, Truman had emphasized the need to accept refugees from East European nations that had come under Communist rule. Congress did respond to this plea under the administration of President Dwight Eisenhower: The 1953 Refugee Relief Act resulted in the authorization of 209,000 visas for various classes of refugees for a period extending to the end of 1956. Just before the 1953 legislation was due to expire and when practically all refugee visas had already been used, however, a new refugee crisis developed. In November 1956 the government of the Soviet Union invaded Hungary to suppress a government that the USSR considered not sufficiently friendly. As a result of the Soviet invasion, some 200,000 Hungarians found refuge in Austria and Yugoslavia. The Eisenhower administration sought a way to bring many of the Hungarian refugees into the United States. It decided to use the existing authority of the attorney general to grant aliens temporary parole in the United States for emergency reasons. Then in 1958 Congress passed a law granting permanent immigrant status to some 30,000 Hungarian refugees who had been earlier paroled.[97]

A second refugee crisis occurred when Fidel Castro's forces overthrew the regime of Fulgencio Batista in Cuba in January 1959. The immediate response of the U.S. government was to admit some 90,000 Cubans to the United States on visitor visas and then to overlook that they would overstay the period of their visas. When U.S. consular offices in Cuba were closed in January 1961, the admission of further Cuban refugees required that the attorney general's parole prerogative again be exercised. A total of 548,000 Cubans entered the United States as parolees from

1961 through 1980. Procedures for changing the status of Cuban parolees into that of permanent legal residents were contained in the Cuban Refugees Act of 1966.[98]

Shortly after Castro assumed power in Cuba, John F. Kennedy was elected president of the United States. As the nation's first president of Roman Catholic faith, Kennedy was determined to reform immigration law and do away with the national origins quotas. In 1958, prior to his campaign to become president and while still senator from Massachusetts, Kennedy had written *A Nation of Immigrants,* in which he had set forth his proposals for immigration reform. In July 1963 President Kennedy presented to Congress his proposals to eliminate the national origins quotas and the Asia Pacific triangle while preserving a nonquota status for immigration from the Western Hemisphere. Kennedy's assassination in November 1963 did not significantly change the momentum toward immigration reform. President Lyndon Johnson announced his support of reform in his January 1965 address to Congress.[99]

The resultant Immigration Act of 1965 represented a radical change in U.S. immigration policy, although it did reflect some compromises with the interests that continued to favor the national origins quotas and additional concessions to those who opposed unlimited immigration from the Western Hemisphere. The 1952 Immigration Act had given priority to those who had strong educations or high skill levels. The new act placed less emphasis on skills and more on family reunification. The American Legion and the Daughters of the American Revolution advocated reunification as a means of diluting the impact of the abolition of national origins quotas. These organizations believed that if priority were given to persons with relatives already here, only people from nations that had had high quotas under the 1952 law—namely, the nations of northwest Europe—would easily be able to enter the United States. Representatives of Asian American organizations opposed the emphasis on family reunification because they believed it would unfairly curtail immigration from Asia.[100] Attorney General Robert Kennedy accepted this argument with respect to Asian immigration. He told a House subcommittee that under the provisions of the bill he expected only 5,000 Asians to enter during the first year and practically none thereafter. Attorney General Kennedy declared that the most important impact would be an increase in immigration from such European nations as Greece, Italy, and Portugal.[101] President Johnson signed the bill into law in October 1965 after it had passed the Senate by a voice vote and the House of Representatives by an overwhelming vote of 320 to sixty-nine.[102]

The Immigration Act of 1965 had several major provisions. First, the national origins quotas were abolished in favor of uniform quotas of

20,000 immigrants each for nations in the Eastern Hemisphere; the total quota for the Eastern Hemisphere nations was 170,000. For the first time, a quota of 120,000, to begin in 1968, was established for Western Hemisphere nations, but there were no separate quotas for individual nations within the Western Hemisphere. The preference system applied only to immigrants from Eastern Hemisphere nations; it reserved 74 percent of all places for family preferences. A small number (only 10,200 of the 170,000) were to enter the United States in a preference category for refugees fleeing communism or from the Middle East. The remaining 20 percent would enter the United States in occupational preference categories. Prospective immigrants from Western Hemisphere nations were allowed to enter on a first-come, first-served basis. Applicants intending to be gainfully employed had to obtain labor certification from the secretary of labor, which was to be granted only if there were not sufficient qualified workers available to fill the particular job in the particular locality the applicant sought. In addition, except in the case of professionals, applicants could not receive certification unless they had actual job offers. In a significant exemption, however, parents of a U.S. citizen who was a minor were not required to have labor certificates.

Events soon caught up with the meager provision for refugees in the 1965 Immigration Act. Beginning in 1970 the attorney general used his power of parole to allow the entry of refugees from the Soviet Union, most of them Jews and Armenians, who could not be accommodated under the quota of the 1965 legislation. Then with the fall of the government of South Vietnam to the Communists in 1975, the attorney general again used the power of parole to admit a massive number of refugees from Vietnam, Laos, and Kampuchea. Congress passed the Indochinese Refugee Act in 1977 and the Refugee Parolees Act of 1978 to permit legal entry to these parolees.[103]

Congress eventually decided that refugee policy must be placed on a more realistic basis. The result was the Refugee Act of March 17, 1980. The new act separated out refugee admissions from the regular admission process and broadened the definition of "refugee" to conform with the definition in the 1967 United Nations Protocol on the Status of Refugees. Under the new definition a refugee was declared to be "any person who is outside any country of such person's nationality . . . and who is unable or unwilling to avail himself or herself of the protection of that country because of persecution or a well-founded fear of persecution due to race, religion, nationality, membership in a particular group, or political opinion."

The new law gave tremendous power to the president in consultation with Congress. Beginning October 1, 1982, the executive branch was required to state in advance the ceilings on the total number of refugees it wished to admit each year and on the number from each region of the world. Congress was then required to hold a hearing on these numbers. To assure that the president would adhere to these ceilings, the parole power of the attorney general was also curbed: Parole could be granted only for a "compelling reason" with respect to a particular individual. In addition to refugees, that is, persons outside their own country but also outside the United States, the new law also concerned itself with asylees, defined as persons already in the United States who feared persecution if they were to return to their country of origin. The 1980 act authorized the attorney general to grant asylum protection to such persons. It further stated that 5,000 asylees could apply each year for permanent resident status.[104]

During this era of change, two key policy shifts primarily affected immigration to the United States from Mexico. The first of these was the abolition of the Mexican Labor Program at the end of 1964, during Johnson's presidency. The program, which had begun during World War II, had gradually grown; between 1956 and 1959 the annual number of workers admitted was always at least 400,000. Nevertheless, there were always many more applicants to the program than could be admitted. The chief opposition to the program came from the AFL-CIO and various Mexican American groups, who claimed that the existence of the program reduced the wage for farm labor for American citizens. During the Kennedy administration it was agreed to increase the minimum wage of workers in the program so that the wage of citizen farm workers could rise. This made the program less attractive to employers, and in 1963 Congress passed a one-year extension of the program with the understanding that it would not be continued thereafter. In a prescient warning the Mexican government declared that the end of the program would not end the migration of Mexican farm workers to the United States; the result would simply be to make their entrance illegal.[105]

The Immigration Act of 1976 also had major implications for Mexico. The purpose of the act was to treat immigration from the Western Hemisphere on the same basis as immigration from the Eastern Hemisphere. To this end, an individual limit of 20,000 immigrants was established for each Western Hemisphere nation, in addition to the retention of the existing hemispheric limit of 120,000. This served to reduce immigration from Mexico considerably because Mexico had always been the leading Western Hemisphere nation in terms of nonrefugee immigrants. Furthermore, the preference system established in the 1965 law for immigrants from the Eastern Hemisphere was extended to immigrants from all nations in the Western Hemisphere. And in a provision important to undocumented Mexicans who wished to legalize their status, the previous labor-certification exemption for the parents of minors who were U.S. citizens was repealed.

Although he signed the 1976 bill into law, President Gerald Ford was not pleased with its impact on Mexican immigration to the United States. Citing the United States' "very special and historic relationship with our neighbor to the south," he promised to "submit legislation to the Congress in January to increase the immigration quotas for Mexicans desiring to come to the United States." But by January Ford was no longer president. Although the new president, Jimmy Carter, also supported a higher quota for Mexico, Congress did not act to change the quota.[106]

These two events, the abolition of the Mexican Labor Program in 1964 and the passage of the 1976 Immigration Act, had much to do with the rise in the illegal immigration of Mexicans to the United States. By the early 1970s this phenomenon increasingly attracted the attention of Congress, government officials, and the public. In 1973 Representative Peter Rodino of New Jersey introduced a bill imposing sanctions on employers who hired undocumented workers. His bill passed the House, but a companion bill did not pass the Senate.

In his annual report of the INS for 1974, commissioner Leonard Chapman wrote, "It is estimated that the number illegally in the United States totals 6 to 8 million persons and is possibly as great as 10 or 12 million."[107] In 1976 Chapman declared dramatically, "We're facing a vast army that's carrying out a silent invasion of the United States."[108] To provide more scientific estimates of the number of undocumented persons in the United States, Chapman commissioned a private research firm, Lesko Associates. The company first prepared an estimate of the number of illegal aliens from Mexico based on a mathematical formula that included the annual number of apprehensions of Mexicans as a crucial variable. Lesko then convened a panel of experts and asked them to reach a consensus, via the so-called Delphi method (in which experts approach a consensus during a series of consecutive pollings), concerning the total number of undocumented individuals. The use of Lesko's mathematical formula resulted in a figure of 5,204,000 undocumented Mexicans in the United States for 1975. The use of the Delphi method for estimating the total number of illegal aliens resulted in an average figure of 8.1 million. A key element in the mathematical formula was the assumption that only 2 percent of the undocumented immigrants who successfully entered the United States each year either legalized their status, voluntarily returned to Mexico, or died.[109] This assumption was contrary to the opinion of most scholars, who had good evidence for their belief that a high proportion of all Mexicans who entered the United States each year did so only on a seasonal basis.

The estimates made by Lesko Associates aroused intense controversy. In response to an inquiry from Congressman Herman Badillo of New York, Vincent Barabba, the director of the U.S. Bureau of the Census,

wrote in December 1975, "We have examined the Lesko study and analyzed the formula used to estimate the current illegal Mexican alien population of the United States. In our opinion the estimates of the current
illegal alien population shown in this study are based on weak and un-
tenable assumptions, and add very little to our knowledge of the size of
the illegal alien population."[110] The Lesko estimates were also attacked
by Jorge Bustamante, one of Mexico's leading experts on Mexican immigration to the United States.[111]

On August 5, 1977, President Carter proposed legislation to Congress
to simultaneously reduce the flow of illegal aliens, grant a legalization of
status to many of the undocumented immigrants then in the United
States, and increase the legal quota for immigrants from Mexico. Congress did not act on Carter's proposals but instead appointed the Select
Commission on Immigration and Refugee Policy to study the issue of
immigration and make recommendations on policy.

Concern with Illegal Immigration: April 1980 to the Present

The Select Commission on Immigration and Refugee Policy took almost
two years to prepare its final report, which was released on March 1, 1981.
The commission was chaired by the Reverend Theodore M. Hesburgh,
president of the University of Notre Dame; its executive director was
Lawrence Fuchs, a distinguished historian from Brandeis University.
Many other well-known social scientists served on its staff. The commission made recommendations on all aspects of U.S. policy concerning
immigrants, nonimmigrant admissions, refugees, and asylees but did
not suggest major changes in policy on topics other than illegal immigration. Public attention focused on its recommendations with respect
to that issue.

The commission's position on employer sanctions and legalization of
status for undocumented persons was similar to that previously taken
by President Carter. The commission recommended that legislation be
passed making it illegal for employers to hire undocumented workers
and that a program to legalize undocumented workers be adopted, with
eligibility to be determined by date of entry and length of continuous
residence. The commissioners were divided on whether a successful
program of employer sanctions would necessitate the creation of a new
form of personal identification for U.S. citizens and legal permanent
residents or whether existing means of identification (such as a social
security card, birth certificate, or alien identification card) would be
adequate.[112]

In July 1981 President Ronald Reagan announced a series of proposals with respect to illegal immigration that were, in rough outline, in accord with those of the select commission. In spring 1982 Republican senator Alan Simpson from Wyoming and Democractic congressman Romano Mazzoli from Kentucky introduced a bill into Congress designed to legalize the status of many existing illegal aliens and impose employer sanctions against the future hiring of illegal aliens.

Hispanic interest groups were strongly in favor of legalizing the status of undocumented immigrants, but these groups opposed employer sanctions because they feared that in practice such sanctions would provoke discrimination against Hispanics who were either U.S. citizens or legal immigrants. Restrictionists, for their part, were most concerned with instituting employer sanctions. They saw legalization of status for many of the undocumented to be the political price they would have to pay. Employers of significant numbers of undocumented workers did not want to lose their labor force; a generous amnesty program was in accord with their interests. In addition, these employers did not want to face penalties unless it could be proven that they had knowingly hired illegal aliens. And because they did not want to make such proof easy, they were not likely to favor any new system of worker identification that might make it more difficult for their undocumented workers to present fake documents or to use documents belonging to another person.

Interest in the Simpson-Mazzoli bill was not confined to the United States. On December 8, 1983, the Mexican senate passed a resolution concerning the bill addressed to Thomas O'Neill, the Speaker of the U.S. House of Representatives. The resolution declared the chamber's

> alarm and concern for the repercussions which will impact both countries if the Simpson-Mazzoli legislation is passed, since this transcendent matter should not be considered from a unilateral perspective, but rather should be treated from a bilateral and even multilateral perspective, taking into account the far-reaching migratory phenomenon of undocumented persons between our two countries.[113]

The president of Mexico, Miguel de la Madrid, also took a stand. In an article published in 1984 in *Foreign Affairs*, he expressed the following thoughts:

> Labor relations are also a matter of concern. The situation of Mexican migrant workers in the United States has been, and continues to be, of special interest. We have reiterated our support for the rights and interests of Mexican nationals abroad. We have no intention of meddling in the legislative processes of the United States. But we express our concern over measures such as the Simpson-Mazzoli bill which could affect the social, labor, and

human rights of numerous Mexicans, whose daily work and efforts represent considerable benefit to the U.S. economy.[114]

By summer 1984 both the Senate and the House of Representatives had passed quite separate versions of the Simpson-Mazzoli bill. In October 1984 the conferees from the two bodies of Congress admitted that they had not been able to reconcile their differences. In fall 1985 the Senate passed a new version of the bill. Over a year later, in early October 1986, the House passed its version by a narrow vote. This time Senate and House conferees were able to work out their differences. The compromise bill was approved by the House by a vote of 238 to 173 and by the Senate by a vote of sixty-three to twenty-four. On November 6, 1986, President Reagan signed the Immigration Reform and Control Act of 1986 (IRCA) into law.

The main features of the legislation were (1) sanctions for the knowing employment of undocumented workers, with evidence to be based on existing documents; (2) a legalization program for many of the undocumented; (3) a limited program of guest workers for agriculture; (4) a provision that warrants be obtained from a judge before INS officials could make raids in open agricultural fields; and (5) authorization for increased funding of the border patrol.

The most tangible effect of the 1986 act was its legalization program. The law allowed three classes of undocumented persons to legalize their status. The first class was made up of persons who had resided continuously in the United States since January 1, 1972. They were allowed immediately to adjust their status to that of permanent legal resident.

In the second class were persons who had resided continuously in the United States in an unlawful status since before January 1, 1982. If these persons paid the required fee ($185 for individuals and a maximum of $420 per family) during a period extending from May 5, 1987, to May 5, 1988, they were eligible to become temporary residents. As a temporary resident alien, an individual would be allowed to live and work in the United States but would not be allowed to receive benefits from federally funded, means-tested entitlement programs. After one and a half years as a temporary resident, an individual could apply to become a permanent legal resident upon demonstrating that he or she either had a minimal knowledge of or was pursuing a course of study in the English language and U.S. history and government. If accepted as a permanent resident alien, the individual would not be entitled to benefits from most federally funded, means-tested entitlement programs until five years after becoming a temporary resident.

The third class consisted of special agricultural workers who had either (1) worked for at least ninety days in agriculture in the United States during the year ended May 1, 1986, or (2) worked ninety days during each of the three years prior to May 1, 1986. Under the program for special agricultural workers (SAW), immigrants were given an eighteen-month period to register to legalize their status upon payment of the same fee charged for those who had resided in the United States since before 1982. Special agricultural workers could adjust their status to that of permanent legal resident without any further qualifications; those who had worked only in 1985–1986 were eligible to become permanent residents on December 1, 1990; those who had worked all three years were eligible to become permanent residents on December 1, 1989.

As of September 30, 1992, some 2.71 million persons had been granted permanent legal residence as a result of IRCA. Some 65,000 gained permanent legal status by reason of having been in the United States since 1972. Some 1.1 million were legalized as special agricultural workers and around 1.6 million by virtue of continuous residence since before 1982. The great majority of all these persons, approximately 2 million, were Mexicans.[115]

There appears to be good evidence that the legalization program for special agriculture workers was subject to considerable fraud. The INS had earlier estimated that nationwide only 400,000 special agricultural workers would be approved.[116] The almost 700,000 persons who applied as special agricultural workers from California appeared to be much higher than the number of such workers—estimated at less than 100,000—presumed to be eligible for legalization without fraud for that state.[117] Nevertheless, for the nation as a whole approximately 80 percent of the applications for legalization of seasonal agricultural workers were approved.[118]

The impact of employer sanctions on stemming the flow of undocumented immigrants was problematic. To avoid sanctions employers had to be able to prove that they had examined relevant documents such as a social security card or a birth certificate and a driver's license from a U.S. state. There were many reports of the presentation of fraudulent documents to employers and the impersonation of individuals with genuine documents.[119] Following the act's passage, there was a substantial reduction in the number of illegal aliens apprehended by the INS. It was uncertain how much of this reduction came about because of the deterrent impact of employer sanctions and how much because of the number of newly legalized persons who could now freely travel to and from Mexico without fear of INS apprehension.[120] Nevertheless, one careful study of the available evidence indicated that free travel among newly legalized persons could not entirely account for the lower number of apprehensions.[121]

The 1980s also produced major problems for asylees. These problems began almost immediately following the enactment of the Refugee Act of 1980. In early April a massive boatlift was initiated from Mariel, Cuba, to Key West, Florida. Essentially, Castro had decided that anyone who wished to emigrate to the United States was free to do so. In addition, he released onto the boats a large number of individuals who had been in prison because of convictions for nonpolitical crimes and those who had been confined to mental hospitals. Over the next six months, some 123,000 Cubans arrived seeking asylum. During the same period some 6,000 persons arrived by boat from Haiti also seeking asylum in the United States. But the newly enacted Refugee Act allowed for the possibility of only 5,000 asylees per year, and the claim of each applicant for asylum had to be treated on an individual basis. To solve the problem the Carter administration established a new temporary status of "Cuban-Haitian entrant" with final status to be determined later.

Since Carter did not win his bid for reelection, the final fate of the Cuban-Haitian entrants rested with the Reagan administration. Although many persons had believed that the Refugee Act of 1980 superseded the Cuban Refugees Act of 1966, the Reagan administration decided in 1984 that it did not. Accordingly, it was ruled that the Cubans, with the exception of the criminals, were admissible as refugees. The Immigration Control and Reform Act of 1986 later legalized the status of the remaining Cuban-Haitian entrants other than criminals.[122]

Reagan developed a restrictive policy toward asylees from nations without Communist governments but maintained a liberal policy toward asylees from Communist nations. Consider the policy toward Haiti, a non-Communist nation: The U.S. Coast Guard was instructed to intercept ships from Haiti carrying persons who wanted to petition for asylum in the United States and to prohibit these ships from reaching U.S. territory. Next consider policy with respect to Central American nations: In 1978 the Marxist Sandinista Party had overthrown the pro-American dictatorship of Anastasio Somoza in Nicaragua. In El Salvador a Marxist group, the Frente Farabundo Martí para la Liberación Nacional (FMLN), began a civil war against the conservative, pro-American government. Guatemala also experienced considerable civil unrest at this time. During the Reagan administration the United States provided funding for the Contras, a guerrilla army based in Honduras attempting to overthrow the Sandinista regime in Nicaragua. The U.S. government also gave large amounts of military aid to the government of El Salvador.

These conflicts in Central America predictably resulted in the flight of individuals to the United States. A large number of those who escaped the civil wars in these nations simply accepted their status as undocumented immigrants in the United States. Many others, however, applied for asylum. During the 1980s the approval rate for Nicaraguan asylum requests was over 80 percent, whereas the approval rate for persons from El Salvador and Guatemala was only about 2 to 3 percent. Moreover, the number of requests for asylum overwhelmed the system set up to consider them. By the end of fiscal 1991, the backlog of unresolved asylum cases was approximately 141,000.[123] The massive backlog of cases was advantageous to most of the petitioners since the mere act of filing for asylum gave them the legal right to work in the United States. Accordingly, even if an individual believed the chances of being granted asylum were poor, it paid to file and have a legal work permit until the case could be settled.

Less than four years after the Immigration Reform and Control Act of 1986 became law, President George Bush signed into law the Immigration Act of 1990, which substantially liberalized the immigration quotas. Unlike the 1986 act, which went through interminable debates in Congress, the 1990 act was passed quickly and received little public attention—perhaps because it was discussed in Congress following the invasion of Kuwait by Iraq, when Americans focused on whether the United States would send troops to repel the Iraqi army.

The 1990 act was extremely complicated; many aspects of the legislation are beyond the scope of our discussion. The act preserved the distinction between refugee and regular immigration that had been established in the Immigration Act of 1980. With one small exception, the new act was concerned only with nonrefugee immigration. The legislation decreed different regulations for two separate time periods: (1) fiscal 1992 through fiscal 1994 and (2) fiscal 1995 and following years. In the subsequent summary I concentrate on the provisions that either are identical in both time periods or went into effect in fiscal year 1995.

Perhaps the most important item was the increased provision for employment-based immigration. Before passage of the 1990 act, the quota for employment-based immigration had been only 54,000. The new act raised this to 140,000 beginning in fiscal 1992; of these no more than 10,000 could be unskilled workers.

The new law left the family-based preference quota at approximately the same level as under preceding legislation, namely, at 226,000 per year (compared to 216,000 under preexisting legislation). Moreover, the 1990 law did not change earlier legislation that had allowed the immediate relatives of U.S. citizens to enter the United States outside of any quota. Within the new family preference quota system, the highest preference went to the category of unmarried sons and daughters of U.S. citizens, the second highest preference was for spouses and minor children of legal permanent residents, the third preference category was for married sons and daughters of U.S. citizens, and the fourth and lowest preference category was for brothers and sisters of U.S. citizens. These preference rankings for family-sponsored immigrants were essentially the same as in preceding law.

Beginning in 1995, the act established a new category of quota immigrants, dubbed "diversity" immigrants. The attorney general was instructed to draw up a list of nations with low numbers of immigrant admissions in recent years. A total of 55,000 visa applicants from these selected nations would then be chosen by lottery to become permanent legal immigrants. To be eligible for the lottery, individuals would be required to have a high school education or its equivalent or two years' experience in an occupation requiring at least two years of training or experience. The program for "diversity" immigrants replaced a temporary program of similar nature legislated for fiscal years 1992 through 1994; in that program, however, 40 percent of all visas granted were reserved for natives of Ireland. It would appear that the first lottery for the 1992–1994 program could not have been fairly administered, as it was impossible to eliminate the numerous multiple entries prior to conducting the lottery. Indeed, one of the lottery winners admitted to sending in more than 1,000 applications.[124] It remains to be seen whether future lotteries can allow each individual applicant the same probability of receiving an immigrant visa.

Similar to preceding legislation, the 1990 law also set a limit on the quota immigration from any one nation. This limit was 7 percent of all quota immigration. In determining this national limit, however, only 23 percent of the visas allowed for spouses and unmarried children of lawful permanent residents were to be counted in the aggregate quota for all nations. This proviso was designed to help eliminate the large backlog of visa applications for spouses and unmarried children of legal permanent residents from certain nations such as Mexico.

One important temporary provision of the 1990 Immigration Act for the 1992–1994 period was a section allowing the annual admission of up to 55,000 persons who were either the spouses or children of aliens legalized under IRCA. This provision was in response to a widely voiced criticism that conditions for legalization under the 1986 law were strictly individual. Most undocumented husbands had come to the United States several years before their wives and children, and few of the husbands who had qualified as special agricultural workers had wives or children who had qualified for the same reason. The 1986 act thus resulted in many cases in which only the husband could meet the conditions for legalization of status.[125] Another provision in the new law prohibited the deportation of spouses or unmarried children of aliens who had been granted legalized status under the earlier act; this provision also gave such persons work authorization.

The 1990 law allowed persons from El Salvador who had been resident in the United States since September 19, 1990, to register for what was termed "temporary protected status" for a period of eighteen months beginning January 1, 1991. Those granted such status could not be deported and were to be given work authorization. The law further authorized the attorney general to grant temporary protected status to undocumented aliens from designated countries subject to armed conflict or natural disasters. Although the law did not deal with refugees, it did deal with asylees, increasing the number of asylees who could transform their status into permanent legal residents from 5,000 to 10,000 annually. Another noteworthy provision of the Immigration Act of 1990 was the creation of the U.S. Commission on Immigration Reform, a bipartisan commission charged with proposing future reform in immigration law.

The 1990 Immigration Act thus appeared to satisfy each of the ethnic pressure groups that wanted to liberalize regulations on immigration by members of their group abroad. In particular, the new legislation was beneficial to persons from Mexico, El Salvador, and Ireland.

The Bush administration faced two major immigration problems during its tenure. In June 1989 the government of the People's Republic of China violently suppressed massive student protests in Tiananmen Square in Beijing. A large majority of the 40,000 Chinese students in the United States had openly sympathized with the protesters and feared political persecution when they returned to China following the completion of their studies in this country. President Bush vetoed a bill granting asylee status to these students for fear that such legislation would antagonize the Chinese government. He did, however, issue an executive order on November 30, 1989, allowing all Chinese students to remain in the United States until June 1994. Then, on October 9, 1992, shortly before the presidential election in which he was a candidate, he signed a second bill, the Chinese Student Protection Act, allowing the students to become permanent legal residents under the unused slots of the quota for skilled workers contained in the Immigration Act of 1990. As of November 30, 1993, visas for permanent legal status had been granted to 43,277 persons under the provisions of the 1992 act.[126]

In 1991 President Bush's policy with respect to Haitians seeking asylum in the United States, which was the same as that of President Reagan, came under fire. At the request of the Haitian Refugee Center, a federal district judge in Miami ruled on December 4, 1991, that it was illegal for the U.S. Coast Guard to intercept Haitians at sea and send them back to Haiti. He ordered the practice stopped. The government appealed the decision to the U.S. Supreme Court, which on January 31, 1992, overruled the federal judge and ordered that his stay be revoked.[127]

Bush was defeated for reelection in 1992 by Democrat Bill Clinton. Shortly before his inauguration, the president-elect was faced with a political crisis connected to immigration law. Clinton had proposed that

Zoe Baird be named attorney general of the United States. It came to light, however, that in 1990 Baird and her husband had hired an undocumented Peruvian couple as household help. This was of course in violation of the Immigration Reform and Control Act of 1986. The nomination drew fire from many quarters, though some opinion leaders remarked that what Baird had done was not at all unusual. Clinton eventually withdrew Baird's nomination.[128]

In his campaign for the presidency, Clinton had attacked Bush's policy toward would-be immigrants from Haiti. But as president-elect he found that there was considerable opposition to a shift in policy. Accordingly, he announced on January 14, 1993, that he would continue the policies of his predecessors.[129] On June 21, 1993, the Supreme Court made its final ruling that the president of the United States had the constitutional right to order the interception of Haitian refugees at sea and use the coast guard to forcibly return them to their homeland. Only Justice Harry Blackmun dissented from the majority.[130]

On July 27, 1993, Clinton announced that he was requesting Congress to streamline procedures so that the tremendous backlog of asylum cases, estimated to number 250,000, could be cleared. He proposed that all claims for asylum be resolved within ten days with virtually no review by the courts. To accomplish this goal, he asked for an appropriation of $82 million. At the same time he asked for $90 million extra to expand the work of the U.S. Border Patrol and provide it with 600 new agents.[131]

Shortly thereafter, the Clinton administration became embroiled in yet another crisis relating to undocumented immigration. The crisis occurred at a time when Doris Meissner, Clinton's nominee for head of the INS, had not yet been confirmed by Congress. On September 19, 1993, Silvestre Reyes, chief of the border patrol in El Paso, Texas, announced his Operation Blockade, designed to curtail severely the number of undocumented immigrants entering the United States in his sector. The blockade involved the expenditure of an additional $250,000 for overtime salary payments to border patrol agents under his command and the shift of agents to the city of El Paso from other areas within the district. In addition, Reyes changed the distribution of agents within the city. Formerly, about one-quarter of the agents within El Paso had been stationed at some distance from the border. In Operation Blockade all of these agents were stationed directly at the border. Moreover, they were told their primary duty was to deter undocumented individuals from crossing the border rather than to make arrests. The transfer of agents from within the city to posts directly on the border also answered an earlier criticism that El Paso border patrol agents, congregated on the campus of Bowie High School, were arresting too many Mexican American high school students who could not be readily distinguished from undocumented immigrants.[132]

Another innovation of Reyes's plan was that apprehended illegal aliens would not simply be transported back to Ciudad Juárez, the large Mexican city directly across the Rio Grande from El Paso. Instead, they were to be taken to the town of Palomas, adjacent to Columbus, New Mexico, some 110 miles away from Ciudad Juárez[133]—even though 60 percent of the undocumented immigrants normally apprehended in El Paso were Juárez residents who were attempting to commute to jobs in El Paso rather than reach other U.S. cities.[134]

The increased numbers of border patrol personnel were used not only to prevent crossings at sites other than inspection points but also to make more thorough searches of cars and pedestrians crossing at the official inspection stations. Much of the anger against the blockade arose because those who had legal border-crossing documents faced tremendous delays as a result of inspections. Mexicans normally accounted for about one-quarter of El Paso's $4 billion annual retail trade; when they kept their business in Mexico, merchants in El Paso suffered substantially. Since the blockade also appeared to be quite effective in deterring illegal entrance into the United States, many residents of Ciudad Juárez were unable to get to their jobs in El Paso, leaving their U.S. employers without their accustomed help.[135]

The blockade was officially terminated on October 4, 1993, by which time the extra funds allocated for the operation had been completely expended. Silvestre Reyes nonetheless indicated that the innovative procedures of Operation Blockade would continue indefinitely,[136] although the name of the operation was to be changed to avoid the connotations of war: The program was renamed Operation Hold the Line.[137]

Whatever its official name, the operation received tremendous publicity in Mexican newspapers and was widely denounced as an instance of American xenophobia. On October 8 Mexico's foreign minister, Fernando Solana, observed, "This situation threatens to create tensions between the two societies that can escape the control of the two governments, damaging the general ambience of the bilateral relation."[138] The following day Mexicans protesting the blockade strangled traffic on the free bridge between Ciudad Juárez and El Paso by setting fire to a tractor.[139]

The Clinton administration tried to repair the damage to the relationship between the United States and Mexico by sending Janet Reno, who was attorney general and thus directly responsible for the activities of the INS, to Mexico City on October 11 to confer with Foreign Minister Solana.[140] Solana later proposed that the United States should, upon request, provide to the residents of each Mexican border city an official permit that would allow free entrance to the twin city on the U.S. side of the border and serve as a legal permit to work there. The United States said it would consider the proposal,[141] but had taken no further action by late 1995.

Meanwhile, Mexican activists made plans for Operation Dignity, a two-day boycott on all U.S. consumer products. Not all Mexicans supported the boycott; the president of the chamber of commerce in Tijuana indicated the opposition of his group to the idea, presumably because a boycott would hurt tourism.[142] Boycott supporters in Tijuana pronounced the campaign a success in that it had temporarily reduced the crossings of Mexicans from Tijuana into the United States by more than 60 percent and considerably cut retail sales in the southern part of San Diego County.[143]

The issue of undocumented immigration continued to engage public attention during 1994. Two matters deserve mention. First, in September 1994 the bipartisan Commission on Immigration Reform presented its report to Congress. Although the commission made a variety of recommendations, one received widespread attention: its proposal that the president immediately initiate and evaluate a pilot program to allow employers to use a computer verification system to check the status of potential hirees who might have falsified work documents.[144]

The second major happening of 1994 involved California's Proposition 187, placed before voters in the November election. The "save our state" (SOS) initiative proposed five legal measures concerning undocumented immigrants in the state. The first of these was that the children of undocumented immigrants be barred from the California public educational system from kindergarten through university and that public educational institutions begin to verify the legal status of both students and their parents. The second measure was that all providers of publicly paid nonemergency health care services verify the legal status of patients if those providers wished to receive reimbursement from the state. Under the third measure, all persons seeking benefits from the state would have to verify their legal status. The fourth proposal was that all service providers be required to report suspected illegal aliens to California's attorney general and to the INS and that police determine the legal status of those they arrested. The final measure proposed that the creation and use of false documents be considered a state felony.[145]

Perhaps the most consequential of these five measures was the ban on enrollment of undocumented persons in the public schools, although there was a lack of agreement concerning the numbers and cost involved. The state estimated that as of October 1994 almost 400,000 undocumented persons were enrolled in California's public educational system, whereas the Urban Institute put the number at only slightly higher than 300,000. The state estimated that the total cost for the education of undocumented immigrants in California was $2.15 billion; the more conservative estimate of the Urban Institute was just $1.3 billion.[146] Despite this disagreement in the estimated cost, it was incontrovertible that the total cost for the public education of undocumented persons was sizable relative to the total California state budget of $40 billion per year.[147]

The Republican governor of California, Pete Wilson, campaigning for reelection, was a vigorous supporter of Proposition 187. His Democratic opponent, Kathleen Brown, was against it, as was President Clinton. In the face of public opinion polls that showed a large majority of the state's voters in favor of the proposition, most of California's Mexican and Mexican American community mobilized to oppose the measure. In the month before the actual vote, many high school students, particularly those in Los Angeles County, left school to march in protest; television cameras recorded these students waving Mexican flags along with banners denouncing the proposition. Many political analysts believed that such television pictures only increased the vote in favor of the SOS initiative. Others declared that the new generation of Hispanic students who participated in the marches would inaugurate an era of activism and make Mexican Americans a more potent source of political influence in the state by encouraging citizenship and voting. In Mexico there were also sharp feelings about Proposition 187. Outgoing president Carlos Salinas stated that "Mexico affirms rejection of this xenophobic campaign." Just before the proposition came to a vote, protesters in Mexico City vandalized a McDonald's restaurant and several activists urged that Mexicans boycott Disneyland.[148]

On November 8, 1994, California voters approved Proposition 187 by a substantial margin: 59 percent to 41 percent. Exit polls showed that the measure was approved by 64 percent of non-Hispanic whites, 57 percent of Asian Americans, 56 percent of African Americans, and even by 31 percent of Hispanics.[149]

The provision in Proposition 187 that kept undocumented persons out of the California public educational system was in direct violation of the decision of the U.S. Supreme Court in *Plyler v. Doe*, which had declared unconstitutional a Texas law banning undocumented persons from attending the public schools. The provisions regarding denial of medical care were also in violation of federal law as embodied in the Omnibus Budget Reconciliation Act of 1986, which had stipulated that the states provide family-planning services and pregnancy-related health care to all indigent persons, regardless of legal status. (For further details, see Chapter 5.) Opponents of Proposition 187 immediately filed suit in federal court against implementation of provisions they believed violated the Constitution of the United States and federal law. On December 14, 1994, federal district judge Mariana Pfaelzer ruled in Los Angeles that most of the provisions of Proposition 187 could not be put into effect until a trial determined their constitutionality and conformance with federal law. As of late 1995 the only part of Proposition 187 allowed to take effect was that which declared the manufacture or distribution of false identification papers to be a state felony.[150]

Although President Clinton opposed Proposition 187, he took other actions during 1994 that were more pleasing to proponents of restrictive immigration policies. In August he reacted negatively to a new inflow of Cubans who came into Florida by boat, avoiding inspection. He issued a decree ending a thirty-year-old policy of automatically granting refugee status to all Cubans who succeeded in reaching U.S. territory. Despite Clinton's edict, the Cubans continued to come, and the U.S. government detained some 30,000 would-be asylees at its naval base in Guantánamo, Cuba, and elsewhere. Finally, on September 9, 1994, the United States negotiated an agreement with Cuba. The Cuban government agreed to use its powers to prevent its citizens from leaving Cuban ports; the U.S. government in turn agreed to accept a minimum number of 20,000 Cubans a year as immigrants. Most would have the refugee status.[151]

In 1994 Clinton also dealt with the problem of Salvadorans who had been granted temporary protected status under the Immigration Act of 1990. In 1992 Bush had extended the original eighteen-month period of protected status; Clinton had done the same in 1993. But the civil war in El Salvador had ended in 1992. Accordingly, Clinton announced on December 2, 1994, that temporary protected status for persons from El Salvador would end on December 31, 1994. This did not mean that the Salvadorans would have to leave immediately, but all work permits for those with temporary protected status would end on September 30, 1995. The president's action affected between 90,000 and 190,000 individuals.[152] News that the United States was contemplating the end of temporary protected status was received unfavorably in El Salvador. The nation's president, Armando Calderón Sol, asked that temporary protected status continue. His foreign minister, Oscar Santamaria, said, "We are not prepared to take these immigrants. . . . If our petition is not heard, it will jeopardize our national stability."[153]

Also on December 2, 1994, Meissner, director of the INS under the Clinton administration, announced a more stringent handling of applicants for asylum: They would no longer be able to receive a work permit until their petition had been granted or six months had elapsed. This reversed a previous policy in which applicants could obtain work permits within ninety days of requesting asylum.[154]

Conclusion

U.S. immigration policy has always been a topic of sharp controversy, revolving around the various values outlined in Chapter 2.

Chapter 4 reports events up to the end of 1994—though certainly much has occurred since then. In our time immigration is almost always in the news.

Notes

1. David Ward, "Immigration: Settlement Patterns and Spatial Distribution," in Stephan Thernstrom, ed., *Harvard Encyclopedia of American Ethnic Groups* (Cambridge: Harvard University Press, 1980), p. 503.

2. Maldwyn Allen Jones, *American Immigration*, 2d ed. (Chicago: University of Chicago Press, 1992), p. 34.

3. Ibid., p. 10.

4. Patrick J. Blessing, "Irish," in Thernstrom, *Harvard Encyclopedia of American Ethnic Groups*, pp. 525–526.

5. Arthur A. Goren, "Jews," in Thernstrom, *Harvard Encyclopedia of American Ethnic Groups*, pp. 571–575.

6. Ward, "Immigration: Settlement Patterns," p. 503.

7. Jones, *American Immigration*, pp. 56–57.

8. Ibid., pp. 57–59.

9. Ibid., p. 69.

10. Marcus Lee Hansen, *The Atlantic Migration, 1607–1860* (Cambridge: Harvard University Press, 1941), p. 66.

11. Jones, *American Immigration*, pp. 72–76.

12. Hansen, *Atlantic Migration*, pp. 108–112.

13. Ibid., pp. 112–115.

14. Ibid., pp. 115–117.

15. Ibid., pp. 94–97.

16. Jones, *American Immigration*, p. 86.

17. Hansen, *Atlantic Migration*, pp. 172–178.

18. Ibid., p. 179.

19. Ibid., pp. 180–198.

20. Blessing, "Irish," p. 525.

21. Ibid., p. 529.

22. Ibid., pp. 529–530.

23. Jones, *American Immigration*, pp. 134–135.

24. Vernon M. Briggs Jr., *Immigration Policy and the American Labor Force* (Baltimore: Johns Hopkins University Press, 1984), pp. 21–22.

25. Jones, *American Immigration*, pp. 135–138.

26. Richard A. Easterlin, "Immigration: Economic and Social Characteristics," in Thernstrom, *Harvard Encyclopedia of American Ethnic Groups*, p. 480.

27. H. M. Lai, "Chinese," in Thernstrom, *Harvard Encyclopedia of American Ethnic Groups*, pp. 218–223.

28. E. P. Hutchinson, *Legislative History of American Immigration Policy, 1798–1965* (Philadelphia: University of Pennsylvania Press, 1981), p. 58.

29. Jones, *American Immigration*, p. 158.

30. Hutchinson, *Legislative History*, pp. 63–66.

31. Briggs, *Immigration Policy*, p. 28.

32. Hutchinson, *Legislative History*, p. 71. Great Britain was included in the resolution because Hong Kong was the principal port of emigration for Chinese bound for the United States.

33. Ibid., pp. 75–76.

34. Ibid., pp. 80–82.

35. Ibid., pp. 79–80.

36. Ibid., pp. 104, 130.

37. Harry H. L. Kitano, "Japanese," in Thernstrom, *Harvard Encyclopedia of American Ethnic Groups*, p. 562.

38. Briggs, *Immigration Policy*, pp. 33–34; Kitano, "Japanese," p. 563.

39. H. Brett Melendy, "Filipinos," in Thernstrom, *Harvard Encyclopedia of American Ethnic Groups*, pp. 354–359.

40. Easterlin, "Immigration," p. 480.

41. Jones, *American Immigration*, pp. 219–220; John Higham, *Strangers in the Land: Patterns of American Nativism, 1860–1925* (New York: Atheneum, 1973), pp. 79–87.

42. Higham, *Strangers*, pp. 102–103.

43. Jones, *American Immigration*, p. 222.

44. Hutchinson, *Legislative History*, pp. 116–121.

45. Jones, *American Immigration*, p. 224.

46. Hutchinson, *Legislative History*, pp. 121–128.

47. Jones, *American Immigration*, p. 224.

48. Hutchinson, *Legislative History*, p. 154.

49. Higham, *Strangers*, pp. 163–164.

50. Ibid., pp. 142–144; Easterlin, "Immigration," pp. 484–485.

51. Higham, *Strangers*, p. 147.

52. Ibid., pp. 125, 153.

53. Hutchinson, *Legislative History*, pp. 163, 167.

54. William S. Bernard, "Immigration: History of U.S. Policy," in Thernstrom, *Harvard Encyclopedia of American Ethnic Groups*, p. 492.

55. U.S. Department of Justice, Immigration and Naturalization Service, *An Immigrant Nation: United States Regulation of Immigration, 1798–1991* (Washington, D.C.: Government Printing Office, 1991), p. 34.

56. Bernard, "Immigration," p. 492.

57. Robert A. Divine, *American Immigration Policy, 1924–1952* (New York: Da Capo Press, 1972), p. 8.

58. Jones, *American Immigration*, pp. 54–55; Higham, *Strangers*, pp. 226–233.

59. Higham, *Strangers*, pp. 155–157, 271–272.

60. Ibid., pp. 272–277.

61. Ibid., pp. 275–276.

62. Hutchinson, *Legislative History*, pp. 176–181.

63. Briggs, *Immigration Policy*, p. 43.

64. Divine, *American Immigration Policy*, pp. 21–23.

65. Briggs, *Immigration Policy*, p. 45.

66. Ibid., pp. 43–44.

67. Ibid., pp. 44–45.

68. Divine, *American Immigration Policy*, pp. 28–30.

69. Ibid., pp. 30–33.
70. Ibid., pp. 47–48.
71. Ibid., p. 51.
72. Ibid., pp. 52–54.
73. Briggs, *Immigration Policy*, p. 47.
74. Arthur F. Corwin, "A Story of Ad Hoc Exemptions: American Immigration Policy Toward Mexico," in Arthur F. Corwin, ed., *Immigrants—and Immigrants: Perspectives on Mexican Labor Migration to the United States* (Westport, Conn.: Greenwood Press, 1978), p. 144.
75. David M. Heer, *Undocumented Mexicans in the United States* (New York: Cambridge University Press, 1990), p. 26.
76. Thomas J. Espenshade, *A Short History of U.S. Policy Towards Illegal Migration*, Policy Discussion Paper, Program for Research on Immigration Policy, PRIP-UI-8 (Washington, D.C.: Urban Institute, 1990), p. 3.
77. Divine, *American Immigration Policy*, pp. 78–79, 88–89.
78. Abraham Hoffman, "Mexican Repatriation During the Great Depression: A Reappraisal," in Corwin, *Immigrants—and Immigrants*, pp. 225–247.
79. Melendy, "Filipinos," pp. 354–356.
80. Divine, *American Immigration Policy*, pp. 92–104.
81. U.S. Department of Justice, *An Immigrant Nation*, p. 15.
82. Briggs, *Immigration Policy*, pp. 98–99.
83. Divine, *American Immigration Policy*, pp. 146–152.
84. Ibid., pp. 152–154.
85. Ellen Percy Kraly, "U.S. Refugee Policies and Refugee Migration Since World War II," in Robert W. Tucker, Charles B. Keely, and Linda Wrigley, eds., *Immigration and U.S. Foreign Policy* (Boulder: Westview Press, 1990), pp. 76–77.
86. Ibid., p. 107.
87. Ibid., pp. 88–89.
88. Divine, *American Immigration Policy*, pp. 120–128.
89. Ibid., pp. 140–142.
90. Kraly, "U.S. Refugee Policies," p. 79.
91. Divine, *American Immigration Policy*, pp. 162–163.
92. Ibid., pp. 164–182.
93. David M. Reimers, "Recent Immigration Policy: An Analysis," in Barry R. Chiswick, ed., *The Gateway: U.S. Immigration Issues and Policies* (Washington, D.C.: American Enterprise Institute for Public Policy Research, 1982), p. 27.
94. Hutchinson, *Legislative History*, pp. 471–472.
95. Vernon M. Briggs Jr., *Mass Immigration and the National Interest* (Armonk, N.Y.: M. E. Sharpe, 1992), pp. 100–102.
96. Arthur F. Corwin and Johnny M. McCain, "Wetbackism Since 1964: A Catalogue of Factors," in Corwin, *Immigrants—and Immigrants*, p. 87.
97. Kraly, "U.S. Refugee Policies," pp. 79–81.
98. Ibid., p. 81.
99. Reimers, "Recent Immigration Policy," pp. 33–34.
100. Briggs, *Mass Immigration*, pp. 110–111.
101. Reimers, "Recent Immigration Policy," p. 35.
102. Ibid., pp. 37–38.

103. Kraly, "U.S. Refugee Policies," pp. 83–84.

104. Briggs, *Mass Immigration,* pp. 124–129.

105. Briggs, *Immigration Policy,* pp. 98–102.

106. Reimers, "Recent Immigration Policy," p. 43.

107. U.S. Department of Justice, Immigration and Naturalization Service, *1974 Annual Report* (Washington, D.C.: Government Printing Office, 1974), p. iii.

108. L. H. Whittemore, "Can We Stop the Invasion of Illegal Aliens?" *South Bend Tribune,* February 29, 1976.

109. Lesko Associates, "Final Report: Basic Data and Guidance Required to Implement a Major Illegal Alien Study," prepared for the U.S. Immigration and Naturalization Service, Washington, D.C., October 1975.

110. Letter of December 23, 1975, from Vincent P. Barabba to Congressman Herman Badillo, cited in Jorge A. Bustamante, "Immigration from Mexico: The Silent Invasion Issue," in Roy Bryce-Laporte, ed., *Sourcebook on the New Immigration: Implications for the United States and the International Community* (New Brunswick, N.J.: Transaction Books, 1980), pp. 139–144.

111. Bustamante, "Immigration from Mexico," pp. 139–144.

112. Select Commission on Immigration and Refugee Policy, *U.S. Immigration Policy and the National Interest: The Final Report and Recommendations of the Select Commission on Immigration and Refugee Policy to the Congress and the President of the United States* (Washington, D.C.: Government Printing Office, 1981).

113. Richard D. Lamm and Gary Imhoff, *The Immigration Time Bomb* (New York: Truman Talley Books / E. P. Dutton, 1985), p. 219.

114. Miguel de la Madrid H., "Mexico: The New Challenges," *Foreign Affairs,* Vol. 63, No. 1 (1984), pp. 62–63.

115. Calculated from data presented in the following publications of the U.S. Department of Justice, Immigration and Naturalization Service: *Statistical Yearbook of the Immigration and Naturalization Service, 1989* (Washington, D.C.: Government Printing Office, 1990); *Statistical Yearbook of the Immigration and Naturalization Service, 1990* (Washington, D.C.: Government Printing Office, 1991); *Statistical Yearbook of the Immigration and Naturalization Service, 1991* (Washington, D.C.: Government Printing Office, 1992); *Statistical Yearbook of the Immigration and Naturalization Service, 1992* (Washington, D.C.: Government Printing Office, 1993).

116. Michael D. Hoefer, "Background of U.S. Immigration Policy Reform," in Francisco L. Ribera-Batiz, Selig L. Sechzer, and Ira N. Gang, eds., *U.S. Immigration Policy Reform in the 1980s* (New York: Praeger, 1991), p. 38.

117. Philip L. Martin and J. Edward Taylor, *Harvest of Confusion: SAWs, RAWs, and Farmworkers,* Policy Discussion Paper, Program for Research on Immigration Policy, PRIP-UI-4 (Washington, D.C.: Urban Institute, 1988), p. 19.

118. U.S. Department of Justice, *Statistical Yearbook, 1991,* p. 71.

119. Marita Hernandez, "INS Reports 'Dramatic' Rise in Fake Work Papers," *Los Angeles Times,* November 17, 1988, p. 1.

120. Hoefer, "Background," p. 42.

121. Frank D. Bean, Thomas J. Espenshade, Michael J. White, and Robert F. Dymowski, "Post-IRCA Changes in the Volume and Composition of Undocu-

mented Migration to the United States: An Assessment Based on Apprehensions Data," in Frank D. Bean, Barry Edmonston, and Jeffrey S. Passel, eds., *Undocumented Migration to the United States: IRCA and the Experience of the 1980s* (Washington, D.C.: Urban Institute Press, 1990), pp. 111–158.

122. Briggs, *Mass Immigration,* pp. 129–133.

123. U.S. Department of Justice, *Statistical Yearbook, 1991,* p. 78.

124. Seth Mydans, "For Winners in Visa Lottery, Round 2," *New York Times,* November 29, 1991, p. A-22.

125. Heer, *Undocumented Mexicans,* pp. 172–174.

126. Robert Pear, "Bush Rejects Bill on Chinese Students," *New York Times,* December 1, 1989, p. A-9; U.S. Department of Justice, Immigration and Naturalization Service, "Adjustment of Status: Certain Nationals of the People's Republic of China," *Federal Register,* July 1, 1993, p. 35832; Independent Federation of Chinese Students and Scholars, "IFCSS Keeps Track of CSPA Implementation," News Release No. 5082 of the Independent Federation of Chinese Students and Scholars, November 30, 1993.

127. Briggs, *Mass Immigration,* pp. 135–137.

128. Joe Davidson, "Baird Says She Regrets Hiring Illegal Aliens," *Wall Street Journal,* January 20, 1993, p. A14; David Lauter and Ronald J. Ostrow, "Under Fire, Baird Withdraws Bid for Attorney General," *Los Angeles Times,* January 22, 1993, p. A1.

129. Stephen Buel, "Clinton Revises Haitian Policy," UPI Newswire, ClariNet Electronic News Service, January 15, 1993.

130. UPI, "Supreme Court Allows Forcible Return of Haitian Boat People," UPI Newswire, ClariNet Electronic News Service, June 21, 1993.

131. David Lauter, "Clinton Asks New Rules on Asylum," *Los Angeles Times,* July 28, 1993, p. A1.

132. Sebastian Rotella, "Texas Border Crackdown Stems Tide, Raises Tensions," *Los Angeles Times,* October 2, 1993, p. A1; Robert Tomsho, "Matter of Principle: High School in El Paso Gives the Border Patrol a Civil-Rights Lesson," *Wall Street Journal,* February 23, 1993, p. A1.

133. Rotella, "Texas Border Crackdown."

134. "Desplomo comercial en El Paso por el bloqueo del SIN," *Diario 29, El Nacional* (Tijuana, Mexico), October 14, 1993, p. 30.

135. Rotella, "Texas Border Crackdown."

136. "Será permanente Operación Bloqueo aún sin fondos: Patrulla fronteriza," *Diario 29, El Nacional* (Tijuana, Mexico), October 20, 1993, p. 30.

137. Frank D. Bean, Roland Chanove, Robert G. Cushing, Rodolfo de la Garza, Gary P. Freeman, Charles W. Haynes, and David Spener, *Illegal Mexican Migration and the United States/Mexico Border: The Effects of Operation Hold the Line on El Paso/Juarez* (Washington, D.C.: U.S. Commission on Immigration Reform, 1994), p. 10.

138. David Aponte, "Creará tensiones tratar a migrantes con medidas policiacas, dice Solana," *La Jornada* (Mexico City), October 10, 1993, p. 3.

139. Rubén Villalpando, Angel Amador Sánchez, and Rodrigo Ibarra, "Estrangulan el puente libre Juárez–El Paso," *La Jornada* (Mexico City), October 10, 1993, p. 1.

140. Notimex, "Refrendó Solana la defensa de indocumentados ante Janet Reno," *Diario 29, El Nacional* (Tijuana, Mexico), October 12, 1993, p. 3.

141. David Aponte, "Propone la SRE crear un documento migratario para residentes fronterizos," *La Jornada* (Mexico City), October 27, 1993, p. 3.

142. Martina M. Miranda, "Comerciantes de Tijuana y de San Diego se openen activamente a la Operación dignidad," *Diario 29, El Nacional* (Tijuana, Mexico), October 26, 1993, p. 5.

143. Horacio Renteria, "Se redujo en más del 60% el cruce de Mexicanos a EU durante dos dias," *Diario 29, El Nacional* (Tijuana, Mexico), November 22, 1993, p. 3; Leonel Sanchez, "Protest Rally at Border Fence Caps Boycott by Mexicans," *San Diego Union-Tribune,* November 22, 1993, p. B1.

144. U.S. Commission on Immigration Reform, *U.S. Immigration Policy: Restoring Credibility* (Washington, D.C.: U.S. Commission on Immigration Reform, 1994).

145. "187 Approved in California," *Migration News,* Vol. 1, No. 11 (December 1994), pp. 1–5.

146. Rebeccah L. Clark, Jeffrey S. Passel, Wendy N. Zimmerman, and Michael E. Fix, *Fiscal Impacts of Undocumented Aliens: Selected Estimates for Seven States* (Washington, D.C.: Urban Institute Press, 1994), p. 90.

147. "187 Approved in California," p. 2.

148. Ibid., pp. 4–5.

149. Ibid., pp. 1, 3.

150. Paul Feldman and Patrick J. McDonnell, "U.S. Judge Blocks Most Sections of Prop. 187," *Los Angeles Times,* December 15, 1994, p. A1; "187—Enforcement Stayed," *Migration News,* Vol. 2, No. 1 (January 1995), pp. 3–4.

151. "US Sets Quota for Cuban Immigrants," *Migration News,* Vol. 1, No. 9 (October 1994), pp. 2–3.

152. "Salvadorans' TPS to Expire," *Migration News,* Vol. 2, No. 1 (January 1995), pp. 1–2.

153. Tracy Wilkinson, "Salvadorans Gird for Losses as Special Status in U.S. Ends," *Los Angeles Times,* December 1, 1994, p. A1.

154. "US Changes Asylum Regulations," *Migration News,* Vol. 2, No. 1 (January 1995), pp. 2–3.

5 Patterns of Immigration to and from the United States

This chapter presents the available data on the current volume of immigration to the United States and goes into considerable detail on the characteristics of immigrants. Before treating these topics, we look at the relationship between the *flow* of immigrants and the *stock* of immigrants as well as the relationship between the flow of immigrants and total population change during a particular period.

The flow of immigrants is defined as the number of foreign-born persons entering the nation as usual residents in a given period. The stock of immigrants is defined as the number of foreign-born persons in the nation at a given point in time. In large part the annual flows of immigrants determine the stock of immigrants at any one time. But two other factors, emigration and death, also determine the stock of immigrants. The best analogy to the stock of immigrants is that it represents the level of water in a bathtub in which both the faucet and the drain remain open. The flow of water into the tub represents the inflow of immigrants and the outflow into the drain represents the exits from the stock of immigrants caused by either death or emigration of the foreign-born. If you look back at Table 4.1, you can see that the stock of the foreign-born population of the United States increased uninterruptedly from 1790 to 1930. In that period the flow of immigrants was always greater than the number of foreign-born persons who either emigrated or died. From 1930 to 1970, however, the stock of foreign-born persons declined; during these decades the number of foreign-born persons who died or emigrated was consistently larger than the number of immigrants. Since 1970 the stock of immigrants has again risen. This implies that the immigrant flow has been greater than the outflow of the foreign-born.

Demographers like to utilize a concept known as the net immigration of the foreign-born. This is defined as the difference between the number of foreign-born persons who immigrate to the nation during a given period and the number of foreign-born persons who emigrate from the nation during the same period. Making use of this term, one can define the change in stock of the foreign-born population during a given time

Koreatown, Los Angeles, California.

Little India, Artesia, Los Angeles County, California.

as equal to the net immigration minus the deaths to the foreign-born population.

The concepts of flow and stock are also useful with respect to the total population of the United States. Here again the two relevant inflows are births and immigration and the two relevant outflows death and emigration. But in this case it is essential that not only the births and deaths but also the acts of immigration and emigration refer to the total population. Thus, in order to count total emigration, we must reckon not only with the the emigration of the foreign-born but also with the number of native-born who leave the nation to seek residence elsewhere. Similarly, in order to count total immigration, we must reckon not only with the immigration of foreigners but also with the number of native-born citizens who, after a period of residence outside the nation, return to reside there again. The total population change within a given period can then be defined as the number of births plus the number of acts of immigration minus the number of deaths and the number of acts of emigration. Demographers define the difference between the number of births and the number of deaths for the total population as natural increase, and they call the difference between the number of events of immigration and the number of events of emigration for the total population as net immigration. Demographers thus commonly subdivide the total population change into a portion attributable to natural increase and a portion attributable to net immigration.

The numbers of births, deaths, and events of immigration or emigration can each be subdivided. One may usefully distinguish the births to native mothers from the births to foreign-born mothers, the deaths to the native population from the deaths to the foreign-born population, and events of immigration and emigration pertaining to the native population from those pertaining to the population born outside the nation. If we make these distinctions, we can calculate what is called the net contribution of immigration of the foreign-born to total population change for a given period: the number of foreign-born immigrants plus the births to foreign-born mothers minus the number of foreign-born persons who died and minus the number of foreign-born persons who emigrated.

It is often but not always the case that the net contribution of immigration of the foreign-born to total population change is substantially larger than the net immigration of the foreign-born. Provided that the current immigrant flow consists mainly of young adults, there will be few deaths to the foreign-born population and many births to foreign-born mothers. In this case the net contribution of immigration of the foreign-born to population change will be considerably larger than the net immigration of the foreign-born.

Without making a distinction between events to the foreign-born or native-born population, we can also calculate what is called the net contribution of immigration to population change: the difference between the actual population change that *did* occur in a particular period given the presence of both immigration and emigration and the population change that *would have* occurred in that time if there had been no immigration or emigration. For the United States, the numerical difference between the net contribution of immigration of the foreign-born and the net contribution of immigration is very slight simply because the net immigration of the native-born is so small.

We are now equipped with most of the conceptual tools necessary to understand the remainder of this chapter. In the next section we consider the most important sector of the inflow of foreign-born persons into the United States—permanent legal immigrants.

The Inflow of Legal Immigrants

Table 5.1 allows us to see how the various provisions of our complicated laws concerning immigration affect the number of immigrants. The table shows the number of immigrants admitted to the United States by major category of admission for fiscal years 1992 and 1991. Admissions for fiscal year 1992 are the first to reflect the Immigration Act of 1990, which substantially increased the number of employment-based immigrants and created additional categories for admission. Because of the importance of the Immigration Act of 1990 for determining the number of immigrants admitted to the United States in fiscal 1992, I have included Table 5.2, which shows the various immigration limits established in the 1990 act for fiscal year 1992.

Now let us look at what Table 5.1 shows concerning immigration for fiscal years 1992 and 1991. In addition to reflecting the Immigration Act of 1990, admissions for fiscal year 1992 also reflect the passage of the Immigration Reform and Control Act of 1986. For fiscal year 1992, IRCA legalizations represented some 17 percent of all immigrant admissions. Admissions for fiscal year 1991, however, were much more heavily impacted by the legalization program of the 1986 act, which accounted for more than 60 percent of all immigrants admitted that year. In future years there will be relatively few additional legalizations of status under IRCA; the INS has stated that as of the end of fiscal year 1992, only 110,000 persons eligible to become permanent legal residents under IRCA had not already become such.[1] Most of these should have been able to obtain permanent legal residence in fiscal 1993.

The impact of the Immigration Act of 1990 is manifest in the differences between the numbers of employment-based immigrants for fiscal 1992 and fiscal 1991. The number of such immigrants almost doubled, reaching some 116,000 in 1992. The 1990 act also resulted in the admis-

TABLE 5.1   Immigrants by Major Category of Admission, Fiscal Years 1992 and 1991

Category of Admission	1992	1991[a]
Grand total	973,977	1,827,167
Total exempt from limitations	558,473	1,551,554
Total IRCA legalizations	163,342	1,123,162
Resident since 1982	46,962	214,003
Special agricultural workers	116,380	909,159
Total others exempt from limitations	395,131	428,392
Immediate relatives of U.S. citizens	235,484	237,103
Spouses	128,396	125,397
Parents	64,764	63,576
Children	42,324	48,130
Amerasians	17,253	16,010
Soviet and Indochinese parolees	13,661	4,998
Refugee and asylee adjustments	117,037	139,079
Exempt for other reasons	11,696	31,202
Total subject to limitations	415,504	275,613
Family-sponsored immigrants	213,123	216,088
First preference	12,486	15,385
Second preference	118,247	110,126
Third preference	22,195	27,115
Fourth preference	60,195	63,462
Employment-based immigrants	116,198	59,525
First preference	5,456	–
Second preference	58,401	–
Third preference	47,568	–
Fourth preference	4,063	4,576
Fifth preference	59	–
Pre-1992 employment preference	651	54,949
Diversity transition immigrants	33,911	–
Legalization dependents	52,272	–

[a] A dash indicates that the category did not exist until fiscal year 1992.

SOURCE: U.S. Department of Justice, Immigration and Naturalization Service, *Statistical Yearbook of the Immigration and Naturalization Service, 1992* (Washington, D.C.: Government Printing Office, 1993), p. 32.

sion of some 34,000 "diversity transition" immigrants (admitted under a temporary diversity program before the permanent program went into effect, in fiscal 1995) and some 52,000 dependents of individuals legalized by IRCA.

An important datum in Table 5.1 is the very high number of persons admitted without quota each year as immediate relatives of U.S.

TABLE. 5.2   Immigration Limits for Fiscal Year 1992

Preference	Description	Limit
Family-sponsored		226,000
First	Unmarried sons and daughters of U.S citizens	23,400 plus numbers not used in fourth family preference
Second	Spouses, children, and unmarried sons and daughters of permanent resident aliens	114,200 plus numbers not used in first family preference
Third	Married sons and daughters of U.S. citizens and their spouses and children	23,400 plus numbers not used in first and second family preferences
Fourth	Brothers and sisters of U.S. citizens (at least twenty-one years of age) and their spouses and children	65,000 plus numbers not used in first, second, and third family preferences
Employment-based		140,000
First	Priority workers and their spouses and children. Priority workers are (1) persons of extraordinary ability, (2) outstanding professors and researchers, and (3) certain multinational executives and managers.	40,040 plus numbers not used in fourth and fifth employment preferences
Second	Professionals with advanced degrees or aliens of exceptional ability and their spouses and children	40,040 plus numbers not used in the first employment preference

(continues)

TABLE 5.2   (Continued)

Third	Skilled workers, professionals without advanced degrees, needed unskilled workers, and their spouses and children	40,040 plus numbers not used in the first and second employment preferences (although the number of unskilled workers is limited to 10,000)
Fourth	Special immigrants and their spouses and children	9,940 (although the number of certain religious workers is limited to 5,000)
Fifth	Employment-creating investors and their spouses and children	9,940
Diversity transition immigrants	Aliens from countries adversely affected by amendments to the Immigration and Nationality Act of 1965 and their spouses and children	40,000, of which 16,000 are reserved for Ireland
Legalization dependents	Spouses and children of aliens legalized under the Immigration Reform and Control Act of 1986	54,255

SOURCE: U.S. Department of Justice, Immigration and Naturalization Service, *Statistical Yearbook of the Immigration and Naturalization Service, 1991* (Washington, D.C.: Government Printing Office, 1992), p. A.2-3.

citizens, that is, as spouses or children of citizens or as parents of citizens aged twenty-one or older. In fiscal 1992 more than 235,000 persons entered as immediate relatives, a number equal to 29 percent of all the non-IRCA immigrants. Why is the number of immigrants in this category so high? Consider first the number of spouses admitted as immediate relatives of U.S. citizens. A large proportion of these spouses were women who married U.S. servicemen stationed overseas. In many other cases they were persons already in the United States, perhaps as students or undocumented aliens, who sought to become permanent resident aliens. By finding U.S. citizens willing to become their spouses, they could become permanent legal residents even though they did not qualify to enter the United States under either the employment-based or the family-preference quotas. Children of U.S. citizens include stepchildren, adopted children, and orphans. Since there is a shortage of adoptable babies in the United States, many infants born abroad who cannot be supported by their natural mothers are adopted by U.S. citizens.

A category of immigrants who come in without quota are Amerasians. These are either children born in Cambodia, Korea, Laos, Thailand, or Vietnam after December 31, 1950, and before October 22, 1982, who were fathered by a U.S. citizen, or they are the spouses, children, parents, or guardians of a child fathered by a U.S. citizen and born in Vietnam between January 1, 1962, and January 1, 1976. In fiscal 1992 some 17,000 persons were admitted to the United States as Amerasians.

Finally, we should take note of the number of refugee and asylee adjustments and the number of parolees from the USSR and Indochina. These persons were also admitted outside of any quota and in fiscal 1992 numbered around 131,000, a number somewhat lower than in 1991.

To what extent is a particular category of admission associated with immigrants from a specific nation? Table 5.3 sheds light on this question. The table presents data on the top nation with respect to the number of immigrants admitted from specific categories in fiscal 1992 and on the top nation with respect to the percentage of all immigrant admissions emanating from the specific category. It also breaks down data on the number of admissions from this category for all nations and on the proportion of immigrants from all nations who entered the United States under the particular category. It is evident that there is a strong association between immigration from particular nations and immigration in a particular category. We see, for example that those born in Mexico made up the majority of IRCA legalizations as well as the majority of persons admitted as legalization dependents (members of the immediate families of persons previously legalized under IRCA). Somewhat surprising, however, is that the top nation with respect to the proportion of all immigrants who were in the category of IRCA legalizations was Haiti. Over 78 percent of all admissions from Haiti were within this one category, compared to only 17 percent for the immigrants admitted from all nations. Moreover, the top nation with respect to the proportion entering under the category of legalization dependents was not Mexico but El Salvador. Around 31 percent of all entrants from El Salvador fell into this

TABLE 5.3   Comparison of Top Nation and All Nations by Major Category of Admission
and Percentage of Total Immigrant Admissions per Category, Fiscal Year 1992

Category	Number Admitted from Category	Percentage Admitted from Category
IRCA legalization		
Top nation	122,470 (Mexico)	78.1 (Haiti)
All nations	163,342	16.8
Immediate relative of U.S. citizen		
Top nation	30,572 (Philippines)	74.0 (Germany)
All nations	235,484	24.2
Amerasians		
Top nation	17,181 (Vietnam)	22.1 (Vietnam)
All nations	17,253	1.8
Refugee and asylee adjustments		
Top nation	33,504 (former USSR)	92.3 (Laos)
All nations	117,037	12.0
Family-sponsored		
Top nation	33,361 (Mexico)	63.1 (Dominican Republic)
All nations	213,123	21.9
Employment-based		
Top nation	11,058 (China)	65.9 (South Africa)
All nations	116,198	11.9
Diversity transition		
Top nation	10,066 (Ireland)	82.3 (Ireland)
All nations	33,911	3.5
Legalization dependents		
Top nation	28,449 (Mexico)	31.1 (El Salvador)
All nations	52,272	5.4

SOURCE: U.S. Department of Justice, Immigration and Naturalization Service, *Statistical Yearbook of the Immigration and Naturalization Service, 1992* (Washington, D.C.: Government Printing Office, 1993), pp. 44–45.

category, compared to only around 5 percent of the immigrants from all nations.

Now let us examine the principal countries of birth for the fiscal 1992 immigrants. Data on this topic are shown in Table 5.4. In comparison with the past, Europe provided only a small proportion—less than 15 percent—of all immigrants. More than 39 percent of all immigrants came from North America. The number of immigrants from Mexico, almost 214,000, or 22 percent of the total, was considerably larger than that from all European nations combined. The number of immigrants

TABLE 5.4   Number and Percentage Distribution of Immigrants by Region and Country of Birth for the Top Twenty Countries of Birth, Fiscal Year 1992

Region and Country of Birth	Number of Immigrants	Percentage Distribution
All countries	973,977	100.0
Africa	27,086	2.8
Asia	356,955	36.6
China	38,907	4.0
India	36,755	3.8
Iran	13,233	1.4
Japan	11,028	1.1
Korea	19,359	2.0
Philippines	61,022	6.3
Taiwan	16,344	1.7
Vietnam	77,735	8.0
Europe	145,392	14.9
Ireland	12,226	1.3
Poland	25,504	2.6
Soviet Union	43,614	4.5
United Kingdom	19,973	2.1
Oceania	5,169	0.5
North America	384,047	39.4
Canada	15,205	1.6
Mexico	213,802	22.0
Caribbean	97,413	10.0
Cuba	11,791	1.2
Dominican Republic	41,969	4.3
Haiti	11,002	1.1
Jamaica	18,915	1.9
Central America	57,558	5.9
El Salvador	26,191	2.7
South America	55,308	5.7
Colombia	13,201	1.4

SOURCE: U.S. Department of Justice, Immigration and Naturalization Service, *Statistical Yearbook of the Immigration and Naturalization Service, 1992* (Washington, D.C.: Government Printing Office, 1993), pp. 30–31.

from Asia, about 357,000, was more than twice the number of immigrants from Europe and represented about 37 percent of all immigrants.

But the percentage distribution by country of birth of the fiscal 1992 immigrants is not necessarily a good guide to the percentage distribution of immigrants by country of birth in future years, assuming that immigration law is not changed. In particular the high number of immigrants from Mexico in fiscal 1992 was due in large part to some 122,000 persons legalized by IRCA and an additional 28,000 persons entering as legalization dependents. By fiscal 1995, when the program for legalization dependents terminated, it is likely that the number of immigrants from Mexico will descend to around 65,000 to 70,000. Moreover, the future volume of refugees from particular nations may also change with changing international conditions.

What were the intended destinations of legal immigrants admitted to the United States in fiscal 1992? The official INS data show that a very high proportion of all immigrants intended to reside in only a few states and metropolitan statistical areas. In rank order these states were California, New York, Texas, Florida, New Jersey, and Illinois. The most important metropolitan statistical areas in rank order were Los Angeles–Long Beach, California; New York, New York; Chicago, Illinois; Anaheim–Santa Ana, California; and Miami–Hialeah, Florida. The Los Angeles–Long Beach metropolitan statistical area, with less than 4 percent of the nation's population, received more than 13 percent of all fiscal 1992 immigrants.[2]

For five metropolitan statistical areas in California, most immigrants were from Mexico, Vietnam, the Philippines, and El Salvador. For the New York City area, the origins of immigrants were very different: The largest numbers came from the Dominican Republic, the former USSR, China, and India. Moreover, immigrants from certain nations were heavily concentrated in only a few of these metropolitan areas, whereas immigrants from other nations were widely dispersed among all areas. For example, more than half of all immigrants from the Dominican Republic intended to reside in the New York metropolitan statistical area, and almost half of all immigrants from El Salvador in the Los Angeles–Long Beach area. In contrast, the intended residences of immigrants from the United Kingdom were widely dispersed among the ten metropolitan areas listed.[3]

The distribution of permanent legal immigrants by age and sex is very different from that of the total U.S. population. Table 5.5 shows this difference in detail for the year 1992. It is evident from the table that for both males and females a higher proportion of immigrants were aged between ten and thirty-nine years than was the total population. But among both males and females, immigrants were less likely to be under age ten or aged forty or higher than was the total population. For both sexes combined, 66.5 percent of all immigrants were aged ten to thirty-nine, whereas only 46.2 percent of the total population in 1992 was in this age group. Yet only 9.9 percent of all immigrants were less than ten years old, as compared to 14.8 percent of the total population. Furthermore, only 19.7 percent of all immigrants were aged forty to sixty-four, as compared to 26.3 percent of the total population, and only 3.8 percent of

TABLE 5.5   Distribution by Age and Sex of Immigrants in Fiscal Year 1992 Compared to Total U.S. Population on July 1, 1992

	Immigrants		U.S. Population	
Age Group	Male	Female	Male	Female
All ages	51.0	49.0	48.8	51.2
Under 5 years	2.0	1.9	3.9	3.7
5 to 9 years	3.1	2.9	3.7	3.5
10 to 14 years	3.9	3.6	3.6	3.4
15 to 19 years	5.0	4.7	3.4	3.3
20 to 24 years	6.2	5.7	3.8	3.7
25 to 29 years	8.2	7.3	4.0	3.9
30 to 34 years	6.7	6.1	4.4	4.4
35 to 39 years	4.7	4.4	4.1	4.2
40 to 44 years	3.2	3.1	3.6	3.7
45 to 49 years	2.2	2.2	3.0	3.1
50 to 54 years	1.7	1.9	2.3	2.4
55 to 59 years	1.3	1.6	2.0	2.1
60 to 64 years	1.1	1.4	1.9	2.2
65 to 69 years	0.8	1.1	1.8	2.2
70 to 74 years	0.5	0.6	1.4	1.9
75 to 79 years	0.2	0.3	1.0	1.5
80 years and over	0.1	0.2	1.0	2.0

SOURCE: Data on the distribution by age and by sex of immigrants in fiscal year 1992 are from U.S. Department of Justice, Immigration and Naturalization Service, *Statistical Yearbook of the Immigration and Naturalization Service, 1992* (Washington, D.C.: Government Printing Office, 1993), p. 52. Data on the age and sex distribution of the U.S. population in 1992 is from U.S. Bureau of the Census, "State Population Estimates by Age and Sex: 1980 to 1992," by Edwin R. Byerly, *Current Population Reports,* Ser. P-25, No. 1106 (November 1993), p. 7.

immigrants were aged sixty-five years or older, in considerable contrast to 12.7 percent of the total population.

Undocumented Immigrants

Although there is no consensus among scholars concerning the number of undocumented immigrants currently residing in the United States, there is much more agreement on the number and characteristics of undocumented persons who resided in the United States in 1980. (Remember from Chapter 3 Warren and Passel's study of the number of undocumented persons counted in the 1990 census.) We also have a great deal of data concerning the persons who legalized their status by means of IRCA. In view of these facts, much of this section of the chapter is devoted to reviewing the characteristics of undocumented persons in the United States in 1980 and the characteristics of the population legalized under IRCA. Before we go on, however, let us consider attempts to answer two questions: How many undocumented persons were counted in the 1990 census? And how many undocumented persons were residing in the United States in October 1992?

The reason we are much less certain about the number of undocumented immigrants counted in the 1990 census than the number counted in the 1980 census is that we no longer possess a significant data source concerning the stock of legal aliens living in the United States. A provision of the Internal Security Act of 1950 had directed that aliens residing in the United States register their addresses with the INS each January. But early in the administration of President Reagan, on December 20, 1981, Congress passed a law eliminating this requirement, saying that the cost of the registration was too great given what it considered a reduced threat to national security from the presence of aliens in the United States.[4]

In Chapter 3 I provided a description of the method by which Warren and Passel estimated the number of undocumented persons counted in the 1980 census. To summarize their methodology, the basic idea was to estimate the number of undocumented persons counted in the 1980 census as the adjusted number of nonnaturalized persons of foreign birth counted in the census minus the adjusted number of persons who were registered as legal aliens in January 1980.[5]

Now suppose we want to estimate the number of undocumented persons in the United States who were counted in the 1990 census. In the absence of a registration of legal aliens, what can we do? Obviously, we should attempt to make use of the concepts developed at the beginning of this chapter concerned with the relationships between stock and flow. We can begin with the stock of foreign-born persons in 1980 subdivided by whether they were undocumented or legally present. Taking as base the stock who were legally present in April 1980, we can add the number of new legal immigrants (permanent and temporary, as long as their length of stay causes them to be considered usual residents according to the definition of the Census Bureau) during the decade, and subtract the emigrants and deaths among those legally present. The resulting number should equal the stock of legally present persons counted in the 1990 census. We can then subtract this number from the total number of foreign-born counted in the 1990 census to obtain the number of undocumented persons counted in that census.

There will be little controversy about the number of deaths to legal immigrants during the decade. We will know the age and sex distribution of the legal immigrants and can simply apply the same age-sex-specific death rates to legal immigrants as apply to the total population. But the number of legal immigrants who emigrated from the United States from 1980 to 1990 will be in dispute. Because we had a registration of legal aliens for January 1980, we can estimate the number of individuals who entered the United States prior to 1980 but who must have emigrated. Without such a registration in 1990, we must assume that the proportion of legal immigrants present in 1980 or immigrating into the United States in the 1980s was the same as occurred during the 1970s. For nations other than Mexico, there may not be too much error in assuming that for each nation of birth the proportion who emigrated during the later decade was the same as the proportion who emigrated during the earlier decade. For Mexico, however, the situation becomes far more complicated.

The reason for this complexity is the ambiguous place of residence of Mexicans legalized under IRCA, particularly of the 1 million legalized as special agricultural workers. Permanent legal aliens do not necessarily lose that status if they never reside in the United States. A decision of the U.S. Supreme Court in 1929 established that those who have been admitted to the United States as permanent legal residents retain that status even if they do not reside in the United States, provided they have been absent from a U.S. job for no more than six months. The Supreme Court reiterated this opinion in another decision handed down in 1974.[6] In the late 1970s Arthur Corwin estimated that the number of permanent legal residents of the United States who were habitual residents of Mexico was around 100,000. Around half of these lived in Mexican border cities and commuted daily into the twin city on the U.S. side of the boundary. The remainder lived in the interior of Mexico and commuted seasonally to jobs in the United States.[7]

We also have evidence from a major survey conducted in Mexico by the Mexican government between mid-December 1978 and mid-January 1979 that altogether 750,000 persons who considered themselves to be residents of Mexico worked in the United States at some time during 1978.[8] If we assume with Corwin that only 100,000 of these were permanent legal residents of the United States, we end up with 650,000 persons who said they lived in Mexico in 1978 but who worked illegally in the United States. We do not know how many of these 650,000 lived at least six months in the United States and therefore should have been counted according to the rules of the U.S. Bureau of the Census as usual residents of the United States.

One assumption that in my opinion is extreme would be that none of the Mexicans legalized under the SAW program became usual residents of the United States. An alternative extreme assumption would be that all

Mexicans legalized under the SAW program became usual residents of the United States. Because the number of Mexicans legalized as special agricultural workers totals 1 million, it follows that with the first extreme assumption the estimate of undocumented persons in the United States would be 1 million higher than with the second extreme assumption.

Karen Woodrow-Lafield, a demographer at the State University of New York at Albany (and formerly on the staff of the Census Bureau as an associate of Passel), estimated the number of undocumented persons who were counted in the 1990 census.[9] She titled the paper in which her results were reported "Undocumented Residents in the United States in 1989–90: Issues of Uncertainty in Quantification." Thus she was well aware of the measurement difficulties inherent in making such an estimate. Nevertheless, for the estimate she considered most likely, she assumed that none of the 1 million Mexicans legalized under the SAW program remained in the United States as usual residents. Using this assumption, she estimated that there were 3.212 million undocumented persons counted in the 1990 census. Had she made the opposite assumption—that all Mexicans legalized under the SAW program had remained in the United States—her estimate of undocumented persons counted in the 1990 census would have been reduced to 2.212 million.

An additional complication is that the definition of an undocumented immigrant became more problematic in the interval between the 1980 census and the 1990 census. By 1990 there were many persons whose status was illegal but who could not be immediately deported. For example, many who entered the United States without documents in the 1980s, particularly those from El Salvador, had immediately applied for asylum. Pending resolution of their requests for asylum, they could not be deported. Moreover, among those denied asylum, many had been granted the privilege of voluntary departure within thirty days. A third complicating factor was the presence of Chinese who were in the United States, either as students or as visitors, at the time of the Tiananmen Square incident in June 1989. According to President Bush's 1989 decree, these Chinese could not be deported until early June 1994 even if their original visas had expired. If we define the term *undocumented persons* as all usual residents of the United States on April 1, 1990, without legal permission for their residence, we will obtain a higher number of undocumented persons than if we define them only as usual residents of the country on an illegal basis who could be legally deported if apprehended.

Furthermore, with the passage of the Immigration Act of 1990, additional numbers of undocumented persons became nondeportable. Specifically, temporary protected status was extended to 194,000 El Salvadorans; in addition, spouses and minor children of persons legalized by IRCA gained freedom from the possibility of deportation.

Another problem in estimating undocumented immigrants occurs because of the large number of people in the United States granted visas as temporary visitors for business (more than 2.6 million in fiscal 1991) or pleasure (more than 14.7 million in fiscal 1991). Some of them, particularly those here on business, may have been in the United States on April 1, 1990, with a planned stay of at least six months and therefore should have been counted in the 1990 census.

Woodrow-Lafield presented a second calculation for the size of the undocumented population in 1990 in which she increased the figure for the legally resident population in 1990 by 1 million. In her calculation she redefined the legally resident population to include individuals without proper documents who could not be legally deported. She also assumed that there were more visitors here on temporary visas who would have been counted as usual residents of the United States at the time of the 1990 census than had been assumed for the first calculation. Consequently, her alternative estimate of undocumented persons for 1990 fell to 2.212 million. It is important to note that if she had also assumed that all Mexicans legalized under the SAW program did become usual residents of the United States, then her estimate of the number of nondeportable undocumented aliens in the United States counted in the 1990 census would have been reduced to 1.212 million.

Further uncertainty surrounds the number of undocumented persons living in the United States as usual residents who were not counted in either the 1980 or the 1990 census. The Bureau of the Census conducted several ethnographic surveys both at the time of a 1986 special census of the central part of Los Angeles County and at the time of the 1990 census to find out why certain people who should have been counted were not. A review of these studies indicates that a substantial number of undocumented persons were not counted in either census. One reason was that many of them lived in illegal housing units. Perhaps the most cited example is from James Diego Vigil's study of El Jardin, a neighborhood located in a working-class suburb of Los Angeles in which almost everyone was either of Mexican birth or Mexican descent. The housing in this neighborhood consisted of small, single-family houses with detached garages. Perhaps compelled by the high price of housing in Los Angeles, many of the householders rented out their garages or other backyard buildings as housing units. A number of the tenants in these garages and other structures were undocumented and were not counted in the 1986 special census because the occupants of the houses did not want to admit that they had violated the law in converting these structures into housing units.[10] Pini Herman and I inspected another neighborhood heavily populated by Mexicans and those of Mexican descent, a section of East Los Angeles where lot sizes were relatively large but there were few garages. We found that on many of the lots, in addition to the main house, there was a second, smaller structure in the backyard. These second structures had been built illegally and may often have housed undocumented persons, but these residents were not likely to have been included in the 1986 special census because, as in El Jardin, the owners of the main houses feared their illegal buildings would be discovered.[11]

Nevertheless, it appears likely that the great majority of undocumented persons in the United States live in legally constructed housing units (even though these units may be in poor condition), and thus they will be included in a decennial census. Two leading experts, Arthur Corwin and John Crewdson, have previously pointed out that the Bureau of the Census had gone out of its way to convince undocumented immigrants that they should be counted in the 1980 census.[12] Moreover, Crewdson also emphasized that local officials in cities with large numbers of undocumented persons were fully aware that federal funding was dependent on the size of the census count and were motivated to take action to ensure that substantial undercount would not occur.[13]

With regard to the undercount of undocumented persons in the 1980 census, Passel and Woodrow stated the following:

> The actual coverage of undocumented aliens in the 1980 Census, either for the entire nation or by state, remains unknown. A number of factors point toward reasonably complete coverage of this group. First, coverage of housing units in the 1980 Census was virtually complete and undercount of all legal residents was on the order of 1 percent. Given these assertions and the marked increase in the number of foreign-born counted in 1980 relative to 1970, it seems unreasonable to claim that undercoverage of undocumented aliens was 3 or more times the undercoverage of the group with the highest measured undercount, black males in their 30s who were missed in 1980 at a rate of 1 in 6.[14]

Despite the controversy surrounding the number of undocumented persons who were not tallied in the census, it is obviously more useful to have an estimate of the total number of undocumented persons in the nation than an estimate of those who were counted in a particular decennial census. In fall 1993 the Statistics Division of the INS, headed by Robert Warren, published such an estimate for the date of October 1992. The division estimated that as of that time there were 3.2 million illegal aliens residing in the United States. Only 31 percent, 1.002 million, were from Mexico. A key assumption the Statistics Division made was that everyone who had been legalized under the SAW program remained in the United States. Another important feature of this INS estimate was a broad definition of *illegal alien* to include nondeportable persons who had been given temporary protected status. The 1993 INS estimate for illegal aliens in October 1992 was almost identical to the number of un-documented persons that Woodrow believed were counted in the 1990 census. But since the INS estimate was for a date 2.5 years later than the Woodrow estimate and was supposed to be a count of the total illegal alien population, it was obvious that its estimate was much smaller than Woodrow's. The most important reason was the INS decision to assume that all workers legalized under the SAW program had remained in the United States.[15]

But social scientists do not always stick to extreme positions. In a paper delivered to a California conference in April 1994, Warren revised estimates published in the 1993 paper. He increased the estimate of the total undocumented population in October 1992 from 3.2 million to 3.379 million. He also revised upward the number of undocumented persons from Mexico from 1.002 million to 1.321 million, primarily be-cause he no longer assumed that all the persons legalized under the SAW program had remained in the United States. His new assumption was that 114,000 of these 1 million Mexicans were not usual residents of the United States. In his revised estimate he assumed a total of 327,000 undocumented immigrants from El Salvador, 129,000 from Guatemala, 97,000 from Canada, 91,000 from Poland, and 90,000 from the Philip-pines. He estimated fewer than 90,000 illegal aliens born in any other nation.[16]

As I have emphasized throughout this section, the assumptions nec-essary to estimate the number of undocumented aliens currently in the United States are controversial, whereas our knowledge of the number of undocumented persons living in the United States who were counted in the 1980 census rests on much firmer ground. Moreover, there can be no dispute concerning the number and characteristics of those who were legalized by IRCA.

We can now go on to examine the characteristics of undocumented persons in the United States (1) according to the data of Warren and Passel for those counted in the 1980 census and (2) according to the data on persons legalized under IRCA. We begin with a look at composition by country of birth. Table 5.6 shows that slightly over half of the undocu-mented population counted in the 1980 census came from Mexico. In contrast, almost 75 percent of all legalization applicants were from Mex-ico. In 1980 only two nations other than Mexico were estimated to have provided at least 50,000 undocumented immigrants: Iran and El Sal-vador. Only three nations besides Mexico supplied 50,000 or more appli-cants for legalization: El Salvador, Guatemala, and Haiti.

I defer until slightly later a discussion of the possible reasons for the discrepancies between the two data sources concerning country of ori-gin. For the moment, we may focus on data on the geographic distribu-

TABLE 5.6   Estimates of Undocumented Aliens in the United States by Country of Birth and Legalization Applicants by Type and Country of Birth (in thousands)

Country of Birth	Undocumented Aliens, 1980	Legalization Applicants[a]		
		Total	Resident Since 1982	Special Agricultural Workers
Total	2,057	3,032	1,760	1,272
Mexico	1,131	2,267	1,228	1,038
Iran	58	15	15	1
El Salvador	51	168	143	25
Haiti	44	60	16	44
Jamaica	39	19	13	6
United Kingdom	38	8	7	1
Guatemala	28	71	53	18
Cuba	27	–	–	–
Colombia	27	35	26	8
Canada	25	12	11	1
China and Taiwan	25	16	12	3
India	18	22	4	18
Philippines	16	29	19	10
Peru	15	20	13	7
Pakistan	–	22	5	17

[a] A dash signifies that data were not published separately because of the small number involved.

SOURCES: The 1980 figures for undocumented immigrants are from Robert Warren and Jeffrey S. Passel, "A Count of the Uncountable: Estimates of Undocumented Aliens Counted in the 1980 United States Census," *Demography*, Vol. 24, No. 3 (August 1987), pp. 380–381. Data on legalization applicants are from U.S. Department of Justice, Immigration and Naturalization Service, *Statistical Yearbook of the Immigration and Naturalization Service, 1991* (Washington, D.C.: Government Printing Office, 1992), p. 72.

tion of the undocumented aliens counted in the 1980 census and of the applicants for legalization. Almost half the undocumented aliens counted in the 1980 census were living in California; similarly, about 54 percent of the applicants for legalization were living in California at the time of their application. In 1980 the Los Angeles–Long Beach metropolitan statistical area had an unusual concentration both of undocumented persons (32 percent of the total) and of applicants for legalization (26 percent). In contrast, the percentage of all undocumented aliens in 1980 who lived in Texas (only 9 percent) was substantially lower than the number of legalization applicants applying from that state (almost

15 percent). Furthermore, the percentage of undocumented persons living in New York State in 1980 (more than 11 percent) was far higher than the proportion of legalization applicants from New York State (less than 6 percent). Another noteworthy datum is the predominance of undocumented Mexicans in the states of California, Texas, and Illinois in 1980 and undocumented immigrants from other nations in New York State, Florida, and the Washington, D.C., metropolitan statistical area. Finally, we should note the large number of persons legalized as special agricultural workers who applied from the two largest U.S. metropolitan areas: 189,000 from the Los Angeles–Long Beach area and 47,000 from the New York City area.[17] The 189,000 legalized through the SAW program from the Los Angeles–Long Beach area may be compared to a total of only 36,945 working there in agriculture according to the 1980 census.[18]

We may also compare the distribution by age and sex of the undocumented immigrants in 1980 with that of the applicants for legalization. These data are shown in Table 5.7. We see that the proportion of males is much higher among legalization applicants (almost 68 percent) than among the undocumented persons counted in the 1980 census (around 53 percent). Not shown in the table is the additional fact that among legalization applicants continuously present since 1982, the proportion male was only 57 percent, whereas among those applying as special agricultural workers the proportion male was 82 percent.[19] Finally, note that the age distribution of undocumented aliens in 1980 is distinctly younger than that of applicants for legalization.

What does a comparison of Warren and Passel's estimates and the number of legalized persons tell us about the accuracy of those estimates? In answering that question, let us first examine why there were so many more legalization applicants in Texas than undocumented persons counted in the 1980 census. I believe the discrepancy was caused at least in part by error in the calculation of the number of undocumented persons in Mexican border communities. I have earlier mentioned Corwin's estimate that there were 50,000 permanent legal residents of the United States who actually resided south of the border and commuted on a daily basis to a job in the United States. In order to avoid daily complications in crossing the border, most of these commuters probably registered themselves as living in the twin city on the U.S. side of the border. For example, Passel's estimate for the number of undocumented Mexicans in Laredo, Texas, was a negative number (minus 1,000).[20] This could easily have resulted even if there were a large number of undocumented Mexicans in Laredo, if the number of legal Mexican immigrants who resided in Laredo at the time of the 1980 census was substantially less than the number who registered themselves as living there in January 1980. In contrast, the greater proportion of un-

TABLE 5.7   Percentage Distribution by Age and Sex of Undocumented Aliens and
Legalization Applicants

Age Group	Undocumented Aliens, 1980		Legalization Applicants	
	Male	*Female*	*Male*	*Female*
All Ages	53.2	46.8	67.7	32.3
Under 15 years	9.4	8.8	1.1	1.1
15 to 24 years	17.0	13.1	13.4	5.8
25 to 34 years	17.4	14.8	28.8	12.2
35 to 44 years	7.0	6.5	15.6	8.3
45 to 64 years	2.2	2.9	8.3	4.3
65 years and over	0.2	0.8	0.6	0.6

SOURCES: Data for undocumented aliens in 1980 are from Robert Warren and Jeffrey S. Passel, "A Count of the Uncountable: Estimates of Undocumented Aliens Counted in the 1980 United States Census," *Demography*, Vol. 24, No. 3 (August 1987), p. 384; data for legalization applicants are from U.S. Department of Justice, Immigration and Naturalization Service, Office of Strategic Planning, Statistics Division, *Provisional Legalization Application Statistics, December 1, 1991* (Washington, D.C., n.d.), table 4.

documented immigrants in 1980 in New York State than legalization applicants might be interpreted as implying that Warren and Passel over-adjusted for the underregistration of legal aliens in January 1980. Alternatively, it may have resulted simply because many of the undocumented immigrants in New York were visa overstayers who had no intention or desire of remaining there permanently and hence did not apply for legalization.

The much higher proportion male among legalization applicants than among undocumented persons counted in the 1980 census does not in my opinion reflect adversely on the accuracy of Warren and Passel's estimates. As can be shown from data I collected in Los Angeles County (presented in Table 5.8), undocumented husbands tended to have been in the United States longer than their wives. Given the condition that one must have maintained continuous residence since January 1, 1982, one would expect a higher proportion of men than women to qualify on that basis. Furthermore, it is likely that a higher proportion of undocumented men than undocumented women who should have been included in the 1980 census were not. Furthermore, the high proportion male among the special agricultural workers is congruent with all other information we have concerning seasonal Mexican migrants to the United States, whether or not they were employed in agriculture. Finally, we may note that we would also expect the average age of the legalization applicants

TABLE 5.8   Legal Status of Mothers and Fathers of Mexican Origin, Los Angeles County, 1980–1981

	Undocumented	Legal Immigrant	Native-born Citizen
Mothers			
Mean age	25.8	27.8	25.3
Percent without conjugal partner	15.3	9.9	29.3
Mean number of persons in household	5.49	5.27	4.76
Mean year of first arrival in United States	1975	1970	–
Mean years of school completed	5.6	7.6	11.6
Percent who completed school in United States	5.3	28.0	–
Percent with no ability to speak English	66.0	27.0	0.5
Percent living in a census tract in which at least 40 percent of the population was black	16.4	7.9	3.6
Percent of mother's children retarded two grades in school	12.2	3.3	1.2
Percent of those in labor force who were unemployed	25.8	16.2	4.3
Percent of those employed who were in white-collar occupations	4.5	21.0	70.0
Percent receiving below minimum wage	54.0	15.8	15.0
Mean annual personal income	$2,507	$3,135	$4,562
Mean annual couple income	$10,475	$14,858	$17,338
Percent with private health insurance	32.6	57.4	50.8
Percent with Medi-Cal for self or baby	15.5	18.8	44.5
Percent receiving food stamps	18.9	15.8	19.3
Percent receiving AFDC payments	1.9	2.9	12.6
Percent with federal income tax deducted from pay	88.4	99.5	99.2
Fathers			
Mean age	29.0	30.6	28.6
Mean year of first arrival in United States	1973	1968	–
Mean years of school completed	5.7	8.3	11.7
Percent who completed school in United States	3.0	26.3	–

(continues)

TABLE 5.8   (Continued)

Percent with no ability to speak English	27.0	7.7	0.0
Percent of those in labor force who were unemployed	8.9	5.1	7.4
Percent of those employed who were in white-collar occupations	3.3	13.5	32.2
Percent receiving below minimum wage	12.9	3.1	1.8
Mean annual personal income	$8,222	$11,472	$12,200
Percent with federal income tax deducted from pay	96.2	98.2	96.3

NOTE: Unpublished data are from the Los Angeles County Parents Survey, conducted in 1980–1981 by the University of Southern California and funded by the National Institutes of Health.

SOURCE: David M. Heer, *Undocumented Mexicans in the United States* (New York: Cambridge University Press, 1990), and unpublished data.

to be higher than that of the undocumented persons counted in the 1980 census. This follows from the requirement for continuous residence since January 1982 for those who did not legalize their status on the basis of being special agricultural workers.

How do the characteristics of undocumented immigrants differ from those of legal immigrants of the same nationality or from those of individuals born in the United States of that nationality? Some pertinent data in answer to this question, provided by my own survey conducted in Los Angeles County in 1980–1981, are shown in Table 5.8. The sampling frame for the Los Angeles County Parents Survey consisted of mothers of babies born in Los Angeles County during 1980–1981 where either the mother or the father of the baby was of Mexican descent. Separate representative samples were drawn of the names and addresses of those mothers born in Mexico and those born in the United States of Mexican descent. Data were collected concerning the characteristics of the mother and the father, if the mother considered him to be her husband. Altogether, interviews were obtained from 903 mothers (or fathers if the mother was not present). Of the mothers of Mexican origin, approximately 48 percent admitted to being undocumented, 25 percent stated that they were either permanent legal residents or naturalized citizens, and 27 percent were born in the United States. From these percentages and official data concerning the proportion of all births in Los Angeles County to mothers born in Mexico, it can be estimated that in 1980–1981 at least 18.6 percent of all births in Los Angeles County took place to undocumented Mexican mothers.[21]

What are some of the salient differences between the undocumented mothers and the undocumented fathers? From the standpoint of policy, perhaps the most important is that the fathers had been in the United States approximately two years longer than the mothers. As was mentioned previously, this implied that under the provisions for legalization mandated by IRCA, a substantial number of husbands could legalize their status, but their wives would not be able to do so. IRCA's lack of regard for family unity aroused sharp opposition from Archbishop Roger Mahony of the Roman Catholic church in Los Angeles. He called for new legislation to provide that if one family member were to qualify for legalization, other family members should receive derivative eligibility.[22] His call was heeded, and the Immigration Act of 1990 did institute a program of legalization for dependents of persons legalized under IRCA.

Another striking difference is the proportion with no ability to speak English. About two-thirds of the mothers had no ability to speak English, as compared to only about 27 percent of the fathers. This large gap is explainable in part by the fathers' longer residence in the United States but perhaps more importantly by the much higher proportion of fathers in the labor force, 98.5 percent versus 29.6 percent of mothers.[23]

Now let us turn to the major differences between the undocumented and legal immigrants. It is significant that for both mothers and fathers legal immigrants had been in the United States about five years longer than the undocumented. This fact may help explain why legal immigrants had a much lower proportion who could speak no English than did the undocumented and why the legal immigrants had a much higher proportion who had completed their schooling in the United States. It may also in part account for the consistently lower socioeconomic status of the undocumented immigrants compared to the legal immigrants in terms of percent unemployed, occupational status, and income. Nevertheless, differences in educational attainment between the two groups must also be significant in explaining other factors in which they vary. For example, the mean years of school completed by undocumented fathers was 2.57 years less than that of fathers who were legal immigrants. Even among fathers who had completed their education outside the United States this difference was 1.31 years.[24]

Among the mothers and fathers of Mexican descent born in the United States, almost none could not speak English. Their average years of schooling were also considerably higher than those of legal immigrants. But the percentage of native-born women who were without a conjugal partner or were receiving AFDC payments was considerably higher than among women born in Mexico.

An important source of information concerning the characteristics of the 1.6 million persons legalized under IRCA by virtue of continuous residence in the United States since 1982 was a survey conducted by Westat for the INS.[25] It is unfortunate that no survey was ever taken concerning the characteristics of the 1.1 million persons legalized under the SAW program. The Westat survey was conducted in spring 1989 among a nationwide sample of 6,193 persons whose status had already been legalized. Mexicans constituted 70 percent of the total sample. Some key characteristics of the total surveyed population and the surveyed population born in Mexico are shown in Table 5.9.

Perhaps the most interesting feature of the table is the high proportion of persons who stated they had never been apprehended by the INS (74 percent for the total sample and 68 percent among Mexicans). It is also interesting to see the strong relationship between nation of origin and usual method of entry. Only 10 percent of Mexicans were visa abusers, whereas among respondents from nations other than Mexico this proportion was almost one-half. Also noteworthy are the low proportions, both for the total population and for Mexicans, ever receiving aid from entitlement programs such as Medicaid, food stamps, or AFDC. Although not shown clearly in Table 5.9, the survey also revealed pronounced differences between Mexicans and persons from other nations in educational attainment and ability to speak English. In contrast to the median of six years of education for those legalized from Mexico, those legalized from Central America had a median of nine years, those from other Western Hemisphere nations a median of twelve years, and those from Eastern Hemisphere nations a median of fourteen years. Moreover, only 10 percent of Mexicans spoke English well, whereas 11 percent of those from Central America, 37 percent of those from other Western Hemisphere nations, and 44 percent of those from Eastern Hemisphere nations could do so.[26] For legalized persons born in Mexico, however, the level of educational attainment and the ability to speak English were both quite similar to what was found in the Los Angeles County Parents Survey.

The Foreign-Born Population of the United States in 1990

As I have emphasized previously, the stock of foreign-born persons who should be included in the decennial census of the United States consists of: (1) permanent legal residents and naturalized citizens who are usual residents, (2) undocumented persons who are usual residents, and (3) persons admitted on temporary visas, such as those issued to international students, provided these persons were present on the census date and were intending to remain in the United States for a period of six

TABLE 5.9   Characteristics of the Total Legalized Population and the Legalized
Population Born in Mexico Resident in the United States Since 1982

	Total	Born in Mexico[a]
Percent whose usual method of entry was		
Without inspection with smuggler	46	50
Without inspection without smuggler	29	35
Border card abuse	3	5
Visa overstay	21	10
Percent never apprehended by INS	74	68
Percent who first entered the United States		
before 1977	33	38
Percent married or living with partner	61	64
Mean size of household	3.5	3.8
Median years of education	7	6
Percent who speak English well	15	10
Percent of legalized males who were in the		
labor force	94	95
Percent of legalized females		
who were in the labor force	68	63
Percent of legalized males in the labor force		
who were unemployed	2	2
Percent of legalized females in the		
labor force who were unemployed	6	7
Percent of employed legalized persons		
who were in white-collar occupations	14	8
Median hourly wage at time of		
application for legalization	$5.45	$5.05
Mean annual family income	$18,196	$17,551
Percent of workers paid below		
minimum wage	10	10
Percent with private health insurance	50	47
Percent covered by Medicaid or Medicare	4	5
Percent receiving food stamps	4	–
Percent receiving AFDC payments	2	–

[a] A dash indicates that the data were not published.

SOURCE: U.S. Department of Justice, Immigration and Naturalization Service, *Immigration Reform and Control Act: Report on the Legalized Alien Population* (Washington, D.C.: Government Printing Office, 1992), pp. 12–20. Data are from a survey conducted in 1989.

months or more (thus considered by the Bureau of the Census to be usual residents).

As would be expected from previous data discussed for legal and un-documented immigrants, the total stock of foreign-born persons is highly concentrated. Almost 33 percent of all foreign-born persons were in California, whereas only 12 percent of the total population of the United States was in that state. The top six states with respect to the number of the foreign-born population (California, New York, Florida, Texas, New Jersey, and Illinois) contained almost 73 percent of the entire foreign-born population of the United States, though they contained less than 39 percent of the total population. Moreover, almost 15 percent of the foreign-born population lived in Los Angeles County, whereas only 3.6 percent of the total population of the United States lived there. Altogether, the thirteen counties with at least 200,000 foreign-born persons had almost 44 percent of the total foreign-born population but less than 14 percent of the total population. The geographic concentration of the foreign-born population also implied that certain areas would have for higher proportions foreign-born than the percentage for the nation (7.9 percent). Among states California had the highest percentage foreign-born (21.7 percent) and New York the second highest (15.9 percent). Among counties the highest percentage foreign-born was in Dade County, Florida (45.1 percent), and Queens County, New York (36.2 percent).[27]

Table 5.10 shows certain demographic characteristics of the foreign-born population by year of arrival and selected country of birth. The table shows large variation in each of the four characteristics shown. The median age varied from 29.9 years for persons born in Mexico to 58.9 years for persons born in Italy. Since most immigrants come to the United States as young adults, for each country of birth the median age was related to the year of entry (data on year of entry are shown in Table 5.11). The higher the proportion of persons who had entered in recent years, the lower was the median age. The sex ratio (i.e., the ratio of males to females) also varied substantially by country of birth. The highest ratio (138.8) was for persons born in Iran; the lowest ratio (54.8) for persons born in Germany. The low ratio in Germany was in large part due to the high proportion of immigrants who entered the United States as wives of U.S. servicemen. There was also substantial variation in the number of children ever born to women thirty-five to forty-four years of age. Women born in Mexico had the highest fertility (3,289), whereas women from Poland had the lowest (1,649). Although foreign-born women as a whole had higher fertility (2,254) than the native-born (1,927), the fertility of women in fourteen of the twenty-three counties of birth shown in the table was lower than that of native-born women. The foreign-born population was much more likely to live in large households of five or more persons than was the native-born: almost 23 percent for the foreign-born compared to slightly more than 10 percent for the native-born. The highest proportion living in households of five persons or more was among Mexicans (47.7 percent); the lowest proportion (5.6 percent) was among those from the United Kingdom or Germany.

TABLE 5.10   Demographic Characteristics of the Native Population and Foreign-Born Population by Year of Arrival and Country of Birth, 1990

Nativity and Country of Birth	Number of Persons (in thousands)	Median Age	Sex Ratio	Children Ever Born per Thousand Women thirty-five to forty-four years old	Percent of Households with five or more persons
Native-born	228,943	32.5	94.9	1,927	10.1
Foreign-born	19,767	37.3	95.8	2,254	22.8
Entered between					
1980 and 1990	8,664	28.0	110.3	2,200	27.1
Entered before 1980	11,104	46.5	85.8	2,282	20.9
Mexico	4,298	29.9	122.9	3,289	47.7
Philippines	913	38.8	76.5	1,866	31.8
Canada	745	52.9	70.3	1,772	5.8
Cuba	737	49.0	93.7	1,765	13.5
Germany	712	52.8	54.8	1,816	5.6
United Kingdom	640	49.7	67.2	1,761	5.6
Italy	581	58.9	93.1	2,126	12.5
Korea	568	34.9	75.3	1,789	18.3
Vietnam	543	30.3	110.9	2,451	39.8
China	530	44.8	98.2	1,812	22.8
El Salvador	465	29.1	106.9	1,826	41.6
India	450	36.4	121.7	1,993	21.2
Poland	388	57.1	89.3	1,649	6.2
Dominican Republic	348	33.6	83.4	2,513	32.2
Jamaica	334	35.7	81.1	2,171	19.0
USSR	334	54.6	82.3	1,690	6.3
Japan	290	37.8	59.7	1,650	7.5
Colombia	286	35.3	86.6	1,821	21.6
Taiwan	244	33.2	88.8	1,670	16.3
Guatemala	226	29.8	105.5	2,567	39.8
Haiti	225	34.6	99.1	2,421	33.4
Iran	211	35.0	138.8	1,821	13.5
Portugal	210	40.1	100.1	2,106	18.1

SOURCE: U.S. Bureau of the Census, *1990 Census of Population, The Foreign-born Population in the United States,* 1990 CP-3-1 (Washington, D.C.: Government Printing Office, 1993), pp. 1–128.

Table 5.11 presents certain social characteristics of the foreign-born and native populations. About 44 percent of the foreign-born population in 1990 had entered the United States in 1980 or later. Among persons born in Italy, only about 6 percent had entered the United States in 1980 or later, whereas among persons from El Salvador 75.2 percent had

TABLE 5.11   Social Characteristics of the Native Population and Foreign-Born Population by Year of Arrival and Country of Birth, 1990

Nativity and Country of Birth	Number of Persons (in thousands)	Percent Who Entered Between 1980 and 1990	Percent Who Do Not Speak English Well	Percent of Persons Twenty-five Years and Older with	
				High School Diploma or Higher	Bachelor's degree or Higher
Native-born	228,943	–	2.3	77.0	20.3
Foreign-born	19,767	43.8	47.0	58.8	20.4
Entered between 1980 and 1990	8,664	–	59.9	59.4	23.7
Entered before 1980	11,104	–	37.2	58.5	18.7
Mexico	4,298	49.9	70.7	24.3	3.5
Philippines	913	49.0	31.8	82.5	43.0
Canada	745	16.6	5.0	72.6	22.1
Cuba	737	25.5	60.1	54.1	15.6
Germany	712	11.2	13.1	75.9	19.1
United Kingdom	640	24.1	1.1	81.3	23.1
Italy	581	6.4	42.0	39.3	8.6
Korea	568	56.1	62.0	80.1	34.4
Vietnam	543	61.8	68.2	58.9	15.9
China	530	53.5	72.1	60.6	30.9
El Salvador	465	75.2	72.4	32.7	4.6
India	450	55.7	27.1	87.2	64.9
Poland	388	30.0	46.8	58.1	16.3
Dominican Republic	348	53.1	68.7	41.7	7.5
Jamaica	334	46.3	1.7	67.9	14.9
USSR	334	39.4	52.1	64.0	27.1
Japan	290	52.7	56.2	86.4	35.0
Colombia	286	51.2	61.1	66.8	15.5
Taiwan	244	65.4	57.9	91.6	62.2
Guatemala	226	68.3	70.7	37.5	5.8
Haiti	225	58.9	55.3	57.6	11.8
Iran	211	49.6	38.8	86.7	50.6
Portugal	210	21.6	56.0	32.1	4.6

SOURCE: U.S. Bureau of the Census, *1990 Census of the Population, The Foreign-born Population in the United States,* 1990 CP-3-1 (Washington, D.C.: Government Printing Office, 1993), pp. 129–192.

arrived in the United States during that period. In general if the place of birth was a developed nation, the proportion who had come to the United States in 1980 or later was much smaller than if the place of birth was a less-developed nation. As would be expected, there was a substantial difference between the proportion of the foreign-born and the native-born who did not speak English well (47 percent compared to 2.3 percent). By country of birth there were extremely large differences in the proportion who had a poor command of English, ranging from around 1 percent for persons born in the United Kingdom to more than 72 percent among persons born in El Salvador. There were also wide variations in educational attainment by country of birth. The proportion of persons aged twenty-five or older who had completed high school ranged from a low among Mexicans of around 24 percent to a high among persons born in Taiwan of almost 92 percent. Similarly, the proportion of those twenty-five years and older with a bachelor's degree or higher ranged from a low of less than 4 percent among Mexicans to a high of almost 65 percent among persons born in India. Altogether the foreign-born had a substantially lower percentage of persons twenty-five years or older who had a high school diploma (58.8 percent) than the native-born (77.0 percent), but the percentage of foreign-born with a bachelor's degree or higher was about the same percentage as the native-born (around 20 percent for each group).

Table 5.12 presents certain labor force characteristics for the native and foreign-born populations. Although the differences are not strikingly large, the foreign-born population had a somewhat higher proportion unemployed than the native population (7.8 percent versus 6.2 percent), a slightly lower proportion of persons in managerial or professional occupations (22.2 percent versus 26.8 percent), a slightly lower proportion of self-employed (6.8 percent versus 7.0 percent), and a substantially lower proportion of persons in government jobs (9.8 percent versus 15.2 percent). What is most striking in the data shown in Table 5.12, however, are the differences by country of birth. The proportion unemployed ranged from a high of 9.7 percent among those born in the Dominican Republic to a low of 1.5 percent for Japanese. Similarly, the percentage in managerial and professional occupations varied from a high of 48.3 among persons born in India to a low of 5.8 among those from either Mexico or El Salvador. The proportion of self-employed among all employed persons went from a high of 18.0 percent among Koreans to a low of 3.3 percent among individuals from the Philippines. Finally, the percentage in government jobs varied from a high of 15.8 percent among those born in the Philippines to a low of 3.2 percent among persons born in El Salvador. The low proportion of government workers among immigrants born in El Salvador is probably related to the high proportion of the population from El Salvador that was undocumented.

Table 5.13 presents income characteristics. The median family income for foreign-born persons ($31,785) was only slightly less than that for the native-born ($35,508). Nevertheless, the proportion of the foreign-born in poverty (18.2 percent) was substantially greater than the proportion for native persons (12.7 percent). As might be expected,

TABLE 5.12   Labor Force Characteristics of the Native Population and Foreign-Born Population by Year of Arrival and Country of Birth, 1990

Nativity and Country of Birth	Number of Persons (in thousands)	Percent of the labor force unemployed	Percent of employed persons in managerial and professional occupations	Percent of employed persons self-employed	Percent of employed persons in government jobs
Native-born	228,943	6.2	26.8	7.0	15.2
Foreign-born	19,767	7.8	22.2	6.8	9.8
Entered between 1980 and 1990	8,664	9.6	17.0	5.1	7.5
Entered before 1980	11,104	6.4	25.7	8.0	11.4
Mexico	4,298	7.9	5.8	4.5	5.3
Philippines	913	3.5	28.3	3.3	15.8
Canada	745	2.2	37.9	9.5	11.6
Cuba	737	4.3	22.8	7.3	10.8
Germany	712	2.3	32.7	9.1	13.2
United Kingdom	640	2.2	39.9	8.3	11.7
Italy	581	2.5	20.3	10.1	9.5
Korea	568	3.3	25.5	18.0	8.0
Vietnam	543	5.3	17.0	5.8	9.6
China	530	3.2	28.9	7.8	12.1
El Salvador	465	8.0	5.8	3.4	3.2
India	450	3.8	48.3	6.3	16.2
Poland	388	2.9	20.8	7.9	7.3
Dominican Republic	348	9.7	10.8	5.1	9.1
Jamaica	334	6.3	21.6	4.0	14.9
USSR	334	5.3	30.9	10.1	9.7
Japan	290	1.5	38.7	7.9	9.7
Colombia	286	6.0	17.0	6.6	7.0
Taiwan	244	2.8	47.4	7.5	13.4
Guatemala	226	7.7	7.0	5.2	4.6
Haiti	225	9.2	13.8	3.5	13.2
Iran	211	4.8	41.9	12.0	9.6
Portugal	210	5.5	9.3	5.1	5.5

SOURCE: U.S. Bureau of the Census, *1990 Census of Population, The Foreign-born Population in the United States,* 1990 CP-3-1 (Washington, D.C.: Government Printing Office, 1993), pp. 193–256.

the median family income of foreign-born persons who entered in 1980 or later ($24,595) was considerably lower than that among foreign-born persons who had entered the United States before 1980 ($35,733); similarly, the percentage of those in poverty among the more recent immigrants (26.2 percent) was far higher than among the earlier immigrants

TABLE 5.13 Income Characteristics of the Native Population and Foreign-Born Population by Year of Arrival and Country of Birth, 1990

Nativity and Country of Birth	Number of Persons (in thousands)	Median Family Income	Percent of Persons in Poverty
Native-born	228,943	$35,508	12.7
Foreign-born	19,767	31,785	18.2
Entered between			
1980 and 1990	8,664	24,595	26.2
Entered before 1980	11,104	35,733	12.0
Mexico	4,298	21,585	29.7
Philippines	913	47,794	5.9
Canada	745	39,995	7.8
Cuba	737	32,007	14.7
Germany	712	41,757	7.7
United Kingdom	640	45,681	6.6
Italy	581	37,673	8.0
Korea	568	33,406	15.6
Vietnam	543	30,496	25.5
China	530	34,225	15.7
El Salvador	465	21,818	24.9
India	450	52,908	21.6
Poland	388	35,742	9.7
Dominican Republic	348	19,694	30.0
Jamaica	334	34,338	12.1
USSR	334	28,799	25.0
Japan	290	47,034	12.8
Colombia	286	30,342	15.3
Taiwan	244	45,325	16.7
Guatemala	226	22,574	19.6
Haiti	225	25,556	21.7
Iran	211	40,273	15.7
Portugal	210	37,367	7.0

SOURCE: U.S. Bureau of the Census, *1990 Census of Population, The Foreign-born Population in the United States,* 1990 CP-3-1 (Washington, D.C.: Government Printing Office, 1993), pp. 257–320.

(12.0 percent). The table shows substantial differences by country of birth. Median family income ranged from a low of $19,694 among immigrants born in the Dominican Republic to a high of $52,908 among those born in India. Moreover, the percentage in poverty ranged from a high of 30 percent among individuals born in the Dominican Republic to a low of 5.9 percent among those born in the Philippines.

The data on labor force characteristics shown in Table 5.12 and the data on income characteristics shown in Table 5.13 are obviously related. The link becomes all the more clear when we consider the low economic status of immigrants born in Mexico. Because the number of persons born in Mexico is such a large proportion of the total foreign-born population (21.7 percent), their economic status is worth particular attention. Among individuals born in Mexico, less than 6 percent of those who had jobs were employed in managerial and professional occupations, the median family income was less than $22,000, and the proportion in poverty was almost 30 percent. The low economic status of Mexicans is of course also related to low educational attainment and lack of ability to speak English, characteristics that appeared in Table 5.11.

Sojourners and Settlers: Emigration from the United States

In his much-cited book *Birds of Passage: Migrant Labor and Industrial Societies,* economist Michael Piore elaborated a distinction between two types of immigrant: the sojourner and the settler.[28] According to Piore, the sojourners, on the one hand, were interested in saving a given sum of money and would return to their native land after they had saved that amount. Thus, he claimed, the labor supply of sojourners was backward sloping. That is, the higher their wages, the sooner they would return home. Settlers, on the other hand, planned to remain permanently in the nation of immigration. Higher wages would not induce them to return to their country of birth. There is no doubt that the distinction between sojourner and settler is important if only because we now have excellent evidence that many immigrants to the United States have been sojourners rather than settlers. Moreover, evidence has accumulated that in particular a large proportion of undocumented Mexican immigrants in the United States have been sojourners.[29] Among undocumented Mexican immigrants, the typical sojourner has been a male who is either young and unmarried or older and married but has decided to leave his wife and children in Mexico. Many of these undocumented Mexican sojourners spend the spring and summer in the United States, return to Mexico during the fall, and spend the winter there.

Nevertheless, initial intentions can change. Those who had intended to settle can become discouraged and return to their native land, and those who came as sojourners can decide that they want to settle. In this connection I am reminded of a conversation I had with one of my former undergraduate students. He had been born and raised in a well-to-do family in Nicaragua. After the Marxist Sandinista Party came to power in 1978, his family decided to leave Nicaragua until a different government could rule the nation. The United States accepted the family as refugees, and they moved to Miami, where my student's father established an automobile dealership. Then in 1990 the Sandinista regime gave up its power after Violeta Chamorro won an election. Shortly after Chamorro's ascent to the presidency, I asked my student whether his father would be moving back to Nicaragua. He replied negatively, explaining that his father's business in Miami was too good to give up.

We have looked at the motives for emigration. Now we need to ask how we can measure emigration from the United States. The best way would be to do so directly, that is, to require that everyone leaving the United States with the intention of a stay of six months or more register this move with the U.S. government. From 1908 through 1957, according to provisions of the Immigration Act of 1907, U.S. law did require that data on the number of non–U.S. citizens leaving the United States be collected. Moreover, the government also collected statistics on the emigration of U.S. citizens between 1918 and 1950. The purpose of the 1907 law was to enable the government to have an idea of net immigration to the United States, since it was correctly presumed that the impact of net immigration on the country's economy and society was greater than the impact of the total number of immigrants. The reason advanced in 1957 for discontinuing the registration of departures of noncitizens from the United States was that the figures obtained were an underestimate of the total number of noncitizen emigrants.[30]

A second way of estimating emigration from the United States among noncitizens would be to have an annual registration of all aliens living in the United States. If we estimate correctly the number of deaths to aliens each year and also know the number of aliens who become naturalized citizens, we can use the number of registered aliens to estimate the number of previous immigrants who must have later emigrated. To understand this method, we need to have a clear definition of the meaning of *cohort*. Demographers define a cohort as the group of persons who experienced the same event during an identical period. Demographers most commonly discuss birth cohorts: all individuals born in the same period, for example, the same year. But we may also refer to an immigration cohort.

Now let us get back to explaining how data from the registration of legal aliens can be used to estimate emigration. Consider the cohort of persons who immigrated to the United States in 1970. From their distribution by age and sex and assuming that death rates by age and sex for immigrants are identical to those of the total population, it is easy to estimate the number of deaths that occurred to this immigrant cohort following their admission to the United States. We also have an accurate count of members of this immigrant cohort who had become naturalized citizens. Now suppose we have data for 1980 concerning the number of registered aliens. Then we can obtain the number from the 1970 immigrant cohort who must have emigrated during the following decade simply by subtracting from the number who immigrated in 1970 three other figures: the number of deaths, the number of naturalizations, and the remaining stock of resident aliens in 1980. From 1951 through 1981 the United States did require that all aliens living in the United States register their addresses each January. As explained earlier in this chapter, however, the requirement for annual registration was abolished in 1981.

Another means of estimating emigration from the United States is to utilize data collected by U.S. consular offices abroad. There is no compulsory registration of U.S. citizens living abroad, but many voluntarily register with the U.S. consulate because they want the consular officers to know who and where they are. In addition to recording the number of these citizens who voluntarily register, each U.S. consulate overseas also estimates how many U.S. citizens living in the area have not registered, although they make no attempt to count the number of former immigrants to the United States who have later emigrated.

Still another method, recently utilized by the U.S. Bureau of the Census for its current population survey, is called multiplicity or network sampling. In July 1987, June 1988, and November 1989, the Census Bureau asked survey respondents about the number of living parents, brothers, sisters, and children and whether any of these specified relatives were living outside the United States.[31] The bureau then asked additional questions about these relatives living abroad. The resulting data on these relatives must be weighted by the inverse of the probability that any of the emigrant's network of immediate relatives fall into the sample. The size of the network eligible to report the emigrant is known as the multiplicity associated with the emigrant and is equal to the total number of parents, siblings, and children in the United States.

The November 1989 survey indicated that there were 353,000 Americans "living abroad temporarily," defined as persons who were either members of the armed forces overseas or civilian U.S. government employees overseas or dependents of either and who had been reported by a relative in the survey. In addition, there were 981,000 emigrants, defined as all other relatives living abroad and reported in the survey. Of these emigrants 466,000 were known to be native-born and 478,000 were known to be foreign-born. The children of these persons living abroad were not counted in these figures, but their numbers can easily be calculated from additional questions included in the questionnaire. Altogether the survey counted 109,000 children of the 353,000 Americans living temporarily abroad and 292,000 children of the 981,000 emigrants.

Because the multiplicity-survey method cannot count emigrants with no surviving immediate relatives left in the United States, it was probably more successful in counting native-born U.S. citizens who have emigrated than immigrants who had later emigrated. Moreover, among previous immigrants who then emigrated, the chance that no one would report them would probably be much higher for persons who had recently immigrated to the United States compared to persons who had immigrated earlier. Even with respect to counting native-born citizens, however, the multiplicity surveys appear to be lacking: Whereas the 1989 survey estimated only 462,000 Americans, including children, to be living temporarily abroad, the count from administrative records of the U.S. government was 1.028 million. Karen Woodrow, who authored the paper on the results of these three surveys, was of the opinion that the true stock of emigrants from the United States was at least 2 million and could be as much as 3 million rather than the 1.3 million, including children, estimated by the survey.[32]

A final method used to estimate emigration from the United States is the analysis of the data on immigration collected by other nations. But such data must be used with great care since their definitions of those who are immigrants may not apply in determining who is an emigrant from the United States. Moreover, many nations do not collect data on the return of their own citizens. The data from other nations are thus most useful in analyzing the emigration of U.S. citizens and least useful in analyzing the emigration of non–U.S. citizens.

In my opinion, and in the opinion of other social scientists, the status of our statistical data concerning emigration from the United States is deplorable.[33] The consequences of net immigration to society are much more important than the consequences of immigration per se. Nevertheless, because of our lack of current data concerning emigration, we cannot accurately estimate net immigration. What can be done about this situation? Robert Warren and Ellen Percy Kraly have suggested that the government institute a sample survey of passengers leaving the United States by air or sea.[34] Questions from this survey could differentiate those whose usual place of residence was the United States from other departing passengers. Among individuals whose usual place of residence had been the United States, additional questions could be asked concerning destination and duration of stay at that destination. Such a survey would exclude most persons traveling between the United States and Canada or the United States and Mexico. Perhaps the best way to survey such travelers on a sample basis would be to institute a cooperative arrangement with the governments of those two nations. The United States would agree to administer a questionnaire to a sample of people arriving in the United States from either Canada or Mexico and the Canadian and Mexican governments would agree to administer sample surveys of those departing the United States for Canada and Mexico.

So far we have talked only about method, and I have perhaps left the impression that we have no recent data on emigration worthy of presentation. Such an inference would be incorrect. The data calculated for 1970–1980 based on the number of immigrants and the number of aliens who registered in January 1980 provide valid estimates of noncitizen emigration during that particular decade. Although I do not believe that the estimates of the stock of native-born U.S. citizens living abroad by place of residence as calculated from the November 1989 multiplicity survey are valid, I do think the percentage distribution of these numbers by place of destination is valid, and I present each of these two sets of data below.

Table 5.14 shows data on the number of legal immigrants to the United States and noncitizen legal resident emigrants from the United States for 1970–1980 by area of origin or destination. Presented also is the ratio of immigrants to emigrants for each area. The table indicates that for all areas combined, the ratio of emigrants to immigrants was approximately 0.3. But the ratios varied widely by continent and nation; the ratio for Canada was approximately 0.87, whereas the ratio for Asia was less than 0.18. From the data shown in Table 5.13, we can generalize that the ratios tend to be highest for the most-developed regions of the world (e.g., Canada and Europe) and lowest for the less-developed (e.g., Asia, Mexico, and South America). These facts imply that the origin of net immigration is more highly concentrated in the less-developed nations than is the origin of immigration in general.

The November 1989 current population survey reports data on the place of residence of the 466,000 native-born U.S. citizens living abroad. The data exclude Americans living abroad temporarily (i.e., members of the armed forces and U.S. civilian government employees and their dependents); they also exclude children not directly reported by a U.S. relative. As I mentioned earlier, the data concerning absolute numbers are no doubt a severe undercount. But there should be relatively little bias concerning the percentage distribution: Almost 17 percent were living in Canada, and around 30 percent lived somewhere in North America. Almost 38 percent lived in either Europe or the USSR and 17 percent in Asia.[35] We can generalize that the majority of native-born American emigrants appear to be living in a developed nation. In contrast, of course, the overwhelming majority of current immigrants to the United States come from one of the less-developed nations.

If some immigrants are considered more desirable than other immigrants, we want to know whether the immigrants who stay in the United

TABLE 5.14   Estimates for the United States of Legal Immigration and Noncitizen Legal Resident Emigration by Area of Origin or Destination, 1970–1980 (numbers in thousands)

	Legal Immigrants		Noncitizen Legal Resident Emigrants		Ratio of Emigrants to Immigrants
	Number	Percent	Number	Percent	
Total	3,938	100.0	1,177	100.0	0.299
Europe and USSR	805	20.4	346	29.4	0.430
Asia	1,335	33.9	239	20.3	0.179
Africa and Oceania	121	3.1	62	5.3	0.512
North America	1,414	35.9	455	38.7	0.322
Canada	112	2.8	97	8.2	0.866
Mexico	614	15.6	120	10.2	0.195
Other	688	17.5	238	20.2	0.346
South America	263	6.7	75	6.4	0.285

SOURCE: Robert Warren and Ellen Percy Kraly, *The Elusive Exodus: Emigration from the United States* (Washington, D.C.: Population Reference Bureau, 1985), p. 6.

States are more or less desirable than those who come and later leave. Little research has been done on the selectivity of emigration other than with respect to country of birth. I do, however, want to report the results of one interesting study that examines selectivity of emigration by sex.

Guillermina Jasso and Mark Rosenzweig analyzed data from successive decennial censuses of the United States.[36] Essentially the data either confirm or reject the viewpoint that males tend to be sojourners more often than females. Since the data were taken from counts of the foreign-born population from the decennial census, Jasso and Rosenzweig's results refer to undocumented as well as legal immigrants. Their research consisted of an analysis of characteristics of the same immigration cohorts over time. The most recent immigration cohort Jasso and Rosenzweig examined was the cohort that first entered the United States between 1965 and 1970. This cohort could be studied from both the 1970 census and the 1980 census. Jasso and Rosenzweig showed that among persons in the 1965–1970 immigration cohort who were born in the Eastern Hemisphere and were aged twenty to forty-four years in 1970, the proportion female was 49.0 percent at the time of the 1970 census but had increased to 54.3 percent when this same cohort was enumerated in the 1980 census. Thus for immigrants from the Eastern Hemisphere it would appear that a higher proportion of males than females had later emigrated. But among individuals of the identical immigration cohort and identical age in 1970 born in the Western Hemisphere, the proportion female decreased slightly, from 55.9 percent in 1970 to 55.4 percent in 1980. Both the change for Eastern Hemisphere immigrants and the change for Western Hemisphere immigrants need to be compared with the change in the proportion female among the cohort of native-born persons aged twenty to forty-four years in 1970. Among this native-born cohort the proportion female was slightly reduced, from 50.7 percent in 1970 to 50.5 percent in 1980.

The results Jasso and Rosenzweig obtained for immigrants from the Western Hemisphere are surprising. Many were from Mexico, and many Mexican immigrants were undocumented. Furthermore, there is massive evidence that a high proportion of undocumented Mexican immigrants are male sojourners.[37] So all prior research would suggest that the proportion female among the Western Hemisphere immigrants should have increased over the ten-year period rather than decreased.

How are we to explain Jasso and Rosenzweig's results for Western Hemisphere immigrants? Is prior understanding simply wrong? Alternatively, are there errors in the census data that mitigate the validity of the results of these two researchers? To clarify the matter, let us again consider the results with respect to native-born persons. Jasso and Rosenzweig found that in the native-born cohort aged twenty to forty-four years in 1970 the proportion female actually declined over the decade. This is unlikely to be a valid result because we know that death rates at each age are higher for females than for males. But there is a conventional explanation for this change recorded for the native-born cohort: The percentage of young adult males not counted in the census is higher than that of young adult females or of older adult males. The true percentage female among native-born persons twenty to forty-four years old in 1970 was somewhat lower than the recorded figure of 50.7 percent, and the trend to a lower proportion female in 1980 was spurious.

Similarly, we must suspect that the figures for Western Hemisphere immigrants may be biased by differential undercount in the two censuses. A key fact that may help explain Jasso and Rosenzweig's findings is that in the 1970 census there appears to have been a severe undercount of persons born in Mexico.[38] Specifically, data from the 1980 census show 929,000 Mexican-born individuals who had immigrated to the United States in 1969 or earlier, whereas the 1970 census showed only 760,000 Mexican-born immigrants. Furthermore, it is obvious that some of those enumerated in 1970 would have died or emigrated by 1980. It is therefore probable that there would have been at least 1 million Mexican-born persons in the United States in 1970 if the coverage of the census had been complete. We also know why this undercount in the 1970 census occurred: According to a report by the U.S. Commission on Civil Rights, one reason for inadequate coverage is that the INS conducted raids in search of illegal aliens in Los Angeles at the same time the 1970 census was being conducted.[39] How does this large undercount of persons born in Mexico help explain Jasso and Rosenzweig's results? If we also assume that among those born in Mexico not counted in the 1970 census there was a high proportion of males, it would follow that the two censuses would record a decline in the proportion female for the 1965–1970 immigration cohort even though the true proportion had increased.

As the preceding example illustrates, the validity of social science findings is determined not only by the results themselves but by their congruence with preexisting data and theory. Surprising results may eventually be found to be correct; if so, they upset existing theory. But there is often an alternative explanation that offers no contradiction to existing theory. Consensus on certain matters may come only after much further research designed to explain initial puzzling findings. This example also backs up Myrdal's argument that social science is best advanced when researchers with differing values and policy preferences reveal their preferences while simultaneously examining the available data. Alternative explanations ignored by one researcher may be quickly advanced by a second who sees the first researcher's interpretation as reducing the strength of arguments in favor of a certain policy position.

The Net Contribution of Immigration of the Foreign-Born to Population Change

At the beginning of this chapter, we defined the concept of the net contribution of immigration of the foreign born to population change. The concept is important because it measures the total amount of population change that can be attributed either to the direct or indirect effect of a given volume of foreign-born immigrants. To reiterate our previous definition, the net contribution of immigration of the foreign-born to total population change during a stated period is calculated as the number of foreign-born immigrants plus the births to the foreign-born immigrant mothers minus the deaths to the foreign-born immigrants and minus the number of foreign-born immigrants who emigrated. Now that I have introduced the concept of an immigrant cohort, I wish to add that a precise definition of the net contribution of immigration of the foreign-born to population change demands that the events of birth, death, and emigration in the original definition refer only to the cohort that has immigrated during the period.

In this section I would like to illustrate the utility of this concept with respect to projections of the size of the U.S. population. What impact will net immigration into the United States have on the size of the nation's population? We can examine this effect by comparing Census Bureau forecasts with a scenario in which the assumptions about future natality and mortality would be identical to those in Census Bureau predictions but in which there would be no net immigration into the United States. Unfortunately, as I mentioned earlier, the concept of the net contribution of immigration to population change, which can be calculated from Census Bureau figures, is not quite identical to the net contribution of the foreign-born to population change, which is what we would ideally like to measure. The difference is minuscule, though, since the volume of net immigration to the United States in fact differs little from the net immigration of the foreign-born, as the net emigration of U.S. citizens is very small. But before we can discuss the Census Bureau results with respect to the net contribution of immigration to future population growth in the United States, we must first understand two terms, *population projection* and *population forecast.*

A *population projection* can be defined as the arithmetic spelling out of the consequences for future population size and age-sex composition of a particular set of assumptions concerning each of the components of population change (i.e., births, deaths, immigration, and emigration). Nowadays almost all population projections are prepared by what is called the cohort-component method. This means that the existing population is divided into birth cohorts subdivided by sex and that annual future events of birth, death, immigration, and emigration are postulated separately for the males and females of each birth cohort.

A *population forecast* is a subtype of population projection in which the set of assumptions utilized is one the author believes is most likely to occur. About every two or three years, the Bureau of the Census projects the size of the U.S. population and its composition by age and sex. The bureau prepares a fairly large number of different projections, but only one projection is based on the most likely set of assumptions and can therefore be considered the forecast.

A recent set of population projections the Bureau of the Census has prepared, issued in November 1992, contains ten different projections.[40] Each of these projects the population of the United States to the year 2050 from the base year of 1991. The forecast is based on the assumption that net immigration into the United States will maintain the constant level of 880,000 persons per year. One of the alternative projections uses the same set of assumptions concerning future natality and mortality as does the forecast projection but is also based on the assumption that there will be no net immigration. Two additional projections deviate from the forecast projection in supposing that annual net immigration will be constant either at a substantially lower level (350,000 per year) or at a substantially higher level (1.37 million per year) than in the forecast.

Table 5.15 compares the population sizes in each of these four projections for five-year intervals beginning with the year 1995 and ending with the year 2050. The differences among the four projections are not large for the early years but become quite pronounced for the later years. By 2050 the forecast predicts a population size of 383 million, whereas the assumption that no net migration will occur yields a projection of only 301 million. According to this forecast, then, net immigration will contribute almost 82 million people to the United States during this period of fifty-nine years. Additionally, the projection with the highest assumption concerning net migration shows total U.S. population in 2050 at 424 million, implying a net contribution of immigration to population growth of more than 123 million. Finally, the projection assuming a low but still positive level of net immigration shows a population of 339 million in 2050, implying a net contribution of immigration to population growth of almost 38 million.

Differences in the projected volume of immigration will also have substantial influence on the projected composition of the U.S. population by age. Table 5.16 illustrates these differences for the year 2030, for

TABLE 5.15   Net Contribution of Immigration to the Future Size of the U.S. Population, 1995–2050

	Population Size According to Type of Assumption Concerning Net Migration			
	Forecast[a]	*None*	*Low*[b]	*High*[c]
1995	262,754	259,078	261,229	264,165
2000	274,815	265,984	270,345	278,965
2005	286,324	271,807	278,644	293,467
2010	298,109	277,497	287,022	308,443
2015	310,370	283,320	295,720	324,049
2020	322,602	288,752	304,227	339,786
2025	334,216	293,168	311,930	355,089
2030	344,951	296,313	318,564	369,700
2035	354,913	298,352	324,624	383,696
2040	364,349	299,606	329,321	397,385
2045	373,504	300,378	334,011	410,681
2050	382,674	301,010	338,650	424,161

[a] Assumes net immigration to be 880,000 per year.

[b] Assumes net immigration to be 350,000 per year.

[c] Assumes net immigration to be 1.37 million per year.

SOURCE: U.S. Bureau of the Census, "Population Projections of the United States by Age, Sex, Race, and Hispanic Origin: 1992 to 2050," prepared by Jennifer Cheeseman Day, *Current Population Reports,* Ser. P-25, No. 1092 (November 1992), pp. 18–62.

TABLE 5.16   Possible Effects of Net Immigration on U.S. Population Size, Age
Composition, and Dependency Ratios

	Figure for 1992	*Figure for 2030 According to Type of Assumption Concerning Net Immigration*			
		Forecast[a]	*None*	*Low*[b]	*High*[c]
Population size (in thousands)					
Total	254,922	344,951	296,313	318,584	369,700
Under 18 years	66,163	80,777	66,752	73,712	87,543
18 to 64 years	156,518	194,335	163,080	177,405	210,230
65 years and over	32,241	69,839	66,481	67,467	71,927
Percentage distribution by age					
Total	100.0	100.0	100.0	100.0	100.0
Under 18 years	26.0	23.4	22.5	23.1	23.7
18 to 64 years	61.4	56.3	55.0	55.7	56.9
65 years and over	12.6	20.2	22.4	21.2	19.5
Dependency ratios					
Under 18 / 18 to 64	0.423	0.416	0.409	0.416	0.416
65+ / 18 to 64	0.206	0.359	0.408	0.380	0.342
Under 18 and 65+ / 18 to 64	0.629	0.775	0.817	0.796	0.759

[a] Assumes net immigration to be 880,000 per year.
[b] Assumes net immigration to be 350,000 per year.
[c] Assumes net immigration to be 1.37 million per year.
SOURCE: U.S. Bureau of the Census, "Population Projections of the United States by Age, Sex, Race, and Hispanic Origin: 1992 to 2050," prepared by Jennifer Cheeseman Day, *Current Population Reports,* Ser. P-25, No. 1092 (November 1992), pp. 12–62.

which the population forecast predicts a considerable change in age composition compared to 1992. As shown in the table, the proportion of the population aged sixty-five and older is projected to rise from only 12.6 percent in 1992 to 20.2 percent in 2030, whereas the population under age eighteen is forecast to decline from 26.0 percent to 23.4 percent. Variations in the projected volume of immigration will have substantial consequences for the proportion aged sixty-five or older in 2030: The higher the volume of immigration projected, the lower will be the proportion of this cohort. With no net immigration 22.4 percent of the total population would be aged sixty-five or above; with the forecast volume of net immigration, the proportion of those sixty-five or older falls to 20.2 percent. In the projection with the highest volume of net immigration, the proportion of the population in the highest age bracket is reduced to 19.5 percent. In contrast, the higher the volume of net immigration, the higher will be the proportion of the population under age eighteen. With no net immigration this proportion would be only 22.5 percent, with the forecast volume of net immigration it is 23.4 percent, and in the projection with the highest volume of net immigration it is 23.7 percent.

For the most part, those under age eighteen and those sixty-five and older are not economically active; they consume but do not produce. Accordingly, demographers like to compute dependency ratios. The child dependency ratio is defined as the ratio of the population under age eighteen to the population aged eighteen to sixty-four. The old-age dependency ratio is defined as the ratio of the population aged sixty-five and older divided by the population aged eighteen to sixty-four. Finally, the total dependency ratio is defined as the population *either* under age eighteen *or* sixty-five years old or older divided by the population aged eighteen to sixty-four. Table 5.16 shows that a positive volume of net immigration will produce a higher child dependency ratio than if no net immigration is assumed. Furthermore, Table 5.16 indicates that the higher the volume of net immigration, the lower will be the old-age dependency ratio in 2030. With no net immigration this ratio will be 0.408, with the forecast level it will be 0.359, and in the projection assuming the highest level of net immigration it is reduced to 0.342. The total dependency ratio will also vary inversely with the assumed level of net immigration. With no net immigration the total dependency ratio will be 0.817, with the forecast level of immigration it will be 0.775, and with the highest level of immigration it would decline to 0.759.

The Context of Reception:
Legal Rights Dependent on Immigration Status

In this section we look at the ways in which U.S. law gives different privileges to various types of immigrant. We first consider the rights—or lack of rights—for undocumented immigrants, then the rights accorded to nonrefugee permanent legal residents, and, finally, the extra rights accorded to refugees.

Until recently, no undocumented immigrant had the legal right to live or work in the United States. If apprehended by the INS, such a person was either deported (involving a legal process before a judge) or was simply required to leave under the escort of border patrol officers. More recently, however (as mentioned in Chapter 4), substantial numbers of undocumented persons gained the right to remain in the United States either temporarily or permanently. Under the Immigration Act of 1990, the spouses and unmarried children of individuals legalized under IRCA who were in the United States illegally as of May 5, 1988, cannot ever be required to leave and have also been given legal work authorization. This same act gave El Salvadorans in the United States illegally since September 19, 1990, the right to stay and work in the United States for the eighteen-month period beginning January 1, 1991, and ending June 30, 1992. Thereafter, the attorney general of the United States was authorized to grant further stays of deportation to nationals of El Salvador according to criteria that would apply to undocumented immigrants from anywhere in the world. These criteria allowed the attorney general to stay deportation and authorize work permits for nationals of countries whose governments faced ongoing armed conflict or natural disasters; such governments unable to handle the return of their nationals had to notify the United States to request this status for their nationals. But President Clinton terminated the temporary protected status for El Salvadorans as of December 31, 1994. A third class of undocumented persons who cannot be deported and who have the legal right to seek work are petitioners for asylum whose cases have not been settled. Finally, there are those whose petitions for asylum have been denied but who have been given the privilege of a temporary stay of deportation; these persons may stay in the United States until a judge decides they must leave.

What happens when an individual is apprehended as an illegal alien? An overwhelmingly high proportion of such persons admit to an illegal status and agree to be removed from the United States under a procedure termed "voluntary departure with safeguards," the alien remaining in custody until the INS has transported him or her beyond the border of the United States. A very small number refuse the offer of voluntary departure and are offered a deportation hearing before an immigration judge. The judge then determines whether the individual had a legal right to be in the United States. An important consequence of deportation is that a deported alien may not be admitted to the United States for a period of five years following deportation unless the attorney general waives such a prohibition. In contrast, an apprehended alien who accepts the procedure of voluntary departure and pays the expense of departure can be legally admitted in the future without penalty.[41]

Perhaps the most important right of undocumented immigrants is the right to attend elementary and secondary schools. In response to a 1975 Texas law that banned the use of state funds to educate illegal aliens, the Supreme Court in June 1982 made a landmark decision in the case known as *Plyler v. Doe*. By a vote of five to four, the Supreme Court ruled that the Texas law was in violation of the Fourteenth Amendment of the Constitution, which stipulated that no state could "deny to any person within its jurisdiction the equal protection of the laws." *Plyler v. Doe* did not apply to higher education, though it is likely that the Supreme Court will soon have to consider this issue, too.[42] Moreover, the 1994 passage of Proposition 187 in California opens up the possibility that the Supreme Court might even decide to reverse *Plyler v. Doe.*

In the judicial system undocumented aliens have the same rights as U.S. citizens: the right to a defense attorney at public expense, the right to trial by jury, and the right to appeal unfavorable decisions to higher courts. The only difference is that an undocumented alien will ordinarily be deported after a criminal sentence has been completed.[43]

Undocumented immigrants also currently enjoy the right to receive emergency and pregnancy-related medical care funded through the Medicaid program, provided the usual Medicaid eligibility criteria have been met. This right dates to July 1986, when a federal district judge in New York City ruled that such care could not be denied. Subsequently, the U.S. Congress, in the Omnibus Budget Reconciliation Act of 1986, enacted legislation that granted undocumented immigrants the right to this limited form of medical care.[44] Undocumented persons are not, however, legally eligible to receive a social security card or benefits from entitlement programs such as unemployment compensation, AFDC, food stamps, supplemental security income (SSI), student financial aid programs, public housing, and so on.

Undocumented immigrants gain important privileges if they become parents of a child born in the United States. The Fourteenth Amendment to the Constitution stipulates that all persons born in the United States are U.S. citizens. Moreover, immigration law allows those aged twenty-one years or older to petition to have their parents become permanent legal residents. Legalization of status under such circumstances is automatic and does not depend on quota, so undocumented aliens in the United States who wish to legalize their status need wait no longer than twenty-one years after having an American-born child. American-born children are eligible to receive benefits from entitlement programs even though their parents are not.

The rights of permanent legal residents are in many respects identical to those of U.S. citizens. Perhaps the most important exception relates to political rights. Voting is a privilege only of U.S. citizens, and the right to hold many political offices is restricted to U.S. citizens—in some cases (e.g., the right to become president) to native-born citizens.

But the status of permanent legal resident does not necessarily mean that the individual may remain in the United States permanently. Permanent legal residents convicted of crime are deportable, as are permanent legal residents who become public charges within five years after entry, unless "the causes for dependency rose after entry."[45] In fiscal 1992 about 2,500 permanent legal residents were deported or required to depart under docket control.[46]

Furthermore, there is an important difference between citizens and permanent legal residents in regard to returning to the United States and maintaining a usual residence outside the United States. Permanent resident aliens who are absent from the United States for one year or more ordinarily lose their status as permanent legal resident. Naturalized citizens who establish permanent residence outside the United States within five years of naturalization also may lose their right to remain in the United States, whereas native-born citizens never lose this right.[47]

Permanent legal residents are considerably disadvantaged in comparison to U.S. citizens with respect to sponsoring their relatives to become permanent legal residents of the United States. Only U.S. citizens can petition to bring in an immediate relative (i.e., a spouse, unmarried minor child, or parent) without a quota restriction. U.S. citizens have further advantages over permanent legal residents in sponsoring relatives under the system of family-preference quotas.

It is unlawful for employers to discriminate in favor of citizens over permanent legal residents, an issue addressed in the Immigration Reform and Control Act of 1986. But it was not to be considered discrimination if an employer chose to hire a citizen over an equally qualified alien.

In general permanent legal residents have the same privileges as citizens with respect to benefits from entitlement programs, though the public charge provision, mentioned earlier, somewhat restricts this right among those who have been legal residents in the United States for less than five years. Moreover, within the first three years following entry to the United States permanent legal residents sponsored by a relative cannot apply for benefits from entitlement programs without taking into account the income and resources of their sponsor.[48] Finally, individuals legalized through IRCA were not allowed to receive benefits from entitlement programs until five years after they were granted temporary legal status.[49]

Unlike regular legal immigrants, refugees are not sponsored by relatives who are citizens or legal residents of the United States. Nor are they sponsored by employers. The ability of at least some refugees to earn a living in the United States is thus marginal at best. Accordingly, the U.S. government has instituted numerous programs to assist refugees. The first job of course is to bring them into the United States and settle them into a community. The government contracts with private resettlement agencies to accomplish this task. The resettlement agencies also provide refugees with job training and English-language programs.[50] The federal government currently reimburses the states for the entire cost of AFDC granted to refugees for the first four months and for general assistance for the first twelve months. Prior to 1990 federal reimbursements for refugee support were even more liberal: up to thirty-six months of AFDC or public assistance. Federal resettlement assistance declined from $4,500 per refugee in 1982 to $2,000 per refugee in 1990.[51]

Becoming a U.S. Citizen

Many permanent legal residents choose to become citizens; many others do not. In general, to become a naturalized U.S. citizen one must be at least eighteen years old, have been lawfully admitted for permanent legal residence, and have continuously resided in the United States for at least five years. Beyond these requirements one must demonstrate the ability to speak, read, and write the English language; have a knowledge of U.S. government and history; and be of good moral character. Finally, one must take an oath of allegiance to the United States, thereby renouncing allegiance to one's original nation of citizenship. In contrast to the general rule, wives of U.S. citizens usually may seek naturalization after only three years of residence in the United States, and children under the age of eighteen become naturalized citizens automatically upon the naturalization of their parents.[52]

Perhaps the chief perceived cost of seeking U.S. citizenship is renunciation of one's previous citizenship, which may substantially reduce one's rights in that nation. Consequently, many who have become permanent legal residents never seek to become U.S. citizens. Perhaps the next most important obstacle is the necessity to demonstrate the ability to speak, read, and write the English language.

The INS recently completed a telling study concerning who among the immigration cohort of 1977 had become naturalized citizens by the end of fiscal year 1991 and who had not.[53] The study was confined to persons aged sixteen and over at time of admission to the United States as permanent legal residents because no central record is kept of naturalization of children attendant on the naturalization of their parents. The INS matched individual naturalization records with the original records of becoming a permanent legal resident. It answered a leading question: Which individuals among the immigration cohort of 1977 became naturalized citizens fifteen years following their admittance to the United States as permanent legal residents? But the study could not answer another important question: What happened to the members of this immigration cohort who did not become naturalized citizens? The possibilities, of course, were that they could have emigrated, died, or remained in the United States as permanent legal residents.

Because the INS knew the age and sex of members of the 1977 immigration cohort, it was easy for staff researchers to estimate their death rate; they estimated that only 3 percent of this cohort could have died during the fifteen years following their entrance into the United States. To answer this second question, then, we need to know how many members of this immigration cohort emigrated during the fifteen-year period and how many remained in the United States as permanent legal aliens. As you are aware, however, since the INS has not been able to estimate emigration from the United States since the discontinuance of the annual alien registration program in 1981, it is impossible to answer this question from INS data. Finally, because of the lack of data, we cannot directly answer a third question, a hypothetical question that is probably the most important of all, namely: If no one had died or emigrated, what proportion of the cohort would have become naturalized citizens by the end of the fifteen-year period? If we could answer the second question, we could easily answer this third question using standard demographic techniques.[54]

You may also wonder whether the INS researchers should have waited longer than fifteen years to examine the proportion who naturalized. Obviously, their study cannot tell us the proportion who ever naturalized. Nevertheless, the results the INS researchers did obtain strongly suggest that the proportion who would naturalize over an entire lifetime would not be substantially greater than the proportion who had naturalized within fifteen years, because only 0.7 percent of all persons who became naturalized citizens did so in fiscal 1991 and only 1.2 percent in fiscal 1990. In fact the number of naturalizations for the 1977 immigration cohort peaked in fiscal 1983 and fell continuously thereafter.

The INS researchers found that 38.7 percent of the entire cohort had become naturalized citizens by the end of fiscal 1991. They also found a strong inverse relationship between the proportion who had naturalized and their age in 1977. Among those who had been teenagers or in their twenties at the time of admission in 1977, almost 50 percent had become naturalized citizens. The proportion of persons around age forty in 1977 who had naturalized was very close to the percentage among all ages. Among persons sixty-five or older in 1977, in contrast, fewer than 10 percent had naturalized (many of this group had of course died).

The INS study also pointed to large differences by country of birth, as shown in Table 5.17. The highest proportion of those who had naturalized were born in the USSR (62.4 percent); this proportion was more than three-fifths higher than that for people from all nations. The second highest proportion was for persons born in the Philippines (60.7 percent). The proportions were less than 20 percent for persons born in the United Kingdom, Mexico, Italy, Germany, and Canada, with the proportion of Canadians (12.1 percent) less than one-third of those who had naturalized from all nations. The INS researchers also discovered substantial differences in proportions who had naturalized dependent

TABLE 5.17   Percentage Naturalized by End of Fiscal 1991 for the Immigration Cohort
Aged Sixteen Years Old and Over in 1977 by Country of Birth

	Immigration Cohort of 1977	
Country of Birth	*Number Admitted as Permanent Legal Residents*	*Percent Naturalized by End of Fiscal 1991*
Total	352,071	38.7
USSR	4,535	62.4
Philippines	31,686	60.7
China	14,421	58.1
Korea	19,824	54.3
Guyana	4,115	53.9
India	15,053	49.8
Jamaica	7,896	37.6
Haiti	4,268	35.4
Cuba	57,023	34.6
Colombia	6,138	34.0
Greece	6,577	29.9
Trinidad and Tobago	4,516	25.0
Portugal	6,964	22.7
Ecuador	4,063	22.2
Dominican Republic	8,955	20.5
United Kingdom	8,982	17.0
Mexico	30,967	16.2
Italy	5,843	15.1
Germany	4,899	13.4
Canada	9,000	12.1
Other nations	96,366	43.9

SOURCE: U.S. Department of Justice, Immigration and Naturalization Service, *Statistical Yearbook of the Immigration and Naturalization Service, 1992* (Washington, D.C.: Government Printing Office, 1993), p. 130.

on category of admission: They found high rates for persons admitted as refugees and under the category of members of the professions or dependents of such persons.

At this point, I would like to return to the third important question posed earlier, namely, the hypothetical question: If no one had died or emigrated, what proportion of the cohort would have become naturalized citizens by the end of the fifteen-year period? As I said, we cannot answer this directly with INS data, but we can make some guesses by examining other sources of data, in particular data on emigration and data from the 1990 census of the United States. My personal conclusion is that the conditional probability of naturalization for a permanent legal resident, given that he or she does not emigrate or die, is quite high—certainly well above 50 percent.

Table 5.18 presents 1990 census data concerning the proportion of the foreign-born population who were naturalized citizens, categorizing them by country of birth. Before discussing in detail the substance of these data, let me remind you of certain facts that affect the interpretation. First, permanent legal residents who have been in the United States for less than five years are not in general eligible to become U.S. citizens. This reduces the proportions naturalized shown in Table 5.17, especially

TABLE 5.18 Naturalized Citizens Among the Foreign-Born Population of the United States by Country of Birth, 1990

Country of Birth	Number of Persons (in thousands)	Percent Who Are Naturalized Citizens
Total	19,767	40.5
Mexico	4,298	22.6
Philippines	913	53.9
Canada	745	54.1
Cuba	737	51.0
Germany	712	71.9
United Kingdom	640	49.6
Italy	581	75.8
Korea	568	40.6
Vietnam	543	42.7
China	530	44.1
El Salvador	465	15.4
India	450	34.9
Poland	388	62.4
Dominican Republic	348	27.6
Jamaica	334	38.4
USSR	334	58.9
Japan	290	28.2
Colombia	286	29.0
Taiwan	244	38.7
Guatemala	226	16.9
Haiti	225	27.4
Iran	211	27.2
Portugal	210	44.0

SOURCE: U.S. Bureau of the Census, *The Foreign Born Population in the United States: 1990,* CPH-L-98, prepared by Susan J. Lapham (Washington, D.C., 1993), pp. 19–21.

for those nations of birth where much of the immigration has been very recent. Second, no undocumented persons can become naturalized citizens until they have legalized their status. In this connection, you should remember that Karen Woodrow estimated that more than 3 million of the 20 million or so foreign-born persons counted in the 1990 census were undocumented. For nations such as Mexico, Guatemala, and El Salvador, from which presumably there were high numbers of undocumented immigrants counted in the 1990 census, the proportion naturalized must accordingly be substantially lower than it would have been if the data had referred only to persons who were here on a legal basis.

Finally, we must consider the question of the accuracy of the data from the 1990 census. You will recall Warren and Passel's finding with respect to census data accuracy concerning the number of naturalized citizens born in Mexico. If their finding holds for the 1990 census, the reported proportion naturalized among persons born in Mexico is considerably inflated. Warren and Passel produced further evidence that in the 1980 census many persons actually born in Mexico had reported they were of Mexican descent but were born in the United States. If this phenomenon also existed at the time of the 1990 census, it would affect the validity of the reported percent naturalized for persons born in Mexico.

As Table 5.18 shows, for all foreign-born persons the percentage who were naturalized was 40.5 percent. This figure is only slightly higher than the proportion of the 1977 immigration cohort who had naturalized within a fifteen-year period. However, if the data from the 1990 census in Table 5.18 had excluded undocumented persons and persons who had been in the United States as legal immigrants for less than five years, the percentage naturalized would have been far higher. Thus it would appear that the 1990 census data on proportion naturalized also substantially underestimate the proportion of legal immigrants who would have become naturalized citizens in a fifteen-year period following admission if none had died or emigrated.

For particular nations, there are some surprising differences between the data shown in Table 5.17 and those shown in Table 5.18. Consider persons born in Canada. According to Table 5.17, only 12.1 percent of the Canadians in the immigration cohort of 1977 had naturalized by the end of fiscal 1991. Yet Table 5.18 shows that in the 1990 census 54.1 percent of all persons born in Canada were naturalized citizens. Why the large discrepancy? The answer would appear to be a very high rate of return migration to Canada. Table 5.14 indicates that the ratio of emigrants to immigrants for Canada for the 1971–1980 period was indeed high (0.866). If this trend continued for the following decade, it would have resulted in a low proportion of naturalized persons among Canadians in the 1977 immigration cohort even in the face of a high conditional probability of naturalization if none had emigrated or died. A similar role for a high rate of return migration may explain the discrepancies between Tables 5.16 and 5.17 for persons from Germany, Italy, and the United Kingdom.

Residential Segregation of the Foreign-Born Within Metropolitan Areas

Within metropolitan areas the residential segregation of the immigrants from a particular nation is a matter of some importance, as it may affect the degree to which that group assimilates into the mainstream of American life. Social scientists disagree whether eventual assimilation is best achieved when a particular immigrant group has a high degree of residential segregation or when it has a low degree. Nevertheless, it is important to establish just how much residential segregation exists.

A large amount of research has chronicled the residential segregation of ethnic groups in the United States, and various indices of residential segregation have been developed. Perhaps the most widely used of these is the index of dissimilarity, a summary measure of inequality between two distributions that is based on the Lorenz curve. In the context of measuring residential segregation, this index can be described as measuring the proportion of persons in one ethnic group who would have to change place of residence in order for the spatial distribution of this given group to be identical to the spatial distribution of a second group. Often the comparison is between one ethnic group and all other persons who do not belong to that particular ethnic group. In addition, it is common practice to compare the extent to which one particular group is residentially segregated from a second group. The index of dissimilarity is usually computed on the basis of census tracts, small areas delineated by the Bureau of the Census that average approximately 3,000 persons. Sometimes the index is computed according to an even smaller area, the city block. Almost invariably the index of dissimilarity computed on the basis of city blocks will be somewhat higher than that computed on the basis of census tracts. This is because there is also considerable residential segregation by city block within each census tract.[55]

It is unfortunate that the Census Bureau does not make it easy to look at the residential segregation of immigrant groups, as a large proportion of the children of immigrants are native-born. Since these children live with their parents, the residential segregation of the foreign-born from the native-born population of a particular national-origin descent group is artificially reduced unless one makes an extra effort to classify minor children according to the place of birth of their parents.

Pini Herman and I recognized the practical need for a broader count of the foreign-born population that would include their minor children. In *A Human Mosaic: An Atlas of Ethnicity in Los Angeles County, 1980–1986,* we provided a new operational definition of the foreign-born population.[56] According to this definition, the foreign-born population included not only those persons born outside the United States but also the estimated number of all persons under age fifteen living with a mother born outside the United States (or, if not living with a mother, living with a father born outside the United States). Based on our definition, Figure 5.1 reproduces a map that demonstrates the spatial distribution of the 1980 population of Los Angeles County that was born in Mexico.

The three panels of Table 5.19 present data on indices of dissimilarity for various ethnic groups in Los Angeles County in which the foreign-born population is also defined as described above.[57] Panel A of Table 5.19 provides an introduction to the subsequent two panels. It shows the indices of dissimilarity for ethnic groups in Los Angeles County without regard to distinctions between native and foreign-born segments. The comparisons are between each ethnic group versus all persons not in that particular ethnic group. Although blacks are the most highly segregated, with an index of dissimilarity of .764, the table shows that each ethnic group, with the one exception of American Indians, is substantially segregated from the remaining population.

Panels B and C of Table 5.19 provide data for the foreign-born and native-born segments of most of the ethnic groups shown in Panel A. Blacks and American Indians are not included in the two later panels because of the small number of foreign-born persons in each of these two ethnic groups. Conversely, Vietnamese are not included in the two subsequent panels because practically none were native-born.

Panel B shows the index of dissimilarity with respect to residence for the foreign-born segment of each ethnic group compared to the native-born segment. What was surprising to me were the high values for most of the ethnic groups included. The index of dissimilarity between foreign and native-born segments of non-Hispanic whites was rather low (.267), but the values for all the other groups were moderate or substantial. What is most striking about the data shown in Panel B, however, is that for each of the foreign-born segments the magnitude of residential segregation with respect to the native-born segment is approximately the same as the magnitude of residential segregation with respect to all other persons in the county.

Panel C examines the degree to which each of the native-born segments is residentially segregated from the rest of the population. Even though each of these native-born segments is substantially segregated

FIGURE 5.1

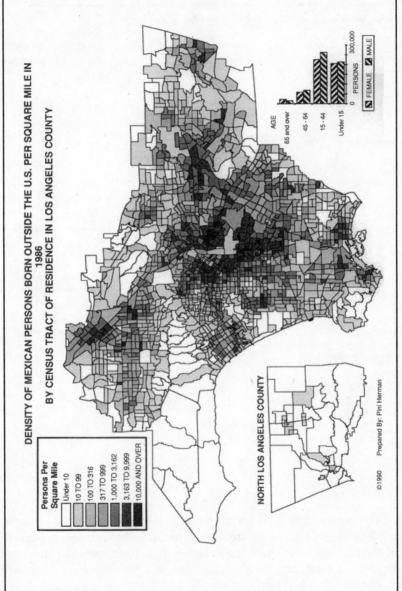

DENSITY OF MEXICAN PERSONS BORN OUTSIDE THE U.S. PER SQUARE MILE IN 1986

BY CENSUS TRACT OF RESIDENCE IN LOS ANGELES COUNTY

Persons Per
Square Mile

Under 10
10 TO 99
100 TO 316
317 TO 999
1,000 TO 3,162
3,163 TO 9,999
10,000 AND OVER

NORTH LOS ANGELES COUNTY

AGE
65 and over
45 - 64
15 - 44
Under 15

0   PERSONS   300,000

FEMALE   MALE

©1990   Prepared By: Pini Herman

SOURCE: David M. Heer and Pini Herman, *A Human Mosaic: An Atlas of Ethnicity in Los Angeles County, 1980–1986* (Panorama City, Calif.: Western Economic Research Company, 1990), p. 67.

TABLE 5.19   Indices of Dissimilarity with Respect to Residence for Ethnic Groups, Los
Angeles County, 1980

Panel A. Both Native-born and Foreign-born Persons

Total Ethnic group	Number of Persons (in thousands)	Index of Dissimilarity Versus All Other Persons
Non-Hispanic white	3,991	.568
Mexican	1,610	.536
Other Hispanic	407	.329
Black	945	.764
American Indian	54	.345
Chinese	94	.559
Filipino	100	.537
Japanese	117	.517
Korean	64	.577
Vietnamese	26	.680

Panel B. Foreign-born Segment of the Ethnic Group

		Index of Dissimilarity Versus	
Foreign-born Ethnic group	Number of Persons (in thousands)	Native Persons in the Same Ethnic Group	All Persons Outside the Specified Foreign-born Group
Non-Hispanic white	495	.267	.355
Mexican	946	.395	.556
Other Hispanic	290	.470	.406
Chinese	78	.586	.612
Filipino	88	.584	.566
Japanese	40	.416	.551
Korean	62	.729	.589

(continues)

from its respective foreign-born segment, it is noteworthy that almost all these native-born segments are also substantially segregated from the rest of the Los Angeles County population. The one exception appears to be the native-born segment of the group labeled "other Hispanic," which consists largely of those whose ancestors were in California or elsewhere in the Southwest at the time the United States acquired these areas from Mexico in 1848. By contrast the foreign-born segment of the group of other Hispanics consists mostly of persons born in El Salvador, Guatemala, or elsewhere in Central America. Therefore, it is not suprising that the native-born segment of this ethnic group has a low degree of

TABLE 5.19 (Continued)

Panel C: Native-born Segment of the Ethnic Group

Native-born Ethnic group	Number of Persons (in thousands)	Index of Dissimilarity Versus All Persons Outside the Specified Native-born Ethnic Group
Non-Hispanic white	3,496	.509
Mexican	664	.469
Other Hispanic	117	.331
Chinese	17	.601
Filipino	12	.649
Japanese	77	.560
Korean	2	.777

NOTE: Indices were computed for 1,612 census tracts.

SOURCE: Pini Herman, David M. Heer, Hsinmu Chen, Fayez Hammad, Yilan Qiu, and Maurice D. Van Arsdol Jr., "Redistribution and Assimilation of New Ethnic Populations in Los Angeles: 1980–1986," paper presented at the Twelfth World Congress of Sociology, Madrid, July 1990, pp. 29–35.

residential segregation with respect to all other persons but a notable degree of segregation from its foreign-born segment.

Let us summarize what we have learned from the three panels of this Table 5.19. First, disregarding native and foreign-born segments, we see considerable residential segregation of each ethnic group in Los Angeles County from all other ethnic groups. Second, within each ethnic group the foreign-born segment is highly segregated not only from the remainder of the population but also from its own native-born segment. Finally, the native-born segment of each ethnic group is in general substantially segregated from all other persons.

Notes

1. U.S. Department of Justice, Immigration and Naturalization Service, *Advanced Report, Immigration Statistics: Fiscal Year 1992* (Washington, D.C.: Government Printing Office, 1993), p. 1.

2. U.S. Department of Justice, Immigration and Naturalization Service, *Statistical Yearbook of the Immigration and Naturalization Service, 1992* (Washington, D.C.: Government Printing Office, 1993), pp. 60–66; U.S. Bureau of the Census, *Statistical Abstract of the United States, 1992* (Washington, D.C.: Government Printing Office, 1992), p. xv.

3. U.S. Department of Justice, *Statistical Yearbook, 1992*, pp. 64–66.

4. U.S. Department of Justice, Immigration and Naturalization Service, *Statistical Yearbook of the Immigration and Naturalization Service, 1990* (Washington, D.C.: Government Printing Office, 1991), p. A.1–18.

5. For a detailed statement of this methodology, see Robert Warren and Jeffrey S. Passel, "A Count of the Uncountable: Estimates of Undocumented Aliens Counted in the 1980 United States Census," *Demography*, Vol. 24, No. 3 (August 1987), pp. 375–393. Other important results from this study appear in Jeffrey S. Passel and Karen A. Woodrow, "Geographic Distribution of Undocumented Immigrants: Estimates of Undocumented Aliens Counted in the 1980 Census by State," *International Migration Review*, Vol. 18, No. 3 (Fall 1984), pp. 642–671, and in David M. Heer and Jeffrey S. Passel, "Comparison of Two Methods for Estimating the Number of Undocumented Mexican Adults in Los Angeles County," *International Migration Review*, Vol. 21, No. 4 (Winter 1987), pp. 1446–1473.

6. Vernon M. Briggs Jr., *Immigration Policy and the American Labor Force* (Baltimore: Johns Hopkins University Press, 1984), pp. 234–235.

7. Arthur F. Corwin, "A Story of Ad Hoc Exemptions: American Immigration Policy Toward Mexico," in Arthur F. Corwin, ed., *Immigrants—and Immigrants: Perspectives on Mexican Labor Immigration to the United States* (Westport, Conn.: Greenwood Press, 1978), p. 139.

8. Centro Nacional de Información y Estadísticas del Trabajo (CENIET), *Los trabajadores mexicanos en Estados Unidos: Resultados de la Encuesta Nacional de Emigracíon a la frontera norte del país y a los Estados Unidos* (Mexico City: CENIET, 1982).

9. Karen A. Woodrow–Lafield, "Undocumented Residents in the United States in 1989–90: Issues of Uncertainty in Quantification," paper delivered at the annual meeting of the American Sociological Association, Miami Beach, August 13–17, 1993.

10. James Diego Vigil, *El Jardin: An Ethnographic Enumeration of a Barrio in Greater East Los Angeles* (Washington, D.C.: U.S. Bureau of the Census, 1987). See also Stephanie Chavez and James Quinn, "Substandard Housing: Garages: Immigrants In, Cars Out," *Los Angeles Times*, May 24, 1987, p. 1.

11. David M. Heer and Pini Herman, *A Human Mosaic: An Atlas of Ethnicity in Los Angeles County, 1980–1986* (Panorama City, Calif.: Western Economic Research Company, 1990), p. 186.

12. John Crewdson, *The Tarnished Door: The New Immigrants and the Transformation of America* (New York: Times Books, 1983), p. 108; Arthur F. Corwin, "The Numbers Game: Estimates of Illegal Aliens in the United States, 1970–81" *Law and Contemporary Problems*, Vol. 45, No. 2 (1982), pp. 274–276.

13. Crewdson, *The Tarnished Door*, p. 108.

14. Passel and Woodrow, "Geographic Distribution of Undocumented Immigrants," p. 666.

15. U.S. Department of Justice, Immigration and Naturalization Service, Office of Strategic Planning, Statistics Division, *Estimates of the Resident Illegal Alien Population: October 1992* (Washington, D.C., 1993).

16. Robert Warren, "Estimates of the Unauthorized Immigrant Population Residing in the United States, by Country of Origin and State of Residence: October 1992," paper delivered at the conference "California Immigration 1994," Sacramento, April 29, 1994.

17. The source of the data on undocumented aliens in 1980 by state is Passel and Woodrow, "Geographic Distribution of Undocumented Immigrants," pp.

656–657. The source for the number of undocumented aliens in 1980 by metropolitan statistical area is a memorandum of August 16, 1985, from Jeffrey S. Passel to Roger Herriot, chief of the Population Division, U.S. Bureau of the Census (copy of the memo in a personal communication to the author from Jeffrey S. Passel). The source of the data on legalization applications is U.S. Department of Justice, Immigration and Naturalization Service, *Statistical Yearbook of the Immigration and Naturalization Service, 1991* (Washington, D.C.: Government Printing Office, 1992), p. 73.

18. U.S. Bureau of the Census, *1980 Census of Population, Detailed Population Characteristics: California,* PC80-1-D6 (Washington, D.C.: Government Printing Office, 1982), p. 1372.

19. U.S. Department of Justice, Immigration and Naturalization Service, Office of Strategic Planning, Statistics Division, *Provisional Legalization Application Statistics, December 1, 1991* (Washington, D.C., n.d.).

20. Personal communication, 1985.

21. David M. Heer, *Undocumented Mexicans in the United States* (New York: Cambridge University Press, 1990), pp. 108–112.

22. Archbishop Roger Mahony, "Statement on Those Who Will Not Qualify for Legalization Under the New Immigration Reform and Control Act of 1986," Archdiocese of Los Angeles, April 13, 1987.

23. Heer, *Undocumented Mexicans,* p. 145.

24. Ibid., p. 123.

25. U.S. Department of Justice, Immigration and Naturalization Service, *Immigration Reform and Control Act: Report on the Legalized Alien Population* (Washington, D.C.: Government Printing Office, 1992).

26. Ibid., pp. 28–29.

27. U.S. Bureau of the Census, *The Foreign Born Population in the United States: 1990,* CPH-L-98, prepared by Susan J. Lapham (Washington, D.C., 1993).

28. Michael Piore, *Birds of Passage: Migrant Labor and Industrial Societies* (Cambridge: Cambridge University Press, 1979).

29. Refer to the data shown previously in Table 5.7. See also Wayne A. Cornelius, "From Sojourners to Settlers: The Changing Profile of Mexican Immigration to the United States," in Jorge A. Bustamante, Clark W. Reynolds, and Raúl A. Hinojosa Ojeda, ed., *U.S.-Mexico Relations: Labor Market Interdependence* (Stanford: Stanford University Press, 1992), pp. 155–195.

30. Robert Warren and Ellen Percy Kraly, *The Elusive Exodus: Emigration from the United States* (Washington, D.C.: Population Reference Bureau, 1985), p. 2.

31. Karen A. Woodrow, "Emigration from the United States: Multiplicity Survey Evidence," U.S. Bureau of the Census, August 28, 1991.

32. Ibid., pp. 5–6.

33. Daniel B. Levine, Kenneth Hill, and Robert Warren, eds., *Immigration Statistics: A Story of Neglect* (Washington, D.C.: National Academy Press, 1985).

34. Warren and Kraly, *The Elusive Exodus,* p. 15.

35. Woodrow, "Emigration from the United States," table 3.

36. Guillermina Jasso and Mark R. Rosenzweig, *The New Chosen People: Immigrants in the United States* (New York: Russell Sage Foundation, 1990), pp. 138–143.

37. Piore, *Birds of Passage.*

38. Heer, *Undocumented Mexicans,* p. 29.

39. U.S. Commission on Civil Rights, *Counting the Forgotten: The 1970 Census Count of Persons of Spanish Speaking Background in the United States* (Washington, D.C.: U.S. Commission on Civil Rights, 1974), p. 45.

40. U.S. Bureau of the Census, "Population Projections of the United States by Age, Sex, Race, and Hispanic Origin: 1992 to 2050," prepared by Jennifer Cheeseman Day, *Current Population Reports,* Ser. P-25, No. 1092 (November 1992).

41. U.S. Department of Justice, *Statistical Yearbook, 1992,* p. 153.

42. David W. Stewart, *Immigration and Education: The Crisis and the Opportunities* (New York: Lexington Books, 1993), p. 38; Thomas Muller, *Immigrants and the American City* (New York: New York University Press, 1993), p. 200.

43. Dianne Klein, "A Hit or Miss Approach to Curbing Deportable Felons," *Los Angeles Times,* November 27, 1993, p. A1.

44. David Simcox, "Overview—A Time of Reform and Reappraisal," in David Simcox, ed., *U.S. Immigration in the 1980s: Reappraisal and Reform* (Boulder: Westview Press, 1988), p. 38; Muller, *Immigrants and the American City,* pp. 202–203; U.S. General Accounting Office, *Trauma Care Reimbursement: Poor Understanding of Losses and Coverage for Undocumented Aliens,* GAO/PEMD-93-1 (Washington, D.C.: Government Printing Office, 1992), pp. 2–3.

45. E. P. Hutchinson, *Legislative History of American Immigration Policy, 1798–1965* (Philadelphia: University of Pennsylvania Press, 1981), p. 450.

46. U.S. Department of Justice, *Statistical Yearbook, 1992,* p. 166.

47. Jasso and Rosenzweig, *The New Chosen People,* p. 122.

48. Milton D. Morris, *Immigration—The Beleaguered Bureaucracy* (Washington, D.C.: Brookings Institution, 1985), p. 46.

49. Federation for American Immigration Reform, "The Immigration Reform and Control Act of 1986," *FAIR Legislative Bulletin* (1986), pp. 7–8.

50. Barnaby Zall, "The U.S. Refugee Industry: Doing Well by Doing Good," in Simcox, *U.S. Immigration in the 1980s,* p. 263.

51. Elizabeth S. Rolph, *Immigration Policies: Legacy from the 1980s and Issues for the 1990s* (Santa Monica: RAND Corporation, 1992), pp. 35–36.

52. U.S. Department of Justice, *Statistical Yearbook, 1992,* pp. 124–126.

53. Ibid., pp. 127–131.

54. A. H. Pollard, Farhat Yusuf, and G. N. Pollard, *Demographic Techniques,* 3d ed. (Sydney: Pergamon Press, 1990), pp. 139–151.

55. Otis Dudley Duncan and Beverly Duncan, "A Methodological Analysis of Segregation Indexes," *American Sociological Review,* Vol. 20 (1955), pp. 210–217.

56. Heer and Herman, *A Human Mosaic,* p. 2.

57. Pini Herman, David M. Heer, Hsinmu Chen, Fayez Hammad, Yilan Qiu, and Maurice D. Van Arsdol Jr., "Redistribution and Assimilation of New Ethnic Populations in Los Angeles: 1980–1986," paper presented at the Twelfth World Congress of Sociology, Madrid, July 1990.

6 Determinants of Immigration

Demographers divide the determinants of the volume of migration into two components. The first concerns the propensity of a given type of individual to migrate, that is, the probability that someone will migrate to a different place of usual residence within a given time. The second concerns the number of individuals who are at risk of migration at each level of propensity. The volume of migration can be calculated as the sum over all levels of propensity of the products obtained by multiplying each separate propensity to migrate by the number of individuals possessing that propensity.

A large part of this chapter is devoted to analyzing variations in the individual propensity to migrate. In trying to project the future volume of immigration into or away from the United States, however, it is extremely important to be aware of the trends in world population size by region forecast for the future by demographers at the United Nations (UN). These forecasts are the necessary basis for estimating the population at risk of immigrating to the United States and emigrating from the United States. The future population at risk of immigrating is of course the population of the whole world minus the population of the United States. The future population at risk of emigrating from the United States is simply the future population of the United States. Accordingly, I begin this chapter with a discussion of the UN population forecasts.

UN Forecasts of Future World Population

Every other year the Population Division of the UN prepares new population projections for each nation in the world.[1] The UN prepares three series for each nation: high, medium, and low. The medium projection is taken the most likely and may therefore be taken to be the forecast. Similar to projections prepared by the U.S. Bureau of the Census, the UN projections employ the cohort component method. Such a method demands assumptions concerning age-sex-specific rates of death, birth, and net immigration for each birth cohort. In making these assumptions, the UN relies heavily on the theory of the demographic transition. Therefore, in

Trinidadian barber shop, Boston, Massachusetts.

order to comprehend the methodology of the UN population projections, we need to understand this theory.

Popularized around the end of World War II by various demographers, including Warren S. Thompson, Frank Notestein, Kingsley Davis, and C. P. Blacker, the theory of the demographic transition suggests how industrialization, or modernization, relates to demographic change.[2] According to the theory, in the first stage of the demographic transition, the preindustrial era, both age-sex-specific birthrates and age-sex-specific death rates are high but balancing so that natural increase is nil. During the second stage, corresponding to an early stage of industrialization, age-sex-specific death rates begin substantial decline with only a small decline in age-sex-specific birthrates, leading to a high rate of natural increase. By the third stage of the transition, a period when industrialization has been further advanced, the age-sex-specific birthrates decline more rapidly than the age-sex-specific death rates, leading to a diminished but still positive rate of natural increase. Finally, in the last stage of the transition, corresponding to an era of mature industrialization, both age-sex-specific birthrates and age-sex-specific death rates are low but balancing so that natural increase is again nil.

For purposes of its population projections, the UN divides the nations of the world into two classes: the more-developed nations and the less-

Vietnamese family, Oakland, California.

developed nations. The more-developed nations include all of Europe plus Australia, Canada, Japan, New Zealand, the United States, and the former USSR. The UN calls the remaining nations less developed, although some might question this status for countries such as Singapore or Taiwan. The UN believes that most of the less-developed nations are currently in the second or third stage of the demographic transition; the developed nations and a small number of the less-developed nations are supposed to have completed the transition. All nations are projected to complete the demographic transition at some point; the least-advanced nations are supposed to complete this transition between 2040 and 2045.

In accordance with demographic transition theory, the UN assumes for all nations that the speed of mortality decline will be higher the more elevated is the level of current mortality. But the UN does not rely solely on the theory of the demographic transition in making its assumptions about change in age-sex-specific birthrates, and it recognizes the effect of government family-planning policies. Given two nations at the same stage of economic development, fertility decline is assumed to be more rapid in a nation with a comprehensive family-planning program than in a nation with no such program. Because the theory of the demographic transition does not take into account that many developed nations have a fertility level too low to allow population replacement without net immigration, in projecting the future course of fertility for such nations, the UN was guided by the fertility assumptions included in the population projections of national statistical agencies. Thus for many nations a continuation of below-replacement fertility was assumed.

The theory of the demographic transition also says nothing about international migration. Yet in preparing a population projection, one must make assumptions about age-sex-specific net immigration. For nations with a long history of either net immigration or net out-migration, the UN assumed a constant flow of age-sex-specific net immigration (or net emigration). For other nations, the net inflow or outflow was expected to be only temporary.

Table 6.1 shows some of the most important results of the medium series for the 1992 UN population projections in a form that distinguishes the forecast population of the United States from that of the rest of the world. The remaining more-developed nations are also set apart from the less-developed nations, and there are entries for all continents and all nations that had at least 50 million persons in 1990.

The most striking indication in Table 6.1 is the tremendous increase in world population outside of the United States. This population is projected to rise from 5.045 billion in 1990 to 8.150 billion in 2025. Almost all of this increase is concentrated in the less-developed nations, where population is predicted to jump from 4.084 billion in 1990 to 7.069 billion in 2025. The developed nations other than the United States increase their population from 1990 to 2030 only from 0.961 billion to 1.081 billion.

A comparison of the data shown in Table 5.15 with that shown in Table 6.1 indicates that the UN forecast for future U.S. population is somewhat lower than the Census Bureau prediction. For the year 2025, the UN forecasts a population of only 322 million, whereas the U.S. Bureau of the Census forecasts a population of 334 million. The published data do not allow an explicit comparison of how the UN assumptions differ from those of the Census Bureau. Despite the discrepancy, we assume the accuracy of the UN forecasts since they are the only such set for all nations.

What implication does this enormous population growth in areas outside the United States have for immigration to the United States? Perhaps

TABLE 6.1   UN Medium-Series Projection of World Population for 1995–2030

	1990 Population	*Projected Population (in millions)*						
		1995	*2000*	*2005*	*2010*	*2015*	*2020*	*2025*
United States	250	263	275	286	296	306	315	322
Rest of world	5,045	5,496	5,953	6,402	6,853	7,303	7,735	8,150
Other developed nations	961	981	1,003	1,024	1,044	1,061	1,073	1,081
Less developed nations	4,084	4,515	4,950	5,377	5,809	6,243	6,663	7,069
Continents and selected nations								
North America (excluding U.S.)	174	191	209	226	243	259	274	288
Mexico	84	94	103	111	118	125	132	137
South America	294	320	344	369	392	414	434	452
Brazil	149	161	173	184	194	204	212	220
Africa	643	744	856	980	1,116	1,265	1,421	1,583
Egypt	52	59	65	71	78	84	88	94
Nigeria	109	127	148	171	197	226	256	286
Asia	3,118	3,408	3,692	3,957	4,214	4,461	4,689	4,900
Bangladesh	114	128	144	161	177	194	209	223
China	1,153	1,238	1,310	1,362	1,410	1,458	1,504	1,540
India	846	931	1,019	1,106	1,189	1,265	1,329	1,394
Indonesia	184	201	218	232	245	258	271	283
Iran	58	67	78	90	104	118	132	146
Japan	124	126	128	130	131	130	129	127
Korea	43	45	47	48	49	50	50	50
Pakistan	118	135	155	176	198	220	241	260
Philippines	62	69	76	83	89	95	100	105
Thailand	55	58	61	64	67	69	71	72
Turkey	56	62	68	74	79	83	88	93
Vietnam	67	74	82	89	97	104	110	117
Europe	509	516	524	531	536	540	542	542
France	57	58	59	60	60	60	61	61
Germany	79	81	83	84	84	84	84	84
Italy	58	58	58	58	58	58	57	56
United Kingdom	57	58	59	59	60	60	60	60
Former USSR	281	289	297	307	317	328	336	345
Oceania	27	29	31	33	35	37	40	41

SOURCE: United Nations, Department for Economic and Social Information and Policy Analysis, *World Population Prospects, the 1992 Revision.* ST/ESA/Ser. A/135. (New York: United Nations, 1993).

none at all. Remember that the population projected for the United States includes a provision for a constant flow of net immigration and that the population projection for the world outside the United States provides for a constant flow of net emigration of equal magnitude. So if future immigration to the United States is the same as that projected by the UN, its volume will not change. But I mentioned in the previous section that the number of immigrants to the United States can be calculated as the sum—over all levels of propensity to immigrate—of the products obtained by multiplying each separate propensity to immigrate by the number of individuals with that propensity. Because of the huge increase in the population at risk for immigration, the only way in which immigration to the United States can be kept at a constant level is for the propensities for immigration to decline. And perhaps the only way in which these propensities will decline is for the United States to use draconian measures to stem both entry without inspection and visa overstay. The chief lesson to be drawn from Table 6.1, then, is that in future years we can expect much more pressure on all laws and regulations designed to restrict immigration to the United States.

We have yet to examine how the population at risk for emigration from the United States will change in the future. This population is of course equivalent to the forecast population of the United States. From Table 6.1 we can see that the forecast population of the United States will also increase substantially, though much less rapidly than the population of the rest of the world. For example, in 1990 the population of the United States was equal to 5.0 percent of the population of the rest of the world; in 2025 this figure is predicted to be only 4.0 percent. Accordingly, if we assume that neither the propensities to immigrate to the United States nor the propensities to emigrate from the United States change, then the decreasing size of the U.S. population relative to that of the rest of the world guarantees that net immigration to the United States must increase.

Now let us get ahead of the game and very briefly consider propensities for immigration. Some demographers hypothesize that propensities to immigrate are affected by either absolute population growth or percentage population growth. The idea is that population growth of the first or second type creates disruption and that disruption would increase the propensity to immigrate to the United States. Tables 6.2 and 6.3 allow an examination of how these two hypotheses would affect immigration to the United States. Results of the UN medium-series projection with respect to the absolute population change during each quinquennium are shown in Table 6.2; results with respect to the projected average annual rate of population change during each quinquennium are shown in Table 6.3. Table 6.2 indicates that the absolute increase in

TABLE 6.2   UN Medium-Series Projection of Absolute Population Change by Quinquennium from 1990 Population Base to 2030

	Absolute Population Change (in millions)						
	1990–1995	*1995–2000*	*2000–2005*	*2005–2010*	*2010–2015*	*2015–2020*	*2020–2025*
United States	13	12	11	10	10	9	7
Rest of world	451	457	449	451	450	432	415
Other developed nations	20	22	22	20	16	12	9
Less-developed nations	431	435	427	431	434	420	406
Continents and selected nations							
North America (excluding U.S.)	18	18	17	17	16	15	14
Mexico	9	9	8	8	7	6	6
South America	26	25	24	23	22	20	18
Brazil	12	11	11	10	10	9	7
Africa	101	112	124	136	148	156	161
Egypt	6	6	6	6	6	5	5
Nigeria	18	21	23	26	28	30	30
Asia	290	284	265	257	247	228	212
Bangladesh	15	16	17	17	16	15	14
China	85	71	52	48	48	46	36
India	85	88	87	83	76	64	65
Indonesia	17	17	14	13	13	13	12
Iran	8	11	13	14	14	14	13
Japan	2	2	2	1	−1	−1	−2
Korea	2	2	1	1	1	0	0
Pakistan	17	20	21	22	22	21	19
Philippines	7	7	7	7	6	5	5
Thailand	4	3	3	3	2	2	1
Turkey	6	6	6	5	4	5	5
Vietnam	7	8	8	8	7	6	7
Europe	7	8	7	5	4	2	−0
France	1	1	1	0	0	0	0
Germany	2	1	1	1	0	−0	−0
Italy	0	0	0	−0	−0	−1	−1
United Kingdom	1	1	1	0	0	0	0
Former USSR	7	8	10	11	10	9	8
Oceania	2	2	2	2	2	2	2

SOURCE: United Nations, Department for Economic and Social Information and Policy Analysis, *World Population Prospects, the 1992 Revision*. ST/ESA/Ser. A/135. (New York: United Nations, 1993).

TABLE 6.3   UN Medium-Series Projection of Average Annual Rate of Population Change by Quinquennium from 1990 Population Base to 2030

	Average Annual Rate of Change (percentage)						
	1990–1995	1995–2000	2000–2005	2005–2010	2010–2015	2015–2020	2020–2025
United States	1.03	0.91	0.76	0.70	0.63	0.58	0.47
Rest of world	1.71	1.60	1.45	1.36	1.27	1.15	1.05
Other developed nations	0.41	0.44	0.43	0.39	0.31	0.22	0.16
Less-developed nations	2.01	1.84	1.66	1.54	1.44	1.30	1.18
Continents and selected nations							
North America (excluding U.S.)	1.94	1.76	1.58	1.42	1.28	1.14	1.00
Mexico	2.06	1.81	1.55	1.33	1.15	0.99	0.83
South America	1.67	1.49	1.35	1.22	1.09	0.95	0.81
Brazil	1.59	1.36	1.22	1.10	0.98	0.83	0.68
Africa	2.93	2.81	2.70	2.61	2.50	2.33	2.15
Egypt	2.20	2.04	1.90	1.72	1.46	1.15	1.11
Nigeria	3.13	3.03	2.95	2.85	2.69	2.48	2.23
Asia	1.78	1.60	1.39	1.26	1.14	1.00	0.88
Bangladesh	2.41	2.35	2.18	1.96	1.75	1.54	1.30
China	1.42	1.12	0.78	0.69	0.68	0.62	0.47
India	1.91	1.80	1.64	1.45	1.23	0.98	0.96
Indonesia	1.78	1.58	1.28	1.08	1.03	0.97	0.88
Iran	2.71	3.11	2.98	2.81	2.54	2.21	1.82
Japan	0.38	0.34	0.27	0.12	−0.09	−0.20	−0.26
Korea	0.82	0.75	0.59	0.40	0.24	0.13	0.05
Pakistan	2.67	2.74	2.54	2.35	2.12	1.84	1.49
Philippines	2.07	1.88	1.70	1.51	1.29	1.01	0.96
Thailand	1.27	0.98	0.92	0.81	0.67	0.53	0.39
Turkey	2.05	1.89	1.61	1.32	1.09	1.11	1.05
Vietnam	2.03	1.99	1.85	1.65	1.41	1.16	1.15
Europe	0.27	0.30	0.27	0.20	0.14	0.07	−0.00
France	0.37	0.35	0.25	0.17	0.12	0.09	0.04
Germany	0.44	0.32	0.22	0.15	0.07	−0.03	−0.10
Italy	0.09	0.08	0.07	−0.02	−0.14	−0.23	−0.34
United Kingdom	0.24	0.25	0.19	0.12	0.10	0.07	0.01
Former USSR	0.51	0.57	0.65	0.68	0.65	0.52	0.47
Oceania	1.52	1.46	1.37	1.29	1.16	1.05	0.91

SOURCE: United Nations, Department for Economic and Social Information and Policy Analysis, *World Population Prospects, the 1992 Revision.* ST/ESA/Ser. A/135. (New York: United Nations, 1993).

world population outside the United States will peak between 1995 and 2000; for Africa, the continent least advanced with respect to the demographic transition, the peak will not come until 2020–2025. Table 6.3, in contrast, suggests that the average annual population change rate for the world outside the United States will be highest in the 1990–1995 quinquennium and will fall continuously thereafter. Moreover, the peak rate for Africa will also be from 1990 to 1995 and will afterward decline. Tables 6.2 and 6.3 therefore give somewhat contradictory results as to when future population growth may enhance the propensities to immigrate to the United States.

A Conceptual Scheme for Determining Individual Propensities to Migrate

In another work I have developed a conceptual scheme for analyzing the determinants of the propensity to migrate.[3] I adapted this scheme from one economist-demographer Joseph J. Spengler developed for the analysis of the determinants of decisions with respect to fertility.[4] In this conceptual scheme I have classified the factors that influence the decision to migrate into those affecting a preference system, a price system, and the total amount of resources in time and money available for all goals.

The preference system describes the relative attractiveness of various places as destinations for potential migrants compared to other destinations that their resources would allow. An area's attractiveness is the balance between the positive and negative values that it offers.

The price system describes the expenditure of resources that is both a precondition to and a concomitant of migration. For many migrants, the price of migration is in large part simply the monetary expense of moving. Because the cost of migration generally varies in direct proportion to the distance traveled, the number of migrants to a given place tends to vary inversely with the distance.

The total resources in time and money available for all goals also affect the decision to migrate. If the only drawback to migration is the expense of the move, then an increase in monetary income should increase the probability of migration.

Another much-used conceptual scheme for discussing the determinants of the propensity to migrate is that of Everett Lee.[5] He summarized the factors entering into the decision to migrate as follows:

1. factors associated with the area of origin
2. factors associated with the area of destination
3. intervening obstacles
4. personal factors

Lee's scheme is complementary to the scheme I employ. In particular, Lee's conceptual scheme has been very useful in analyzing trends in immigration from one nation to another nation over time. In such a study it is helpful to analyze yearly change in migratory volume as a function of economic conditions both in the nation of destination and in the nation of origin.[6]

To apply my conceptual scheme in more concrete terms, I begin with factors associated with the preference system. Among the positive values generated by migration, perhaps the most important is the prospect of a better job. In 1991 the United States had a per capita GNP of $22,130, a very high amount compared to the levels of per capita GNP based on purchasing-power comparability in the less-developed nations. The per capita GNP in these nations ranged from around $500 to around $8,000 in 1991. Most individuals residing in one of the less-developed nations, then, could anticipate a substantially better job if they were to immigrate to the United States and find work there. For residents of the developed nations (among which the per capita GNP in 1991 was typically only marginally lower than in the United States), however, the possibility of finding a better job in the United States is much lower, depending on a very specific job market.[7]

Nevertheless, a job is not the only source of economic support. For women, a "good" marriage provides an alternative. Women in overseas cities where large numbers of U.S. military personnel are stationed have an opportunity to marry someone who may provide much better support than any local man. The mere continuance of marital and family ties is an important cause for immigration. Since U.S. immigration laws encourage the immigration of family units, a sizable proportion of all persons admitted as permanent legal residents to the United States are dependents of a primary wage earner.

Another positive value immigration may achieve is a more favorable physical climate. Retired Canadians may migrate to Florida solely to escape winter cold. Freedom from persecution has always been an important motive for international migration among many religious and racial minorities as well as for intellectuals. Well-known examples include the settlement of New England by the Puritans and the flight of Jews from Russia to escape pogroms in the decades surrounding 1900. More broadly, the mere attempt to preserve life and limb can also be a primary motive for international migration. Such was the case during the civil war in El Salvador during the 1980s, when threats to the lives of the El Salvadorans proved to be a powerful stimulus to immigrate to the United States.

Migration also creates negative values. One of the most important is disruption of interpersonal relationships with kin and friends. The greater the distance of the move, the greater this disruption will be, as return visits and contacts become more costly. To mitigate against this disruption, many migrants travel to the same towns or city neighborhoods to which relatives or other people from their towns of origin have previously migrated. I was made very aware of this fact in a study trip to Puerto Rico in 1964. Our group made a visit to the small town of Peñuelos on the south coast of the island, where we met many Puerto Ricans who talked about their relatives living in the United States. What was surprising was that almost all of these relatives lived in one city: Waterbury, Connecticut.

In addition, the volume of migration from one locale to another tends to rise once a small nucleus of settlers from a particular origin has established itself in a certain locale, a phenomenon termed "chain migration."[8] The important aspect of chain migration is that once it has begun, the negative values associated with disruption of interpersonal relationships markedly decline.[9]

Migration may also cause deprivation because of the necessity to adapt to a new culture, including a new language. Some languages are more similar to English than are others. In particular, languages derived from Latin (such as Spanish, Italian, and French) and languages of Germanic origin (such as German, Dutch, and Swedish) are sufficiently close to English so that native speakers can learn English with relatively little trouble. But native speakers of Asian or African languages often have great difficulty learning English.

Religion is another important cultural component that may differ between the country of origin and the country of destination. With respect to immigration to the United States, potential immigrants who are Christians obviously suffer less disruption from prevailing religious norms than adherents of religions that have few members in the United States. In particular, adherents of Islam, Buddhism, and Hinduism may find it harder to adjust to conditions in the United States. (For example, Muslims celebrate the Sabbath on Friday, a workday in the United States.)

Laws restricting the number of legal entrants to the United States are of course a major negative value for those immigrants who arrive in the United States without a legal permit or fail to leave when their legal permit has expired. Such persons live in fear of being discovered and sent back to their native land. As a result of their illegal status, they are deprived of entitlement programs available to legal immigrants, and their lack of legal status may also keep them from attaining a certain wage or salary level.

Another possible negative value caused by immigration is relative deprivation. The importance of relative deprivation has been emphasized by economists Oded Stark and J. Edward Taylor.[10] Consider this example: A man from a Mexican village contemplates migration to Los Angeles. In his village his socioeconomic status is close to the median; approximately half of his fellow villagers have a lower status and the other half a higher status. Now assume he moves to Los Angeles. By moving there his actual purchasing power may double, but his reference group may now change. If his new reference group consists of everyone living in Los Angeles, he will find that almost all of them have a higher income than he does. But his reference group might change even more than that. If he found himself a job as a gardener in Beverly Hills, his problem of relative deprivation might be very acute; in this case his reference group might consist only of the rich and famous. Stark and Taylor believe that one function of the residential segregation of newly arrived immigrant groups is to lessen feelings of relative deprivation. They explain the prevalence of seasonal and sojourn migration of Mexicans to the United States as a similar attempt to lessen relative deprivation: When seasonal migrants to the United States return to their native villages in Mexico in the late fall, the earnings they bring back provide them an opportunity to be the big fish in a small pond.[11] A desire to reduce relative deprivation may also explain the large number of Mexicans holding the status of permanent legal resident in the United States who work in a U.S. border city but actually reside in Mexico.

A final component of the preference system that merits discussion is what economists call risk aversion. The idea behind this concept is that most people prefer a lower income obtained with certainty than the possibility of a much higher income but with considerable uncertainty whether they will in fact have the chance to enjoy the income or whether it might be drastically reduced. Under many circumstances the desire for risk aversion will lead individuals to forgo migration even though, on average, migration might allow them to increase their income dramatically. This may be the case above all when individuals lack strong networks in possible places of destination, since such networks provide an individual with inexpensive sources of information concerning job opportunities. But as Stark and D. Levhari have pointed out, there are circumstances in which the desire for risk aversion will lead to migration.[12] Consider the case of a small farmer in Mexico who expects poor crops because of drought. As insurance against the possibility of financial loss on his farm, he may persuade his eighteen-year-old son to migrate without documents to California to participate in the harvests there. Since they live in a village from which many residents migrate seasonally to California, his son will have good sources of information about specific job opportunities there. The father will give his son the money to pay for the trip; in return the father will expect remittances from his son that should provide the father with a substantial net profit. In this case the father's desire for risk aversion has provided the occasion for his son's migration.

Let us now examine the price system in more detail. We mentioned earlier in this section that in general the cost of transportation to the United States is a function of distance from the United States. Another aspect of the price system is the price for obtaining knowledge about opportunities in the United States. Individuals with preexisting networks of relatives and friends in the United States have a great advantage over persons without such networks. Furthermore, restrictive legislation with respect to legal immigration also has a major effect on the price system. Undocumented immigrants who succeed in reaching the U.S. border must often pay for forged documents and the services of a so-called coyote who will lead them safely through the barriers imposed by the border patrol. Finally, the price system depends on the migrant's age. If we assume that an individual does not contemplate return migration, then one way of looking at the cost of the trip is in terms of the cost per year that the person will reside at the new destination. Obviously, this cost is less the younger the migrant at the time of the move. The strength of this reasoning is perhaps best revealed if it is assumed that the migrant has borrowed money to make the trip. Then it is clear that the more years the migrant has to pay back the debt, the better off the migrant will be. Economists assume that this is why most migrants are young adults. In my opinion, their argument is sufficient but perhaps not necessary. It is also possible that for biological reasons young adults can more readily adapt to new circumstances than can older ones.

Finally, let us consider in greater detail the total resources in time and money available for all goals. We have already emphasized that the decision to migrate is a positive function of these total resources. In speculation concerning the future volume of immigration from the less-developed nations to the United States, it is interesting to imagine how this future flow may be affected by an increase in per capita income in these nations. On the one hand, a rise in per capita income would increase the total resources in time and money available to potential immigrants. This factor by itself should serve to increase the volume of immigration to the United States. On the other hand, if growth in per capita income in the less-developed nations results in a decline in the relative income gap between those nations and the United States, it should reduce the incentive to migrate to the United States. Accordingly, it is doubtful that economic advance in the less-developed nations would have any immediate effect on propensities to migrate to the United States.[13]

Up to now our discussion has assumed that the United States was the only possible destination for international migrants. As George J. Borjas has forcefully pointed out, this is not the case.[14] Instead, the United States participates in a world immigration market. A resident of Hong Kong may consider migration not only to the United States but also to Canada or Australia. A French-speaking Haitian may consider migration not only to Miami or New York but also to French-speaking Montreal. Similarly, a resident of Jamaica might think of moving either to New York or Toronto. So we must understand that potential immigrants will come to the United States only if the perceived cost-benefit ratio of immigration to this nation is greater than that for (1) immigration to any other nation, (2) internal migration within their own nations, or (3) no migration at all.

Moreover, it is possible that the rewards from immigration to the United States will be less than expected. If this is the case and if the costs of additional migratory movement are not prohibitive, there is a high probability that immigrants will leave the United States and return to their homelands or possibly migrate to some other country.

Structural Determinants of Propensities to Immigrate

The conceptual scheme we have used to analyze the propensity for immigration or emigration is at the level of the individual. In using this scheme, we intend to predict whether an individual will migrate and, if so, where he or she will migrate. We do so on the basis of factors pertinent to that individual alone. Nevertheless, many of the existing studies of immigration are not studies of individuals but studies of aggregates. Generally, this aggregate is a nation and the analysis is of the variation in emigration rates to the United States from other nations. In such studies the independent variables are characteristics of the nation rather than those pertaining to individuals in the nation. For example, instead of data on the current wage a potential immigrant is receiving relative to the wage he or she might expect to receive if he or she immigrated to the United States, we would make use of data on per capita income in a particular nation compared to per capita income in the United States. Moreover, rather than a measure of individual transport cost, we might substitute the distance from the capital city of each nation to a central point in the United States. And we would not use data on the strength of an individual's preexisting network in the United States; instead, we might utilize data on the size of the immigrant stock from that nation resident in the United States relative to the total population of that nation. This might serve as an indicator of the average strength of preexisting network ties. Finally, instead of a dichotomous variable indicating whether the individual immigrant would be allowed to come to the U.S. legally, we might substitute population size. This is a good substitute because U.S. immigration quotas are identical for all nations regardless of the size of their population, and thus individuals from more populous nations have a lower opportunity to immigrate legally.

In addition to these structural determinants, another factor may be significant. Alejandro Portes has emphasized the importance of the hegemonic power of the United States.[15] Portes believes that immigration rates to the United States are increased among those nations in which the United States has exercised its hegemonic power. Portes points out that following the Mexican war of 1848, the United States annexed half of Mexico's territory. Because former citizens of Mexico continued to live in the southwestern United States following annexation, there existed henceforth a stock of Mexicans in the United States who became the preexisting network for additional immigrants.

Portes takes Cuba as another example. The United States fought a war with Spain in 1898 over the issue of independence for certain Spanish colonies, most notably Cuba, Puerto Rico, and the Philippines. Following that war, Cuba was nominally independent but dominated by U.S. economic interests. When Fidel Castro assumed power in Cuba in 1959, the Cuban middle class fled to the United States, not with the idea of permanently residing in this country but to solicit the help of the U.S. government in overthrowing the Castro regime so that they could return to Cuba.

Another obvious example of the link between U.S. hegemony and immigration concerns the Philippines. From 1899 to 1941, when the Philippines were a possession of the United States, a large proportion of Filipinos learned the English language. Consequently, when the U.S. government finally allowed sizable immigration from the Philippines, after passage of the 1965 Immigration Act, the number of Filipinos who had an elevated propensity to immigrate to the United States was much higher than it would have been had the country always been independent. U.S. hegemony was also the essential condition for the establishment of many U.S. military bases in such countries as Germany, Japan, Korea, and the Philippines following World War II. As pointed out previously, much immigration to the United States has been connected to the existence of these military bases because of the tendency of American servicemen to marry local women.

Let us now attempt a more systematic investigation of some of the structural factors that may have had an impact on national rates of legal emigration to the United States. Table 6.4 presents the legal emigration rate to the United States from the twenty nations that supplied the largest numbers of legal immigrants to the United States in 1992. The legal emigration rate is simply the number of permanent legal immigrants to the United States from each nation divided by that nation's

TABLE 6.4   1992 Emigration Rates for Nations with the Most Immigrants to the United States and Possible Structural Determinants of Variation in These Rates

	Emigration rate (per 10,000)	Index of Per Capita GNP, 1991 (per 1,000) (US 5100)[a]	Distance (in thousands of miles)[b]	Population Size (in millions)	Natural Increase Rate (per 1,000)	Immigrant Stock Ratio (per 10,000)
Asia						
China	0.33	7.6	7	1,166	13	4.5
India	0.42	5.2	8	883	20	5.1
Iran	2.22	21.1	7	60	33	35.3
Japan	0.89	87.6	6	124	3	23.3
Philippines	9.58	11.0	8	64	24	143.3
South Korea	4.37	37.6	7	44	11	128.3
Taiwan	7.86	–	7	21	11	117.4
Vietnam	11.23	–	8	69	22	78.5
Europe						
Ireland	34.93	51.6	4	4	6	485.2
Poland	6.64	20.3	5	38	4	101.1
USSR	1.54	26.1	5	284	7	11.8
United Kingdom	3.46	73.8	4	58	3	110.8
North America						
Canada	5.55	87.3	1	27	8	271.8
Cuba	10.92	–	1	11	11	682.4
Dominican Republic	55.96	13.9	2	8	23	463.8
El Salvador	46.77	9.5	2	6	29	831.1
Haiti	17.19	5.5	2	6	29	352.2
Jamaica	75.66	16.6	2	3	20	1,336.6
Mexico	24.38	32.4	1	88	23	490.1
South America						
Colombia	3.85	24.7	3	34	20	83.4

NOTES: [a] A dash indicates that data were not available from the cited sources.

[b] The distance is the mileage from the nation's capital to St. Louis, Missouri, chosen because it is close to the center of U.S. population.

SOURCES: U.S. Department of Justice, Immigration and Naturalization Service, *Statistical Yearbook of the Immigration and Naturalization Service, 1992* (Washington, D.C.: Government Printing Office, 1993), pp. 30–31; World Bank, *World Development Report 1993* (New York: Oxford University Press, 1993), pp. 296–297; Population Reference Bureau, *1992 World Population Data Sheet* (Washington, D.C.: Population Reference Bureau, 1992); U.S. Bureau of the Census, *1990 Census of Population, The Foreign-born Population in the United States,* (1990 CP-3-1) (Washington, D.C.: Government Printing Office, 1993), pp. 2–64; and the Rand-McNally globe.

estimated population. A word of caution is in order concerning the stability of legal emigration rates from year to year: For example, the legal emigration rate from Mexico in 1992 more than doubled because of the inclusion of persons legalized by IRCA. Similarly, the rate of immigrants from Ireland was extraordinarily high because of the temporary advantage they enjoyed in the diversity transition program.

Table 6.4 also presents several variables that may be structural determinants of the legal emigration rate. One of the most important may be the per capita GNP relative to that of the United States. Table 6.4 shows data from the World Bank on the relative size of GNP per capita for most of these nations in 1991 based on purchasing-power comparability. In my opinion an index of GNP based on purchasing-power comparability should be a much more accurate reflection of the attractiveness of the United States than one based on current exchange rates between the dollar and the various national currencies. In general the less-developed nations show much higher values for this index when it is linked to purchasing-power comparability rather than current monetary exchange rates. For example, based on purchasing-power comparability, the per capita GNP for Mexico is 32.4 percent that of the United States; based on current exchange rates it would be only 13.6 percent that of the United States.[16]

Another important structural variable is distance; Table 6.4 shows the approximate distance from each nation's capital city to St. Louis, Missouri, which is near the center of U.S. population. Also shown in the table is the population size for each nation in 1992. As I mentioned before, this is important because current U.S. immigration law is definitely discriminatory against immigrants from nations with a large population. An additional column presents the 1992 rate of natural increase for each nation. In an earlier section of this chapter, we discussed the population growth rate as a measure of disruption, but the natural increase rate is probably a better measure of disruption than the population growth rate because the latter is affected by the current volume of net immigration. Finally, Table 6.4 presents the ratio of the immigrant stock born in each nation and resident in the United States as of the time of the 1990 census to the total population of the nation in 1992. As explained previously, this is meant as an indicator of the strength of average network ties for immigrants from each nation.

Table 6.4 demonstrates a wide range of legal emigration rates, from 0.33 per 10,000 for China to 75.66 per 10,000 for Jamaica. But the table gives data only for twenty nations out of the approximately 200 nations in the world. What about legal emigration rates for these other nations? Going beyond the data shown in Table 6.4, we can show that China does not have the lowest legal emigration rate to the United States. Among the nations of the world with more than 100 million people, two had a lower legal emigration rate to the United States than China: Indonesia, with a rate of 0.16 per 10,000, and Brazil, with a rate of 0.32 per 10,000. Among the other nations with populations of more than 100 million, Bangladesh had a rate (0.34 per 10,000) barely exceeding that of China; the legal emigration rate for the whole continent of Africa (0.41 per 10,000) was not much higher. At the other end of the scale, Jamaica was not alone in its high rate of legal emigration to the United States; its rate was exceeded by English-speaking Guyana, a small nation on the north coast of South America with a population of only 800,000. The legal emigration rate for Guyana was approximately 113 per 10,000. In addition, various other English-speaking nations in the Caribbean basin with very small populations had high rates similar to that of Jamaica.

Now let us look at the relationships between the possible structural determinants and the legal emigration rate. It is obvious that there is a strong negative relationship between distance from St. Louis and the legal emigration rate to the United States. It is also obvious that there is a strong negative relationship between population size and the legal emigration rate to the United States. Nevertheless, for the nations shown in Table 6.4 there is a strong positive relationship between population size and distance from the United States. Accordingly, it is not easy to determine which of these two variables has the greater impact on the legal emigration rate. Indeed it is possible that only one of these two variables has a causal impact on the legal emigration rate to the United States. Furthermore, the data suggest that there may be a curvilinear relationship between per capita GNP and the legal emigration rate to the United States, such that the legal emigration rate tends to be highest when the per capita GNP is neither very high nor very low—though this apparent effect may be the result of correlations between per capita GNP and other structural determinants. There appears to be only a slight relationship between the natural increase rate and the legal emigration rate. The possible effect of this structural determinant, however, may be masked by other possible structural determinants highly correlated with the rate of natural increase. Finally, a strong positive relationship exists between the immigrant stock ratio and the legal emigration rate. On the one hand, this may be an indicator of the importance of networks as a causal determinant of the legal emigration rate. On the other hand, the relationship between these two variables may be spurious; it may be present only because both the immigrant stock ratio and the legal emigration rate are each functions of the same structural determinants, such as distance and population size.

In summary, it is not possible to inspect Table 6.4 and directly deduce from the data which of the possible structural determinants are indeed related to the legal emigration rate to the United States and which are not. To investigate the causal significance of each of these possible structural determinants, we need a multivariate analysis. Moreover, to avoid what is called selection bias, we should base the multivariate analysis on all nations, not merely the twenty that provided the largest number of immigrants. To examine the causal significance of possible structural determinants on measures of the emigration rate to the United States, then, we turn to the work of other investigators.

There appears to be no study in which the legal emigration rate was the dependent variable, perhaps because investigators are more interested in the determinants of immigration propensity other than that provided by the facility with which legal immigration requirements can be met. But one helpful study is that by economists Michael J. Greenwood and John M. McDowell, who analyzed national differences in the natural log of the rate of legal immigration in 1970 among immigrants who reported an occupation.[17] Their sample consisted of thirty-four nations, and they used ten independent variables in their equation. The value of r^2 was .51. Two variables were found to be statistically significant at the .05 level and negatively correlated with the emigration rate. These were distance to the United States and average weekly earnings in the nation of origin; both findings were in accordance with existing theory. Two variables were found to be statistically significant at the .05 level and positively related to the emigration rate. These were the percentage of the labor force in manufacturing in the nation of origin and the percentage of the male population aged twenty to twenty-four in the nation of origin who attended a U.S. university in 1970. The first of these two variables may be related to a fit between the characteristics of immigrants and the needs of the U.S. economy. The positive relationship between the proportion of students at American universities and the emigration rate may be spurious, simply reflecting that nations whose inhabitants have a high propensity to migrate to the United States will also have a high propensity to send students to U.S. universities.

In another major study Jasso and Rosenzweig concentrated on the determinants of the number of persons admitted to the United States as wives or husbands of U.S. citizens.[18] Because these individuals enter the United States outside the quota, analyzing their numbers allows a good opportunity to study the extralegal factors that influence immigration to the United States. Jasso and Rosenzweig's multivariate analysis was based on the immigration cohort of 1971. They included seventy nations in each analysis and used nine independent variables pertaining to the nation of origin in each of the two equations, the first for wives and the second for husbands. In each equation the population size of the nation of origin was one of the independent variables; this meant that the results would be equivalent to results in which the dependent variable was the emigration rate but in which population size was not an independent variable. In the equation predicting the number of persons admitted as wives of U.S. citizens, the value of r^2 was .417; however, only one independent variable had a statistically significant impact at the .05 level: the presence of a U.S. military base. This variable had a positive impact on the number of immigrants admitted as wives of citizens. In the equation for wives, variables such as GNP per capita, population size, distance from the United States, and whether English was the official language were not statistically significant, although the last three of these four variables had signs of the predicted direction. In the equation for husbands, the value for r^2 was low, only .125. The only variable that was statistically significant was distance from the United States, which was negatively related. One might wonder why distance would be a statistically significant factor for husbands but not for wives. Jasso and Rosenzweig attribute this to the government's policy of paying the cost of transportation back to the United States for the wives of U.S. servicemen.

Another interesting component of the research by Jasso and Rosenzweig was an equation predicting the visa backlog from sixty-eight nations as of January 1980. The visa backlog is a measure of unfulfilled desire to come to the United States since it consists only of those who hope to enter under the national quotas. As of January 1980 the visa backlog from all nations was slightly more than 1 million persons. For the equation predicting the visa backlog from each nation, the value of r^2 was .480. Among the statistically significant predictors negatively related to the visa backlog were GNP per capita and distance; both of these results are what existing theory would predict. Among the statistically significant predictors positively related to the visa backlog were population size and the presence of a U.S. military base. The positive relationship of population size to visa backlog is to be expected because U.S. immigration quotas are constant regardless of population size. The positive relationship of the presence of a military base follows from Portes's theory that U.S. hegemony will encourage immigration. More specifically, it may relate to the desire of women brought to the United States as wives of U.S. servicemen outside of the quota to bring their own relatives to the United States within the quota system.

Linda Peterson of the U.S. Bureau of the Census and Robert Warren of the INS produced a third important work of multivariate research.[19] Their study pertains to what they call unauthorized migration to the United States. It covered sixty-nine different nations for which data were available; among the major nations omitted were Cambodia, Cuba, Lebanon, the USSR, and Vietnam. One of their dependent variables, the natural log of the legalization rate, is of special interest. In this rate the numerator was the number of persons from each nation who applied for legalization under IRCA by virtue of having resided in the United States continuously since 1982; the denominator was the population of the native country in 1985. This dependent variable is an excellent indicator of the propensity of persons from a given nation to immigrate illegally to the United States. For this dependent variable, nineteen independent variables were used as predictors.

In the equation in which the legalization rate was the dependent variable, the value of r^2 was .76. Three variables were found to be statistically significant at the .05 level and negatively related to the natural log of the legalization rate. The first of these was an index of increase in per capita food production during the preceding five and one-half years. This relationship is expected from a relative deprivation perspective. The second of these was distance from the United States, measured as the airline distance between the nation's capital or other major city and New York, Los Angeles, or Miami, whichever was closest. Their finding with respect to distance is in accordance with theoretical expectation. The third of these was the natural log of the number of U.S. military stationed in the nation. This result was not in accordance with theory.

Five variables were statistically significant at the .05 level and were positively related to the natural log of the legalization rate. First was the natural log of the visa backlog for the nation as of January 1986. This relationship is expected from theory, and it may also explain the statistically significant negative relationship between the natural log of the number of military personnel stationed in the nation and the legalization rate. As mentioned previously, Jasso and Rosenzweig found that the presence of a U.S. military base was an important cause of the visa backlog. Thus it may not have been legitimate to include both variables in the same equation. The second and third variables positively related to the natural log of the legalization rate were dichotomous variables indicating respectively whether the nation was located in Asia or Africa or whether it was located in Latin America. Essentially, that both of these variables were positive meant that the legalization rate was higher for the less-developed nations than for the more-developed nations. This result is in accord with theoretical expectations. The fourth variable positively related to the natural log of the legalization rate indicated the proportion of the population aged twenty to twenty-nine born in that nation who were in the labor force according to the 1980 census. This variable is difficult to interpret. It may simply be an indicator of the proportion of the population from that nation in that age group who were undocumented immigrants in 1980. This could come about because undocumented immigrants of that cohort, which has a high proportion of males, are likelier to be in the labor force. If so, the relationship would be spurious. The last of the five positively related variables with statistical significance was that measuring the mean years of schooling completed by members of the labor force in each nation. This result is somewhat surprising if one assumes that undocumented immigrants have access only to unskilled jobs.

It is unfortunate that Peterson and Warren were not able to include any variable reflecting the strength of network ties in the United States. They considered using a variable corresponding to what I have previously called the immigrant stock ratio but rejected it because of its high correlation with the dependent variable. It is certainly true that the relationship between the immigrant stock ratio and the legalization rate might be in part spurious because the presence of undocumented immigrants would be reflected not only in the dependent variable but in the independent variable as well.

Summary and Conclusions

Perhaps the main conclusion of this chapter is that the volume of immigration to the United States will increase in future years unless individual propensities to migrate decrease. This is because the population of the world outside the United States, at risk of migration to the United States, will rise so rapidly. By the year 2025 the population at risk to immigrate to the United States will probably be about 60 percent larger than it had been in 1990. Moreover, unless there is stricter enforcement of immigration law, there seems to be no guarantee that the propensities to immigrate to the United States will decline. This is so because in the near future further economic development in Third World nations will increase the proportion of individuals who can afford a move to the United States at the same time that it decreases the incentive to migrate by narrowing the relative wage differential.

We have also seen, however, that immigration to the United States induces many negative values. Among the most important of these may be the loss of accustomed interpersonal relationships, the necessity to learn a new language and adapt to a new culture, the desire to avoid risk to one's income, and feelings of relative deprivation. The propensity to immigrate to the United States, then, may decline long before the nations that currently qualify as less developed catch up to the United States in per capita GNP. Finally, we can probably expect that a fairly constant proportion of immigrants to the United States will not remain permanently but will later emigrate. This implies that net immigration to the United States will always be proportionately less than the number of immigrants arriving.

If the process of economic development in the less-developed nations does not substantially reduce the propensities to immigrate to the United States within the next thirty years, the following three scenarios for the future are possible. First, there would be no change in the laws concerning legal immigration, but draconian measures would be used successfully to curb illegal immigration. Accordingly, total net immigration to the United States, both legal and illegal, would remain at its current level. Second, the United States would not change either its immigration laws or the ways in which it attempted to enforce these laws. As a consequence, the net flow of undocumented immigrants to the United States would rise far above its current level. Third, the United States would change its immigration laws so that a much higher proportion of the persons who most want to immigrate to the United States could do so legally. In this case the net flow of illegal immigration would perhaps decline to a very low level, and total net immigration might be smaller than in the second scenario.

Notes

1. The latest projection is found in United Nations, Department for Economic and Social Information and Policy Analysis, *World Population Prospects, the 1992 Revision* (New York: United Nations, 1993).

2. See Warren S. Thompson, *Population and Peace in the Pacific* (Chicago: University of Chicago Press, 1946), pp. 22–35; C. P. Blacker, "Stages in Population Growth," *Eugenics Review*, Vol. 39, No. 3 (October 1947), pp. 88–102; Kingsley Davis, *Human Society* (New York: Macmillan, 1949), pp. 603–608; and Frank W. Notestein, "The Economics of Population and Food Supplies," in *Proceedings of the Eighth International Conference of Agricultural Economists* (London: Oxford University Press, 1953), pp. 15–31.

3. David M. Heer, *Society and Population*, 2d ed. (Englewood Cliffs, N.J.: Prentice-Hall, 1975), pp. 94–96.

4. Joseph J. Spengler, "Values and Fertility Analysis," *Demography*, Vol. 3, No. 1 (1966), pp. 109–130.

5. Everett S. Lee, "A Theory of Migration," *Demography*, Vol. 3, No. 1 (1966), pp. 47–57.

6. For an excellent example of such research, see Parker Frisbie, "Illegal Migration from Mexico to the United States: A Longitudinal Analysis," *International Migration Review* Vol. 9, No. 1 (1975), pp. 3–13.

7. World Bank, *World Development Report 1993* (New York: Oxford University Press, 1993), pp. 296–297.

8. John S. MacDonald and Leatrice D. MacDonald, "Chain Migration, Ethnic Neighborhood Formation, and Social Networks," *Milbank Memorial Fund Quarterly*, Vol. 52, No. 1 (January 1964), pp. 82–97.

9. Some of the most important research on the significance of social networks for immigrants has been conducted by Douglas S. Massey and his Mexican colleagues. See especially Douglas S. Massey, Rafael Alarcón, Jorge Durand, and Humberto González, *Return to Aztlan: The Social Process of International Migration from Western Mexico* (Berkeley: University of California Press, 1987), pp. 139–171.

10. Oded Stark and J. Edward Taylor, "Relative Deprivation and Migration: Theory, Evidence, and Policy Implications," in Sergio Díaz-Briquets and Sidney Weintraub, eds. *Determinants of Emigration from Mexico, Central America, and the Caribbean* (Boulder: Westview Press, 1991), pp. 121–144.

11. Massey et al., *Return to Aztlan,* pp. 2–4.

12. Oded Stark and D. Levhari, "On Migration and Risk in LDCs,"*Economic Development and Cultural Change,* Vol. 31, No. 1 (1982), pp. 191–196.

13. For an elaboration of this argument, see Peter Gregory, "The Determinants of International Migration and Policy Options for Influencing the Size of Population Flows," in Díaz-Briquets and Weintraub, *Determinants of Emigration,* pp. 49–73.

14. George J. Borjas, *Friends or Strangers: The Impact of Immigrants on the U.S. Economy* (New York: Basic Books, 1990), pp. 3–25.

15. Alejandro Portes, "Unauthorized Immigration and Immigration Reform: Present Trends and Prospects," in Díaz-Briquets and Weintraub, *Determinants of Emigration,* pp. 75–97.

16. World Bank, *World Development Report 1993,* pp. 238–239, 296–297, 306–308, and 319–321.

17. Michael J. Greenwood and John M. McDowell, "The Supply of Immigrants to the United States," in Barry R. Chiswick, ed., *The Gateway: U.S. Immigration Issues and Policies* (Washington, D.C.: American Enterprise Institute for Public Policy Research, 1982), pp. 54–85.

18. Guillermina Jasso and Mark R. Rosenzweig, *The New Chosen People: Immigrants in the United States* (New York: Russell Sage Foundation, 1990), pp. 162–173.

19. Linda S. Peterson and Robert Warren, "Determinants of Unauthorized Migration to the United States," Center for International Research, U.S. Bureau of the Census, 1989, pp. 1–36.

7 Enforcement of Immigration Law

The INS, part of the Department of Justice, has the primary responsibility for the enforcement of U.S. immigration law; the Bureau of Consular Affairs of the Department of State plays an important supplementary role. In this chapter we look at the role of each agency and examine not only the effectiveness of immigration-law enforcement in the manner in which it is currently being conducted but also the side effects of that enforcement. We also discuss to what extent prior illegal immigration helps an individual become a legal immigrant and the extent to which policies designed to mitigate hardships for undocumented immigrants encourage further illegal immigration.

The Activities of the Bureau of Consular Affairs

The Bureau of Consular Affairs is charged with guaranteeing that no person is granted the privilege of a visa for permanent residence in the United States unless that person is fully qualified under the law. Many persons who enter the United States on a temporary visa, such as a tourist visa, abuse that visa, overstaying the time they are legally allowed; a number of these visa abusers desire to remain in the United States more or less permanently. The Bureau of Consular Affairs is also charged to minimize such abuse by denying temporary visas to persons likely to take advantage of the privileges afforded by a temporary visa to remain and work in the United States illegally. To this end an official of the Bureau of Consular Affairs must interview each applicant for a non-immigrant visa.

How well does the bureau perform its duties? Perhaps the most comprehensive survey of this question has been attempted by *New York Times* reporter John Crewdson in his 1983 book *The Tarnished Door.* Crewdson examines the whole problem of enforcement of immigration law by both the INS and the Bureau of Consular Affairs. Crewdson's report on the work of the Bureau of Consular Affairs is startling to anyone who takes for granted the consular officials' conscientious performance of duty.[1] Crewdson focuses his attention on the tremendous pressures consular officials are under to grant temporary visas to visit the United

Men about to cross the U.S. border, Tijuana, Mexico, 1988.

States, particularly from citizens of less-developed nations. He reports that many American consuls with high aspirations for social status but low salaries have accepted bribes to issue temporary visas; according to Crewdson, the going rate in the early 1980s was around $1,000 per non-immigrant visa. Crewdson describes how in 1981 an American vice con-sul in Port-au-Prince, Haiti, was sentenced to prison for selling visas; he quotes State Department estimates that foreign service officers or other U.S. embassy employees sold 20,000 to 50,000 U.S. visas every year, with corruption most prevalent among U.S. consulates in Hong Kong, India, Brazil, and Paraguay.

Apart from the problem of corruption, the Bureau of Consular Affairs is overwhelmed by the numbers of people seeking temporary visas. From 1972 to 1982 the number of nonimmigrant visa cases the bureau handled increased from about 2.5 million to around 7 million. Moreover, although personnel increased by only about 22 percent from 1974 to 1982, consular work (most of which was visa-related) increased by 166 percent. As a result, the amount of time consular officials spent in exam-ining each nonimmigrant visa had to be substantially reduced,[2] proba-bly allowing into the country potential visa abusers who would have been denied entry had more time been devoted to each visa application. If consular officials had not spent less time with each visa applicant,

Border crossers, Tijuana, Mexico, 1988.

however, applicants for nonimmigrant visas would have had to wait to receive a final decision, and many tourists who wanted to come to the United States would have decided to travel elsewhere.

Traditionally, citizens of Canada and Mexico have had fewer restrictions than citizens of other nations with respect to admission to the United States on a temporary basis. Canadians have been able to come to the United States for business or pleasure for a period of up to six months without a nonimmigrant visa. Mexicans have been eligible to apply for border-crossing cards that can be used for admission to the United States for business or pleasure travel not to exceed seventy-two hours and for a destination within 25 miles of the U.S. border. Because the Bureau of Consular Affairs has been well aware of the tendency to abuse these permits in order to live and work in the United States, consulates in Mexico routinely reject applications for border-crossing cards. A recent study by a Mexican social scientist shows that for residents of Mexican border cities there is a strong correlation between an individual's social class and the probability of having received a border-crossing card.[3]

Acting on the premise citizens of less-developed nations were likelier to abuse nonimmigrant visas, Congress recently decided largely to eliminate the visa requirement for citizens of selected economically developed nations. The original provision for such visa exemption was contained in the Immigration Reform and Control Act of 1986. According to that law, visitors for pleasure or business from eight developed nations did not need to apply for a visa. The Immigration Act of 1990 extended the number of developed nations in the visa waiver program from eight to twenty-one. In fiscal 1992 approximately 8.5 million visitors were exempted from a visa requirement.[4] The new legislation has no doubt been a boon to the tourist industry and has probably also helped reduce visa abuse by allowing the Bureau of Consular Affairs to concentrate its efforts on citizens from the nations with a higher probability to abuse visas. Nevertheless, the new policy might also be attacked as being unfair to citizens of nations other than those selected.

The Activities of the INS

The enforcement activities of the INS may be subdivided into three classes: exclusions, apprehensions, and removals. INS inspectors at designated points of entry have the responsibility of deciding whether aliens seeking to enter the United States have the legal right to do so. The U.S. Border Patrol, a subdivision of the INS, has the major responsibility for preventing aliens from entering the United States at places along the Mexican and Canadian border other than designated points and for removing persons who have gained entry without inspection. INS investigations officers are charged with investigating the possible presence of illegal aliens throughout the United States and initiating processes to remove those aliens. Finally, immigration judges, who are employees of the Executive Office for Immigration Review within the Department of Justice, determine whether an alien who is suspected of violating an immigration law but declares innocence has in fact violated the law and must be removed.

INS Inspections

The INS has estimated that in fiscal 1992 some 480 million people entered the United States at a designated point of entry. Of these some 166 million were U.S. citizens and some 314 million were aliens. The first responsibility of the INS inspector is to determine whether someone who seeks entry to the United States is a U.S. citizen. If the person is a U.S. citizen, he or she is allowed free entry into the United States; if not, the inspector must decide whether the presumed alien is legally allowed to enter the United States. If there is any uncertainty, the individual is shunted off to undergo what is called secondary inspection. During secondary inspection a final determination is made whether an individual is legally allowed to enter the United States. In fiscal 1992 some 913,000 aliens were denied entry to the United States after primary and secondary inspection. Approximately 11 million persons were admitted to the United States only after secondary inspection. Nearly 90 percent of the aliens seeking admission to the United States in fiscal 1992 were border crossers from Mexico or Canada. Among U.S. citizens seeking entry, approximately 86 percent were border crossers. Most other citizens and aliens sought admission at U.S. airports. Entry into the United States in fiscal 1992 was concentrated at four points in San Diego County, California, where some 56 million people tried to gain admission.[5]

During fall 1993 I crossed the border from Tijuana, Mexico, to San Diego in my car every week, usually on Thursday at about 4:30 P.M. I chose that time in large part because I knew that crossing then would be much easier than at other times. The wait for me to be inspected on Thursdays at 4:30 P.M. varied from about five minutes minimum to forty-five minutes maximum and generally took fifteen to twenty minutes. In contrast, on Sunday afternoons the wait was usually more than one hour and could be as long as two hours. I never had any trouble getting across. I would be asked whether I was a U.S. citizen and whether I had anything to declare to customs. Upon my negative answer to both questions, I would be waved through. With my blond hair and blue eyes and with no foreign accent, I was never a suspect. Nevertheless, I wanted to get across the border as quickly as possible. I soon learned never to get into an inspection lane directly behind a car with license plates from Baja, California, as the inspectors would always take a long time with such a car and would usually demand that the back trunk be opened. But even if a car had California plates, if its driver appeared to be of Mexican descent, inspectors were likely to take some time before they let the car pass through.

Travelers of course had expectations as to how long they should wait. When it took forty-five minutes to cross, drivers would become angry and many would blow their horns in an attempt to induce the inspectors to let them across more quickly. Not only are inspectors under pressure from their superiors to prohibit entry of anyone not legally allowable into the United States; they are also under pressure from border crossers to perform their inspections as quickly as possible.

How does one attempt to enter the United States at a port of entry without proper documentation? Several ways are possible. First, one may show a counterfeit U.S. birth certificate or counterfeit naturalization document and claim to be a U.S. citizen. Alternatively, one can show a counterfeit green card or counterfeit border-crossing card to enter as an alien. Because it is likely that a counterfeit green card or counterfeit border-crossing card will not look genuine, Mexicans often borrow someone else's border-crossing card, provided they can pass off the photo on the card as their own. Once safely past the border, the im-personator can then mail back the border-crossing card to its real owner.[6]

There is documented proof that at least some inspectors have ac-cepted bribes to allow individuals to pass into the United States and have sold documents such as green cards and border-crossing cards to those with no right to receive them. The most thorough description of such corruption is in Crewdson's *Tarnished Door*, in which he narrates the history of Operation Clean Sweep, a Department of Justice campaign to uncover corruption among its own INS inspectors.[7] The initial impe-tus for the campaign was the prosecution of Frank Paul Castro, an immi-gration inspector at the San Ysidro port of entry in San Diego. The Castro case was presented to a grand jury in May 1971. According to govern-ment prosecutors, Castro had supplemented his annual salary of $24,000 with more than $250,000 in direct bribes for granting entry to the United States and for selling U.S. immigration documents. In 1972 Castro was declared guilty and sentenced to six years in prison. During the Castro prosecution, the INS agents who were most closely involved in preparing the evidence against Castro were told by another INS in-spector that Castro's case was merely the tip of the iceberg and that cor-ruption was rampant among many INS inspectors. As a result, in 1972 Attorney General Richard Kleindienst ordered a general investigation, assigning the three INS agents who had worked on the Castro case di-rectly to the U.S. Attorney's Office. In what became known as Operation Clean Sweep, investigators opened criminal cases against 217 past and present INS officers; 146 of those involved taking bribes from illegal aliens.

Operation Clean Sweep began in the election year in which the Water-gate burglary took place and continued into 1973, when Watergate threatened to topple the Nixon presidency. Facing possible impeach-ment concerning his role in the coverup of the burglary, President Nixon did not need another scandal. Neither did the Democrats. Operation Clean Sweep uncovered an allegation that Lyndon Johnson, while presi-dent of the United States, had arranged with a top official in Washington "for the regular delivery of illegal Mexican farm workers to the LBJ Ranch." Representative Peter Rodino (D.–N.J.), chairman of the House Judiciary Committee and hence in charge of INS activities, also came under attack: An INS agent testified that he had arranged to provide Mexican prostitutes for Rodino. In the wake of the Watergate burglary, Rodino's Judiciary Committee would play the key role of hearing evidence that might lead to Nixon's impeachment, and Democrats were afraid that a scandal for Rodino would affect their case against Nixon. The Nixon administration took the first action against Operation

Clean Sweep, terminating the operation without appearing to do so. On September 25, 1973, Al Murray, the leading Clean Sweep investigator, had just climbed out of his car next to the federal courthouse in San Diego when a government car knocked Murray down, splintering two of his spinal disks. Fearing for his life, Murray fled to Miami, effectively ending Operation Clean Sweep. Little had yet been accomplished. Out of 300 potential criminal cases, there had been only seven indictments and five convictions. Following Nixon's resignation on August 9, 1974, and the accession to the presidency of Gerald Ford, the new commissioner of the INS, Leonard Chapman, officially shut down Operation Clean Sweep, affirming his conviction "that virtually all of the employees of the INS are honest, dedicated, hard-working and loyal public servants."[8]

The Work of the Border Patrol

As mentioned earlier, the major functions of the border patrol are to prevent unlawful entry into the United States at points on the border other than official ports of entry and to apprehend persons who have succeeded in crossing into the United States beyond the border and supervise their departure from the United States. How well the border patrol performs its first function is uncertain; we do know that the number of people the border patrol apprehends each year is currently large and has grown dramatically since about 1970. Table 7.1 shows the total number of deportable aliens the INS located for each decade through 1950 and every year since then. The border patrol apprehended almost all of these aliens. For example, in fiscal 1992, of the almost 1.3 million deportable aliens located, more than 95 percent were apprehended by the border patrol. Moreover, among the 1.2 million deportable aliens located by the border patrol, more than 97 percent were Mexicans.[9] About two-thirds of such apprehensions take place almost immediately after entry into the United States; an additional 25 percent occur within seventy-two hours of entry and only about 10 percent four or more days after entry.[10]

It is very important to understand that the INS figures on deportable aliens located do not refer to the number of persons apprehended but to the total number of events of apprehension. Thus if a given individual is apprehended three times during a year, the number of deportable aliens located will be increased by three—the total number of additional events—rather than by one—the total number of additional individuals apprehended. It is likely that many if not most apprehended persons will make another attempt to cross the border, because it is INS policy with respect to Mexicans and Canadians merely to transport individuals to the nearest border point rather than their hometowns.

From data on the number of apprehensions, can we estimate the number of aliens who successfully reach the United States? Thomas

TABLE 7.1   Deportable Aliens Located, 1925–1992 (in thousands)

Period	Number	Period	Number
1925–1930	128	1971–1980	8,321
1931–1940	147	1971	420
1941–1950	1,377	1972	506
1951–1960	3,599	1973	656
1951	509	1974	788
1952	544	1975	767
1953	886	1976	876
1954	1,090	1976,	
1955	254	transition	
1956	88	quarter[a]	222
1957	60	1977	1,042
1958	53	1978	1,058
1959	45	1979	1,076
1960	71	1980	910
1961–1970	1,608	1981–1990	11,883
1961	89	1981	976
1962	93	1982	970
1963	89	1983	1,251
1964	87	1984	1,247
1965	110	1985	1,349
1966	139	1986	1,767
1967	162	1987	1,190
1968	212	1988	1,008
1969	284	1989	954
1970	345	1990	1,170
		1991–1992	2,456
		1991	1,198
		1992	1,258

[a] In 1976 the U.S. government changed its fiscal year to begin October 1 rather than July 1.

SOURCE: U.S. Department of Justice, Immigration and Naturalization Service, *Statistical Yearbook of the Immigration and Naturalization Service, 1992* (Washington, D.C.: Government Printing Office, 1993), p. 156.

Espenshade has attempted to do so for the apprehensions of Mexican aliens. He provides mathematical proof that if we know the proportion of all persons apprehended in a given month who have not previously been apprehended that month and if we assume that everyone who wants to cross the border eventually does so within a month, we can derive the number of individuals who successfully cross the border from the number of apprehensions. According to Espenshade's formula, the number of people who succeed in entering the United States is equal to the number of apprehensions multiplied by the ratio of first-time apprehensions to repeat apprehensions. Making use of INS data on whether a given alien apprehended was a repeat offender (repeat offenders average around 31.7 percent of all apprehensions), Espenshade concluded that the number of persons who were able to cross into the United States each month averaged about 2.2 times the number of monthly apprehensions. His conclusion coincided with the existing INS belief that for every alien apprehended two to three got away.[11] If Espenshade's assumption that everyone succeeds in entering the United States within a month is correct, his estimate is extremely sensitive to the accuracy of the INS data on whether a given apprehendee is a repeat violator. For example, if we assume that 50 percent of all apprehendees were repeat violators, then the estimated number of successful border crossers each month would fall drastically and would equal exactly the number of apprehensions. Moreover, if 90 percent of all apprehendees were repeat violators, then the number of persons who enter the United States each month would drop much further to constitute only 11 percent of the number of apprehendees.

Most border patrol activity is highly concentrated along a few miles of the border with Mexico, particularly in areas around San Diego, California, and El Paso, Texas. In fiscal 1992 about 52 percent of all apprehensions took place in the region of the San Diego district office and about 20 percent in the region of the El Paso district office.[12] A minute portion of the Mexican border—only 28.5 miles as recently as 1989—is fenced.[13] Since 1989 a 14-mile, 10-foot-high steel fence has been built along the border in San Diego to replace the old 6.6-mile chain-link fence. The new fence extends eastward to a point east of the Otay Mesa port of entry and includes the Zapata Canyon area, which, unfenced, had long been a popular point of crossing. In 1993 the fence was extended into the Pacific Ocean for a distance of 340 feet,[14] and in 1993 the INS announced plans for a new 6-mile fence to be built along the border in Tecate, a port of entry in San Diego County about 30 miles east of the main port of entry at San Ysidro.[15]

The old fence in San Diego was riddled with holes cut through the wire by would-be crossers to make it easy to slip through. As of fall 1993 the new fence had not been cut, though holes had been dug under it in several places and earthen mounds and old refrigerators placed on the Mexican side allow aliens to climb over the fence. One afternoon I watched a teenage boy take time off from his soccer game in Zapata Canyon and easily cross over the steel fence from the large dirt hill behind it. He remained in the United States for a few minutes and then scaled the 10-foot high fence to return to Mexico. No border patrol agents were in sight.

In addition to fencing, selected small areas of the border have other devices to deter unauthorized border crossing. In a 2-mile area where the Tijuana River crosses over from Tijuana into San Diego, there are high-intensity lights, two additional fences within the United States, and metal lining on the northern side of the fences to prevent the digging of holes underneath. At selected points all along the border, the border patrol makes use of portable lights and portable seismic monitors that can indicate pedestrian movement.[16] For their part, undocumented immigrants use various means to thwart the border patrol at unauthorized crossing points. From a woman whose job was to interview Mexicans in Tijuana just before they planned to enter the United States, I heard that the optimum stratagem involved crossing after nightfall in a large group.

Most of the personnel of the border patrol are stationed within a mile or so of the border. In northern San Diego County, however, the border patrol maintains two highway checkpoints: at San Clemente on Interstate 5 and at Temecula on Interstate 15. When these checkpoints are in operation (they are usually closed Sundays and holidays), all northbound vehicles must come to a complete stop for inspection. Agents also patrol public transportation terminals. In San Diego this includes the Greyhound bus station, the Amtrak terminal, and the railroad freight yards.[17]

Two Mexican social scientists who interviewed apprehended Mexicans immediately upon their return across the Mexican border observed that a high number of them were stopped at bus stations en route back to Mexico. These apprehensions, of course, did not reduce the number of undocumented aliens working in the United States but did serve to meet the arrest quotas of the border patrol agents.[18]

INS Investigations

The uniformed members of the border patrol act mainly as police; members of the Investigations Division act mainly as detectives. Traditionally, the most important function of the Investigations Division has been to investigate workplaces where illegal aliens might be located and then gather supporting materials in order to obtain warrants to raid such sites. An additional duty is to collect information to prosecute "coyotes," who guide undocumented immigrants across the border for a fee. A third is to investigate fraud in petitions for immigrant status, particularly with respect to petitions for permanent immigrant status on the basis of marriage to a U.S. citizen.[19] Since the enactment of employer sanctions as part of IRCA, the Investigations Division has also looked into compliance with respect to the provisions that impose civil and criminal penalties for knowingly hiring an illegal alien. As a result of these new responsibilities, the Investigations staff was expanded from 875 to 1,600. One observer considers the hiring of new agents to handle employer compliance with IRCA as especially beneficial, as the hirees were not trained in the tradition of roughshod dealing with undocumented persons, a tradition that would not be appropriate when dealing with citizen employers.[20]

Legal Prosecution

The final step in enforcement of immigration law is prosecution in the courts. The INS legal staff is charged with this responsibility. By subjecting employers to possible civil and criminal sanctions, IRCA greatly expanded the scope of immigration-law violation. As a consequence INS also doubled its legal staff from 225 in 1986 to 450 in 1989.[21] According to one expert, the INS legal staff has played a restraining role with respect to prosecution of employers, "often sending cases back for more documentation, reducing the penalty, or proposing a settlement."[22]

Immigration-Law Enforcement: Effectiveness and Side Effects

Effectiveness

Suppose we want to measure how effectively the current enforcement of immigration law eliminates illegal immigration to the United States. How would we go about it? The tenets of social science research suggest that the best way would be a controlled experiment. Let us imagine a version of such an experiment. We would first use a method of random allocation to place all nations into either the control group, where current immigration-law and current immigration-law enforcement would prevail, or the experimental group, where there would be no restrictions on immigration into the United States. After having observed the results over a time, we would look at four numbers: (1) the average annual net immigration in the control group before the experiment, which we can call ICB; (2) the average annual net immigration in the control group after the experiment, or ICA; (3) the average annual net immigration in the experimental group before the experiment, or IEB; and (4) the average annual net immigration in the experimental group after the experiment, or IEA. We would compute $(IEA - IEB) - (ICA - ICB)$. The magnitude of this value would equal the effect of ending our current immigration law and its current enforcement in favor of unrestricted immigration for nations representing one-half the world's population.

Doubling the magnitude of this value would indicate the effect of ending our current immigration law and its enforcement for all the world's population.

One obvious criticism of the experimental design outlined above is that the results would depend heavily on whether Mexico fell into the control group or the experimental group. This is so because such a high proportion of the demand for immigration to the United States comes from that nation. To counter this criticism, it would no doubt be wise to divide the period of the experiment into two subperiods. In one of the two subperiods, Mexico would be placed in the experimental group; in the other subperiod it would be placed in the control group. All other nations would be randomly assigned into either experimental or control group at the beginning of each subperiod.

Still, other impediments to the validity of the experiment would remain. For one, persons from nations in the experimental group with an interest in immigration to the United States would know that the time period of the experiment was strictly limited. Accordingly, they would make plans to immigrate during the period of the experiment even though they would not have planned to do so at that particular time if free immigration to the United States were always allowed. Thus the number of persons coming to the United States from the experimental group of nations would be falsely inflated. A second impediment occurs because we need to measure the volume of net immigration to the United States. This is difficult because the U.S. government currently has no sure way to measure either net illegal immigration or the emigration of citizens and permanent legal residents. Finally, of course, Congress is unlikely to approve such an experiment.

So let us proceed from the assumption that such an experiment is impossible. What other means do we have to measure the effectiveness of our enforcement of immigration law? A feasible approach is to use multiple regression to look at the possible impact of two specific enforcement variables on the apprehensions of deportable aliens by the border patrol along the Mexican border. Such an approach does not allow us to examine the question of how well we prevent visa overstay or prevent individuals from entering the United States at official points of entry through fraudulent means. Moreover, the results of multiple regression are valid only if we are able to measure all other independent variables that may significantly affect the dependent variable. The two enforcement variables we can examine in a multiple regression equation are border patrol effort and whether the period was before or after the 1986 passage of IRCA. Three related studies, all conducted as part of the Program for Research on Immigration Policy jointly involving the RAND Corporation and the Urban Institute, with funds provided by the Ford Foundation, are examples of this approach.

We begin with the study by Frank Bean, Thomas Espenshade, Michael White, and Robert Dymowski.[23] In this study there were two principal dependent variables: (1) monthly linewatch apprehensions by the border patrol (apprehensions directly on the border) and (2) monthly non-linewatch apprehensions by the border patrol. Border patrol effort for the first dependent variable was measured by border patrol linewatch hours and border patrol capital investment and for the second dependent variable by nonlinewatch hours and capital investment. The effects of IRCA were measured by a series of categorical variables for particular periods following its passage and by the cumulative number of applications for legalization under the SAW program. The cumulative number of SAW applications was included because once individuals have applied for legalization under the SAW program, they may travel freely back and forth between Mexico and the United States. Additional control variables were the size of the young adult population in Mexico, the ratio of the average wage in Mexico to the average wage in the United States, the ratio of the male unemployment rate in the United States to that in Mexico, and categorical variables for each month of the year. For each dependent variable, the measures with respect to border patrol effort were statistically significant, indicating that the greater the effort the more the apprehensions. For example, according to the equation for the first dependent variable, a 5 percent increase in linewatch hours led to a 3.2 percent increase in apprehensions. The categorical variables indicating periods of time after the passage of IRCA were also statistically significant. Overall the number of apprehensions decreased following the passage of IRCA, though the deterrent effect was greatest in the first year after the act's passage and declined in the second and third years.

The second study, by Thomas Espenshade, was similar in many respects to the study Bean and his colleagues conducted.[24] This time, however, the dependent variable was the number of persons who successfully crossed the Mexican border, estimated in the manner I described earlier in this chapter. Espenshade excluded measures of border patrol effort (a tactic necessary due to the change in the dependent variable) but otherwise included the same independent variables as the first study. A final difference was that Espenshade examined figures for only the first two years following passage of IRCA rather than three years. His study showed that successful crossings to the United States from Mexico declined after passage of IRCA, but the decline in the first year was larger than in the second year. Altogether, and including the effect of SAW legalizations, Espenshade estimated that in the two years after it went into effect IRCA reduced the flow of undocumented immigrants from Mexico by 38 percent.

The third study, by Keith Crane, Beth Asch, Joanna Heilbrunn, and Danielle Cullinane, was a variant on the study by Bean and colleagues but with more explicit attention paid to sorting out the effect of employer sanctions from the effect of the SAW program. The authors of this third study concluded that the imposition of employer sanctions reduced apprehensions on the Mexican border by about 20 percent during fiscal year 1987. Their estimates for the two following years were less certain; nevertheless, they believed "employer sanctions may have reduced undocumented immigration by at most one-fifth in FY 1989."[25]

None of the three above-mentioned studies include data for the 1990s, but they all indicate that the deterrent effect of IRCA may have declined during the first three years following its passage. Why should this be so? To answer this question, it pays to look at accounts of counterfeiting documents intended to prove legal presence in the United States. In September 1991, for example, INS agents in Los Angeles arrested nine persons for manufacturing and selling counterfeit documents, including green cards, U.S. birth certificates, and social security cards. According to INS officials, 250,000 fake documents with a market value of $8 million were seized. As John Brechtel, assistant director of the Los Angeles district office of INS, described the situation, "With one $40 document, you've beaten employer sanctions."[26] In January 1993 the INS raided a shoe factory in southern California. Of 600 workers changing shifts at the plant, 233 were unable to show legitimate documents proving they had a legal right to work in the United States. Yet the company in question had fully complied with the law with respect to inspection of documents and thus had not knowingly hired any of the illegal aliens. According to Brechtel, this company had been targeted by counterfeiters, who had supplied false documents to many of its workers.[27]

Side Effects

The activities of the U.S. Border Patrol produce certain side effects in immigration-law enforcement. Officers take certain precautions to ensure that the persons they question are undocumented immigrants and not U.S. citizens or permanent legal residents. They are taught that there must be sufficient "articulable facts" before they stop and interrogate pedestrians or motorists, and in the area covered by the Ninth Circuit Court (California, Nevada, Arizona, and Hawaii), citizens are not required to answer any questions about their nationality.[28]

Despite these precautions, there are occasions when INS agents grossly violate the rights of U.S. citizens. Crewdson recounts the confession of an INS inspections agent at the port of San Ysidro in San Diego. The agent told Crewdson that on one occasion he had been ordered by his supervisor to "break" a thirteen-year-old girl who sought to enter the country as a U.S. citizen and who had carried a U.S. birth certificate with her. After several hours of detention, the girl confessed that she had been born in Mexico. Her birth certificate was then taken from her as counterfeit and she was sent back to Mexico. Two days later the girl reappeared with her angry father with undeniable proof that indeed she was a U.S. citizen.[29]

More recently, the border patrol was accused of harassment by students at Bowie High School, located in a Mexican-American neighborhood next to the Rio Grande in El Paso, Texas. The steel fence adjacent to the high school that borders the river's levee is a popular crossing point for undocumented Mexicans. One incident involved a Mexican-born naturalized citizen on the day he was to graduate from high school in June 1992; he stated that border patrol agents grabbed his arm, pushed him face first into a fence, and then kicked his legs to frisk him. In another incident, in November 1991, a Bowie High School football player claimed that an agent pointed a gun at his head and ordered him out of his car. A third student, a seventeen-year-old female, stated that a border patrol agent "stood on her chest with one boot and kicked her with the other causing deep leg and chest bruises." At the request of the school's principal, two dozen students came forward with stories of abuse or questionable detention by the border patrol and filed a lawsuit against the INS. In December 1992 district judge Lucius Bunton granted the plaintiffs' request for a restraining order against the border patrol, saying, "The government's interest in enforcing immigration laws does not outweigh the protection of the rights of United States citizens and permanent residents to be free from unreasonable searches and seizures."[30]

Further side effects are the result of employer sanctions imposed in 1986. IRCA requires that all applicants for employment and the employer sign an I-9 form, in which the applicant must attest that he or she is legally authorized to work in the United States and the employer must attest to having examined appropriate documents that present evidence of the applicant's legal authorization to work in the United States. The employer is also required to preserve the I-9 form for each employee and to present it upon demand to an INS agent; failure to do so is a punishable offense. In order to prove that the documents they have examined appeared to be genuine and relate to the applicant, employers photocopy these documents and preserve these photocopies with the I-9 form.

The cost of preparing and preserving the I-9 forms is the first side effect of employer sanctions. Research by the General Accounting Office (GAO) concluded that the cost of this activity for all employers in the United States in 1988 would be $69 million at a per hour labor cost of $10 and $138 million at a per hour labor cost of $20.[31] This aggregate cost can be met only by forgoing profits, increasing prices, or reducing wages. A second side effect is that the freedom of employers to hire the person they consider most qualified to do the job is curtailed. The law now forces employers to choose the best candidate from the pool who present work documents that appear to be genuine.

The most publicized possible side effect concerns whether the existence of employer sanctions stimulates discrimination against job applicants whose appearance or speech suggests that they might be illegal aliens. This was the main issue for the Hispanic caucus in Congress during the debates over IRCA prior to its passage into law. At the insistence of the Hispanic caucus, Congress included a provision that the GAO conduct a study to determine whether employer sanctions led to a pattern of "widespread discrimination." If so, Congress would be required to provide an expedited review of employer sanctions and decide whether they should be continued. Congress also incorporated in the act a passage to outlaw discrimination on the basis of national origin or citizenship (except that a U.S. citizen may be preferred over an alien if the applicants are equally qualified).

In March 1990 the GAO issued its required report to Congress.[32] The GAO concluded that employer sanctions had resulted in discrimination on the basis of national origin. Congress was thus required to have an expedited review of employer sanctions. Subsequent to the release of the report, however, GAO director Charles Bowsher testified to Congress that despite the report's findings, he did not believe employer sanctions should be repealed. Instead, he suggested that the law be changed to reduce the number of acceptable documents that could be used to prove legal residence in the United States. If the number of acceptable documents was reduced, Bowsher claimed, discrimination would be reduced.[33] Perhaps in part because of Bowsher's statement, Congress never passed Massachusetts senator Edward Kennedy's bill to repeal employer sanctions.

Two major studies commissioned by the GAO were influential in its conclusion. In the first study, conducted by the Urban Institute, eight pairs of researchers, each consisting of one Hispanic and one non-Hispanic male college student, posed as applicants for low-skilled jobs advertised in the local newspaper in Chicago and San Diego. Each member of the pair spoke English fluently and was instructed to tell the potential employer that he was a U.S. citizen. The Hispanic researchers together had 360 encounters with prospective employers; the non-Hispanic researchers likewise had 360 encounters. The proportion of non-Hispanic encounters resulting in a job offer was 36 percent, whereas the percentage of Hispanic encounters resulting in a job offer was only 24 percent. This first study showed that employers discriminated against Hispanic applicants, but it did not prove that they did so because of IRCA.

The second major study, a mail survey of a random sample of employers, attempted to determine whether the passage of IRCA had affected discrimination. The questionnaire was mailed to 9,491 employers across the nation. Among the firms to which questionnaires had been mailed, only 6,317 were still in business and hiring employees. Of these firms, 4,362 completed a usable questionnaire, yielding a response rate of 69 percent. Employers were asked whether they had undertaken any of several actions as a result of their understanding of the 1986 immigration law. Five percent of the sample of employers stated that they had begun a practice of not hiring persons because of their foreign appearance or accent. Moreover, 14 percent of the employers said that they had begun a practice either to hire only applicants born in the United States or not to hire applicants with temporary work eligibility documents.[34] This study provides strong evidence that IRCA produced discrimination, though the study can be faulted for a relatively low rate of response. One may also question whether employers would always tell the truth. If not, the proportion engaging in discriminatory practices might be different from that obtained in the survey.

We cannot estimate exactly to what extent net immigration to the United States is affected by current immigration laws and the efforts made to enforce them. It is clear that bribery of State Department consular officials and INS inspectors detracts from the effectiveness of immigration-law enforcement. There is also clear evidence that giving the border patrol more human and capital resources will increase the number of apprehensions along the Mexican border. Moreover, employer sanctions, at least in the first three years in which they were in effect, appeared to produce a measurable decline in the number of undocumented immigrants entering the nation from the Mexican border. With respect to side effects, there appears to be little doubt that border patrol activities on many occasions have caused harm to citizens who look like they might be undocumented immigrants. To the cost to the taxpayer of immigration-law enforcement activities must be added the cost to the nation of employer responsibility for filling out and preserving I-9 forms attesting to legal eligibility for work in the United States. Finally, there appears to be good evidence that employer sanctions have induced at least some employers to discriminate against job applicants with a foreign appearance.

How Prior Illegal Immigration Facilitates Legal Immigration

Research conducted in the 1970s and early 1980s indicated that a majority of recently admitted legal immigrants from Mexico had been former undocumented immigrants. The first study of this type was reported in an article by Charles Hirschman about the results of a survey of 822 self-supporting male Mexican immigrants legally admitted to the United States who entered at Laredo or El Paso, Texas, in late 1973 and early 1974. Among these men 62 percent had previously lived here, 40 percent reported the United States as their last permanent residence, and 31 percent had lived here at least three years. Of the 356 men who gained admission to the United States as husbands of U.S. citizens, 75 percent had previously lived here.[35] The second study was conducted in 1984 by Lisa Kubiske of the U.S. embassy in Mexico City. Among 1,225 visa applicants for permanent residence who had applied for visas in Mexico City, 80 percent had lived illegally in the United States.[36]

Why should prior residence in the United States in an undocumented status increase one's chances of becoming a legal immigrant? At the present time the major reason would appear to be the chance to marry a U.S. citizen and thus be eligible to receive permanent legal resident status outside of any quota. Let us look at the data for fiscal 1992 concerning the admission of immigrants from Mexico and from the world as a whole who were admitted neither under the legalization provisions of IRCA nor under the provisions of the 1990 Immigration Act that enabled dependents of persons legalized under IRCA to become permanent legal residents. Among 62,883 such immigrants from Mexico, 24.4 percent were spouses of U.S. citizens. For the world as a whole, the corresponding percent was only 16.9.[37] This comparison is particularly noteworthy because for the world as a whole many of the spouses admitted without quota were wives of U.S. servicemen. But because the United States does not maintain military bases in Mexico, most Mexicans admitted as spouses were probably already in the United States.

Another major advantage to an undocumented immigrant comes from bearing or siring a child in the United States. At age twenty-one the child, who is automatically a U.S. citizen, can petition to legalize the status of both parents, who can then receive permanent legal resident status outside of any quota. An American-born child can also petition to have any undocumented brothers and sisters enter the United States under the quota provisions of the fourth family-sponsored preference.

In the past, undocumented residence in the United States provided even more advantages to persons seeking the status of permanent legal resident. From 1965 to 1977 being the parent of an American-born child of any age allowed one to apply for permanent legal residence without labor certification. Furthermore, from the time of the War on Poverty initiated in the administration of President Johnson until January 1, 1980, free legal aid funded at least in part by the United States Legal Services Corporation was widely available to undocumented immigrants in the United States seeking to legalize their status.[38]

How Extending Rights to Undocumented Residents May Encourage Illegal Immigration

As I noted in Chapter 5, undocumented residents of the United States have acquired a certain collection of rights. In addition about 2.7 million former undocumented residents were able to legalize their status as a result of IRCA. A convincing argument can be made for two propositions: (1) the more rights are given to undocumented immigrants, the larger the number who will in the future be encouraged to come to the United States, and (2) the legalization of status of undocumented immigrants under IRCA has provoked a future increase in the net flow of the undocumented persons into the United States because it has encouraged the idea that additional amnesties will be granted.

In recent years many people have argued that the rights accorded to undocumented immigrants should be reduced. Nevertheless, there may be harmful consequences to the American public if those rights are diminished. For example, since 1987 federal Medicaid funds have been used to provide emergency and pregnancy-related care to indigent illegal aliens. Suppose federal funding for emergency care were to be abolished. One result might be a marked increase in the prevalence of communicable diseases, such as tuberculosis. In Los Angeles, where a high proportion of the total population consists of undocumented immigrants, such diseases could easily spread from undocumented persons to the rest of the city's population. Consider also the law effective in California in 1994 that decreed that one could not obtain a California driver's license without proof of legal residence in the United States.[39] If this law is effective, it may mean that many undocumented immigrants in California will drive without a license and without having passed a driving test. Accordingly, Californians may find more unsafe drivers on the roads and a higher probability that they will be involved in a traffic accident with an unlicensed, uninsured, and unskilled driver.

Notes

1. John Crewdson, *The Tarnished Door: The New Immigrants and the Transformation of America* (New York: Times Books, 1983), pp. 30–37, 136–138.

2. Milton D. Morris, *Immigration—The Beleaguered Bureaucracy* (Washington, D.C.: Brookings Institution, 1985), pp. 96–102.

3. Tito Alegría, "Ciudad y transmigración en la frontera de México con Estados Unidos," *La frontera norte*, Vol. 2, No. 4 (1990), p. 21.

4. U.S. Department of Justice, Immigration and Naturalization Service, *Statistical Yearbook of the Immigration and Naturalization Service, 1992* (Washington, D.C.: Government Printing Office, 1993), p. 96.

5. Ibid., pp. 170–175.

6. Arthur F. Corwin and Johnny M. McCain, "Wetbackism Since 1964: A Catalogue of Factors," in Arthur F. Corwin, ed., *Immigrants—and Immigrants: Perspectives on Mexican Labor Migration to the United States* (Westport, Conn.: Greenwood Press, 1978), p. 75.

7. Crewdson, *The Tarnished Door,* pp. 143–165.

8. Ibid., p. 160.

9. U.S. Department of Justice, *Statistical Yearbook, 1992*, pp. 156, 169.

10. Thomas J. Espenshade, "Undocumented Migration to the United States: Evidence from a Repeated Trials Model," in Frank D. Bean, Barry Edmonston, and Jeffrey S. Passel, eds., *Undocumented Migration to the United States* (Washington, D.C.: Urban Institute Press, 1990), p. 161.

11. Ibid., pp. 162–166.

12. U.S. Department of Justice, *Statistical Yearbook, 1992*, p. 167.

13. Federation for American Immigration Reform, *Ten Steps to Securing America's Borders* (Washington, D.C.: Federation for American Immigration Reform, 1989), p. 10.

14. Sebastian Rotella, "Costs, Risks of Halting Illegal Immigrants Debated," *Los Angeles Times*, November 20, 1993, p. 1.

15. David Aponte, "Levantará EU frente a Tecate otra barda metálica en apoyo a la que construy e junto a Tijuana," *La Jornada* (Mexico City), October 20, 1993, p. 1.

16. Rotella, "Costs, Risks," p. 1.

17. Edwin Harwood, *In Liberty's Shadow: Illegal Aliens and Immigration Law Enforcement* (Stanford, Calif.: Hoover Institution Press, 1986), p. 63.

18. Carlos H. Zazueta and César Zazueta, *En las puertas de paraíso* (Mexico City: CENIET, 1980), p. 62.

19. Harwood, *In Liberty's Shadow,* pp. 77–167.

20. Jason Juffras, *Impact of the Immigration Reform and Control Act on the Immigration and Naturalization Service* (Washington, D.C.: RAND Corporation and Urban Institute Press, 1991), pp. 22–23.

21. Ibid., p. 23.

22. Ibid., p. 26.

23. Frank D. Bean, Thomas J. Espenshade, Michael J. White, and Robert F. Dymowski, "Post-IRCA Changes in the Volume and Composition of Undocumented Migration to the United States: An Assessment Based on Apprehensions Data," in Bean et al., *Undocumented Migration*, pp. 111–158.

24. Espenshade, "Undocumented Migration," pp. 159–181.

25. Keith Crane, Beth J. Asch, Joanna Zorn Heilbrunn, and Danielle C. Cullinane, *The Effect of Employer Sanctions on the Flow of Undocumented Immigrants to the United States* (Washington, D.C.: RAND Corporation and Urban Institute Press, 1990), pp. 5–36.

26. Josh Meyer, "Fake Green Card Ring Was Largest in U.S.," *Los Angeles Times*, September 29, 1991, p. B1.

27. Jeff Cole, "INS Arrests, Deports over 200 Employees of California Firm," *Wall Street Journal*, January 18, 1993, p. A7B.

28. Harwood, *In Liberty's Shadow*, pp. 49–76.

29. Crewdson, *The Tarnished Door*, pp. 170–171.

30. Robert Tomsho, "Matter of Principle: High School in El Paso Gives the Border Patrol a Civil-Rights Lesson," *Wall Street Journal*, February 23, 1993, p. A1.

31. U.S. General Accounting Office, *Immigration Reform: Employer Sanctions and the Question of Discrimination* (Washington, D.C.: Government Printing Office, 1990), p. 110.

32. Ibid., pp. 1–62.

33. Shawn Pogatchnik, "Congress Urged to Adopt Better ID for Legal Workers," *Los Angeles Times*, March 31, 1990, p. A18.

34. U.S. General Accounting Office, *Immigration Reform*, pp. 38–50, 124–125.

35. Charles Hirschman, "Prior U.S. Residence Among Mexican Immigrants," *Social Forces* Vol. 56, No. 4 (1978), pp. 1179–1201.

36. Lisa Kubiske, "A Survey of Immigrant Visa Applicants Handled by the Mexico City Consular District," *FAIR/Information Exchange*, October 15, 1985.

37. U.S. Department of Justice, *Statistical Yearbook, 1992*, pp. 41–42.

38. Wayne A. Cornelius, *The Future of Mexican Immigrants in California: A New Perspective for Public Policy*, Working Papers in U.S.-Mexican Studies, No. 6 (La Jolla: Program in United States–Mexican Studies, University of California, San Diego, 1981), p. 61.

39. "California Laws '94," *Los Angeles Times*, December 31, 1993, p. A3.

8 The Impact of Immigration

In this chapter we examine social science findings on the effect of immigration on a set of values most Americans consider important. These values (previously described in Chapter 2) include the standard of living in the United States, issues of equity, issues concerning the preservation or modification of existing American culture, ethnic and class conflict within the United States, and the power of the United States in international affairs. We begin with the American standard of living.

Standard of Living

In Chapter 2 we emphasized that immigration policies that will improve the standard of living of one group of native Americans may have negative impacts on the standard of living of other groups. In that chapter we also introduced some of the major points of economic theory with respect to the consequences of immigration for the American standard of living. We then distinguished three groups of native Americans (unskilled workers, skilled workers, and owners of land or capital) and brought up the concepts of substitutes and complements in the production process. According to economic theory, the introduction of an additional worker who is a substitute for an existing worker will tend to reduce the marginal productivity of the original worker; the introduction of an additional worker who is a complement to an existing worker will tend to raise the marginal productivity of the original worker. Land and capital are in general complements to either skilled or unskilled workers, and skilled workers are complements to unskilled workers. But unskilled workers are substitutes for other unskilled workers, skilled workers in one occupation are substitutes for additional skilled workers in the same occupation, and additional units of land and capital are often substitutes for existing units. Finally, in Chapter 2 we stressed that native workers who were substitutes for immigrant workers and hence subject to diminished marginal productivity could react in three different ways: (1) They might accept a lower wage, (2) they might quit their jobs and become unemployed, or (3) they might leave the local labor market and seek better jobs elsewhere. In contrast, native workers who were complements to immigrant workers and hence subject to a rise in marginal

Israeli and Iranian garment manufacturers and Japanese garment exporter, garment district, Los Angeles, California.

productivity might (1) gain a higher wage, (2) be attracted into the work force, or (3) migrate into the local labor market if they did not already live there.

Let us now look at the results of some empirical studies that have attempted to examine the effects that a large increase in the immigrant labor force would have on native workers. We begin with studies concerned with the effect of Mexican immigration in California, particularly in Los Angeles County. The justification for such a focus is threefold: First, as of the time of the 1990 census, there were more foreign-born persons in Los Angeles County than in any other primary metropolitan statistical area, and the foreign-born in Los Angeles County constituted almost 15 percent of the total in the nation.[1] Second, in 1990 there were more persons in the United States born in Mexico than born in any other foreign nation, and those born in Mexico constituted about 22 percent of all foreign-born persons.[2] Third, in 1990 a high percentage (about 40 percent) of all foreign-born persons in Los Angeles County

Soviet Jewish girls at Chabad Day Camp, West Hollywood, California, 1994.

were Mexican immigrants, and of all persons born in Mexico who lived in the United States 27 percent were in Los Angeles County.[3] The great majority of Mexican immigrants have had only a few years of formal schooling[4] and thus could be expected to be substitutes for unskilled workers in the area but complements to skilled workers and to land and capital.

The Impact of Mexican Immigration in Los Angeles County

Among the most important studies on this topic are one by two researchers from the Urban Institute, Thomas Muller and Thomas Espenshade, and another by two researchers from the RAND Corporation, Kevin McCarthy and R. B. Valdez.[5] In examining the effects of Mexican immigration, both teams relied heavily on changes in census and survey data from the decade of 1970 to 1980. My own research has also related to this topic.

The Urban Institute study considered trends in unemployment in the five-county Los Angeles metropolitan statistical area. The researchers found that in 1970, prior to the beginning of mass Mexican immigration, the unemployment rate in the Los Angeles area had been higher than in the United States, not only for all persons but also for blacks. By 1980, after a mass influx of Mexican immigrants, the unemployment rate in the area was lower than in the United States both for the total population and for blacks. Thus the researchers concluded that the influx of Mexican immigrants had had no adverse effect on unemployment.[6]

One reason for this lack of impact was the mass net out-migration of non-Hispanic whites. In the Los Angeles consolidated metropolitan statistical area from 1970 to 1980, the non-Hispanic white population declined by 497,000 at the same time that the Hispanic population increased by 1.379 million.[7] Moreover, the out-migration appeared to be selective of those who could be considered substitutes for the Mexican immigrants. The 1980 census revealed that for the state of California as a whole, the net interstate out-migration from 1975 to 1980 for white persons twenty-five years old and over was 18,841. But this overall net out-migration consisted of a net out-migration of 93,699 persons who were not college graduates and a net in-migration of 64,858 college graduates.[8] During 1975–1980, then, persons who were not college graduates and thus were substitutes for newly arrived immigrants from Mexico left California, whereas highly educated persons who were complements to the unskilled Mexican immigrants came into the state. Results from the 1990 census revealed a continuation of this particular pattern of interstate migration for 1985 to 1990. In this later period, among white persons aged twenty-five and over, there was a net interstate in-migration of 112,565 college graduates into California but a net interstate out-migration of 89,951 persons who were not college graduates.[9]

What was the effect of Mexican immigration on wages in the Los Angeles area? Muller and Espenshade analyzed wage growth among all workers in Los Angeles County from 1972 to 1980 and among categories of workers differentiated by the percentage of all workers in the category who were Mexican immigrants. They showed that Mexican immigrants constituted 9.9 percent of all workers in Los Angeles County in 1980 but 47 percent of all workers in low-wage manufacturing industries (e.g., apparel, leather goods, and furniture) and 19.5 percent of all workers in high-wage manufacturing (e.g., metals, machinery, and transportation equipment). There was a very high correlation between the proportion of all workers who were Mexican immigrants and the increase in the wage from 1972 to 1980 in Los Angeles relative to that in the United States. For low-wage manufacturing, the relative increase in the Los Angeles County wage was only 77 percent of that in the United States; for high-wage manufacturing it was only 91 percent; but for all workers it was 109 percent. Muller and Espenshade concluded that some wage depression was attributable to immigrants.[10]

The RAND study added further information concerning the consequences of Mexican immigration for persons of Hispanic origin born in the United States. McCarthy and Valdez showed that for Los Angeles County the average earnings of year-round, full-time workers born in the United States and of Hispanic origin had been 16 percent higher than the national average in 1970. By 1980 they were only 99 percent of the U.S. average.[11] The implication was that many U.S.-born citizens of Hispanic origin had been substitutes for Mexican immigrants.

My collaborators and I were the first to look at the placement of undocumented Mexican immigrants in the Los Angeles County work force relative to that of other ethnic groups. We showed that this placement by occupation, industry, and class of worker in 1980 was more distinct than for that of any other ethnic group. The two groups closest to undocumented Mexican immigrants in placement were legal Mexican immigrants and Hispanic immigrants from nations other than Mexico (in many cases undocumented immigrants from El Salvador and Guatemala). Blacks and Hispanics born in the United States were not similar in placement to undocumented Mexican immigrants but were somewhat less different from undocumented Mexicans than were non-Hispanic whites. The implication of these findings was that a continued flow of undocumented Mexican immigrants would be most harmful to legal Mexican immigrants and Hispanic immigrants from nations other than Mexico and would have relatively minor negative effects on other ethnic groups.

With respect to Hispanics born in the United States, we contended that the effect of a continued flow of undocumented Mexican immigrants would be greatly contingent on skill levels: Skilled persons of Mexican descent born in the United States would be complements to undocumented Mexican immigrants. Bilingual professionals such as teachers, lawyers, nurses, and physicians could expect to benefit from a continued influx of undocumented Mexicans; demand for bilingual foremen would also increase. Unskilled workers born in the United States of Mexican descent, however, would likely be substitutes for undocumented Mexicans and might suffer accordingly. We predicted that many of them would leave Los Angeles County for jobs elsewhere.[12]

None of the studies reviewed so far provide evidence of harm to blacks in California due to high levels of immigration from Mexico. But there is one case study that does reveal competition between blacks and Hispanic immigrants resulting in definite disadvantage to blacks. This case study, by Richard Mines and Jeffrey Avina, concerned the fate of a Los Angeles janitors' union, Local 399 of the Service Employees International Union. The union began organizing Los Angeles janitors in 1946. In the 1970s a small number of large unionized firms, most of whose employees were black, dominated the market for janitorial services in high-rise office buildings. Competing with these large firms at the time were midsized firms with nonunionized workers, most of them Hispanic immigrants. The wage paid to janitors in the standard union contract (in effect, for high-rise buildings) was much higher than that paid nonunion janitors and, moreover, rose rapidly after 1976. By 1982 the standard union contract paid over $12 an hour, whereas nonunion firms paid approximately $4 per hour. Faced with this differential, union firms could not compete with nonunion firms. The number of union workers covered by the standard agreement dropped from 2,500 in 1977 to only 100 in 1985. Total union membership, including union members with wages less than that in the standard agreement, declined from 5,000 to 2,000. The number of black workers in the union fell from 2,500 in 1977 to only 600 in 1985. Of black workers who had lost their jobs, Doris Boyd, a black official for Local 399, said, "A very small percentage of these workers have found jobs. They are unskilled people; they don't know anything but janitorial. Most have had fifteen to twenty years experience. About 700 are out of work right now because of the changes."[13]

A further elaboration of how blacks might lose out to immigrants from Mexico and Central America came from Roger Waldinger's study on the attitudes of employers in the restaurant and hotel industries in Los Angeles County. He interviewed thirty-three employers for their opinions on which ethnic groups provided the most desirable workers. At the time of the interviews, practically no blacks were employed in the restaurants or hotels surveyed. Whites were employed in "front jobs" where contact with customers was emphasized. The "back jobs," such as kitchen and housekeeper jobs, were filled primarily by Hispanic immigrants. A typical comment on the job performance of blacks was as follows:

> If you're talking about service in the hotel industry you have to have a certain attitude. If you come with a chip on your shoulder, negativeness, "I've been a victim," you don't come across as guest-oriented, helpful. You have to smile, use the guest's name, have to be friendly, the attitude shows you want to be friendly in tone and manner. [With blacks] there is an attitude that is there. It's hard to pinpoint because when you say it you're accused of being a racist.

Native whites were also compared unfavorably to immigrants. According to one employer, "They tend to be lazier. They figure they will get paid the same whether they work or don't, whether they bust their butts cleaning the place up and making it look nice, or just kick back." In contrast to these negative statements were positive statements about Hispanic immigrants. One employer remarked, "Yes, the immigrants just want to work, work long hours, just want to do anything. They spend a lot of money coming up from Mexico. They want as many hours as possible. If I called them in for 4 hours to clean latrines, they'd do it. They like to work. They have large families, a big work ethic, and small salaries."[14]

Waldinger's interviews suggest that employers in Los Angeles perceive that the continued immigrant flow works to their own personal financial advantage. Both Muller and Espenshade and McCarthy and Valdez came to similar conclusions. Muller and Espenshade estimated that without the immigration of Mexicans to Los Angeles County during 1970 to 1980, there would have been 53,000 fewer production jobs in manufacturing in the county in 1980 than there actually were. In effect, because employers could pay less money for more productive workers, they were able to expand production beyond what would have been possible without Mexican immigrant workers. Furthermore, they estimated there would have been a multiplier effect from the loss of these 53,000 manufacturing jobs. Altogether, Muller and Espenshade estimated that an additional 37,000 jobs in the county would have been lost if there had been no Mexican immigration. About 12,000 of these represented high-pay nonproduction jobs in manufacturing; the remainder were jobs in industries other than manufacturing.[15] From a similar analysis, McCarthy and Valdez concluded, "Our evidence suggests that Mexican immigration has provided a boost to California's economy, especially in the Los Angeles area, by enabling many low-wage industries to continue to expand at a time when their counterparts nationwide were contracting in the face of foreign competition."[16]

Muller and Espenshade also examined the relationship between the surge of Mexican immigration to Los Angeles and changes from 1967 to 1981 in specific components of the cost of living in Los Angeles County relative to changes in the cost of living in the nation as a whole. They found that prices of items in which Mexican immigrant labor was a heavy component (such as personal care, apparel, entertainment, food away from home, and household goods and operations) rose less in Los Angeles than in the nation. Prices of other items, such as medical care and rent, went up more rapidly, reflecting that health-care workers and owners of land and capital are complements to unskilled labor. Overall, the cost of living in Los Angeles County rose somewhat less from 1967 to 1981 than it did in the nation (168.3 percent versus 180.2 percent).[17]

Both the Urban Institute and the RAND Corportion researchers examined the fiscal impact of Mexican immigrants on state and local governments. Muller and Espenshade concluded that Mexican immigrant households on average received $2,245 more in state and local government expenditures than they contributed to state and local government revenues, whereas the state and local fiscal gap for all households in Los

Angeles County averaged only $139. They attributed much of this difference to the fact that Mexican immigrant households had more than twice the average number of children in school per household than was the case among all households in the county.[18] McCarthy and Valdez came to similar conclusions with respect to the fiscal impact of Mexican immigrants.[19] Neither study examined the effect of Mexican immigrants on federal taxes or expenditures.

The Impact of Immigration on the Nation as a Whole

A large number of researchers have attempted quantitative analyses of the impact of immigrants on the nation as a whole. Many studies have used local labor markets (usually metropolitan statistical areas) as the unit of analysis to see how variation in the number of immigrants in a local labor market has affected the native population in each market. Any number of studies have examined the impact of immigration on the native black population; excellent descriptions of their findings appear elsewhere.[20] Here I attempt only a summary of the main findings. Perhaps the most general conclusion is that variation in the number of immigrants produced little effect on either unemployment or wages of the native population as a whole. A study by Espenshade and Tracy Ann Goodis is of particular note because it showed that variation in the number of immigrants had no effect on black unemployment rates across 247 metropolitan statistical areas.[21] A study by Frank Bean, B. Lindsay Lowell, and Lowell Taylor is also noteworthy because it dealt with the impact of the number of undocumented Mexican immigrants (as measured by Warren and Passel) on the average wage of whites, blacks, and native Hispanics in forty-seven metropolitan areas in the southwestern states. They found small effects but effects consistent with economic theory that undocumented Mexicans should be complements to more skilled workers but substitutes to other unskilled workers. They found that a 10 percent increase in the number of undocumented Mexican immigrants was associated with a 0.1 percent increase in the average wage of white males, a 0.1 percent decrease in the average wage of black males, and no change in the average wage of native Hispanic males.[22]

All studies done to date on the consequences on wages or unemployment across local labor markets can be criticized because they ignore the fact that workers who are substitutes for immigrants in a particular labor market are likely to migrate out and workers who are complements to immigrants are likely to move in.[23] If the volume of resulting out-migration of substitutes and in-migration of complements is of sufficient magnitude, we should expect to see no relationship between the number of immigrants and either the employment or the wage of natives in local labor markets. But this would not mean that there was no effect for the nation as a whole. Borjas has recognized this point, even though he conducted many of the existing studies in which local labor markets were the units of analysis.[24] Former secretary of labor Ray Marshall made the point forcefully in a critique of the studies carried out by the Urban Institute and the RAND Corporation concerning the Los Angeles area. Marshall argued that black blue-collar workers outside Los Angeles County suffered indirect displacement because of the high volume of Mexican immigration to the county. He contended that blacks elsewhere in the United States were well represented in some of the industries that employed large numbers of undocumented Mexicans in Los Angeles. Because undocumented Mexicans in Los Angeles are willing to work for less, options are closed for blacks outside Los Angeles and they become "off-stage victims."[25]

In summary, then, for the nation as a whole the immigration of unskilled workers may have a negative effect on the wages of native unskilled workers. Yet the resultant reduction in the average wage for unskilled workers may preserve or expand certain industries in the United States that otherwise could not have survived foreign competition. Thus the lowering of wages for unskilled workers may create and make available to native workers new jobs as foremen, managers, professionals, and government workers that would not have existed otherwise. To the extent that native unskilled workers can take advantage of these new opportunities, they will gain rather than lose from the immigration of unskilled immigrants. To the extent that they fail to capitalize on these opportunities, they will suffer from a lower wage and may have an increased propensity to rely on entitlements rather than their own earnings as sources of income.

How do the taxes immigrants pay compare to the benefits immigrants receive from government? Researchers have done many studies on this topic, but their conclusions have been vociferously challenged.[26] Let us begin our discussion with some noncontroversial facts concerning the income that natives and various types of immigrants receive from governmental entitlement programs. Fix and Passel tabulated data from the 1990 census on the proportion of individuals fifteen years of age or older who received means-tested public assistance income (i.e., AFDC, SSI, or general relief) in 1989. Natives were contrasted with three types of immigrants: (1) those who arrived in the United States between 1980 and 1990 from eleven nations that send large numbers of refugees to the United States, (2) those who arrived in the United States between 1980 and 1990 from other nations, and (3) those who arrived in the United States before 1980. For recent immigrants from refugee nations, the percentage receiving public assistance income (15.6 percent) was far higher than for individuals in the other three groups. Only 2.8 percent of recent immigrants from nonrefugee countries received public assistance income, as did 4.2 percent of natives and 4.9 percent of immigrants who had come before 1980. Among the subgroup who were aged sixty-five or over, the picture was somewhat different. All refugees aged sixty-five and older and all nonrefugee legal aliens aged sixty-five and over who have been in the United States at least three years are eligible for SSI if their income from other sources, such as social security or pensions, is very low or nonexistent. For persons aged sixty-five and over, 49.6 percent of recent immigrants from refugee countries received public assistance income, as did 25.7 percent of recent immigrants from all other nations. In contrast, only 6.9 percent of natives in this age group and only 11.1 percent of immigrants who had come to the United States before 1980 received such income. The last two groups no doubt relied heavily on income from social security, which is not a means-tested program.[27]

How do immigrants and natives compare with respect to their receipts from the social security system? This question is a crucial one because federal government expenditures for social security in fiscal 1993 amounted to $305 billion and constituted almost 21 percent of all federal outlays.[28] Julian Simon, who has made the most thorough analysis of this question, contends that a large flow of young adult immigrants can be a major factor in solving a forthcoming crisis in the social security system.[29] This crisis is predicted to hit when the large cohorts born during the baby boom following World War II reach retirement age. Beginning around the year 2015 and becoming most acute around 2030, the crisis will occur because the U.S. social security system is largely a pay-as-you-go system in which payments by current workers cover benefits to retired persons. The crucial empirical fact in Simon's argument is the difference in age composition between new immigrants and the native population. As we noted in Chapter 5, the native population has a higher proportion of persons aged sixty-five and older and a lower proportion of young adults than do newly arrived immigrants. Moreover, as shown in Table 5.16, the projected annual volume of net immigration to the United States will make a substantial difference to the ratio of individuals of working age (eighteen to sixty-four years old) to individuals of retirement age (ages sixty-five and over) expected in the year 2030. Accordingly, Simon makes a convincing argument that a large volume of immigration for the next few decades will allow native workers to pay less in social security taxes and allow natives higher pension benefits and a lower age at retirement than would be possible if immigration volume were small or nil.

I have already noted the findings of Muller and Espenshade concerning the high educational expenses for the children of Mexican immigrants in Los Angeles. As I pointed out in Chapter 5, immigrants from nations other than Latin America or Vietnam do not have significantly higher fertility than do native-born U.S. citizens. For all households with an immigrant householder, then, the costs of public schooling per household should not be much larger than the costs for households with a native householder. Moreover, paying taxes to support the education of children is different from paying taxes to support the indigent or elderly in that payments for children's education represents an investment in future human capital, whereas expenditures for the elderly or the indigent in general do not.

The amount of taxes immigrants pay is a topic that tends to arouse even more controversy than does the amount of benefits they receive. In particular, there has been debate about the amount of taxes undocumented immigrants pay and the proportion of undocumented immigrants who pay taxes at all. My own study of undocumented Mexican mothers and fathers in Los Angeles County showed high proportions of both the employed fathers (96.2 percent) and employed mothers (88.4 percent) who have federal income tax deducted from their paychecks (see Table 5.8 for comparisons with other groups).

To estimate the net fiscal cost or benefit of immigration to the United States, it is not enough simply to tally the taxes immigrants pay and the amount of governmental benefits they receive. It is also necessary to consider the indirect effects on the native population. If, because of immigration, unskilled native workers drop out of the labor force or receive lower wages, they will pay less in taxes and receive more in benefits. Conversely, if, because of immigration, skilled native workers and native owners of land or capital receive higher income, they will pay more in taxes and receive less in benefits.

The first scholar to attempt an analysis of the net fiscal impact of immigration taking into account these indirect effects was economist Donald Huddle.[30] Huddle made estimates of the net fiscal cost for the following populations: (1) regular legal immigrants, including refugees, who arrived since 1970; (2) undocumented immigrants; (3) former undocumented immigrants who were legalized under IRCA; and (4) the native population. For 1992, Huddle estimated the net fiscal cost to be $19.5 billion for regular legal immigrants who arrived since 1970; $7.6 billion for undocumented immigrants; and $3.5 billion for former undocumented immigrants legalized under IRCA. He put the indirect costs incurred by the native population at $11.9 billion. In making the estimate for the native population, Huddle included only negative impacts. Altogether, including both direct and indirect impacts, Huddle estimated the net fiscal cost of immigration in 1992 to be $42.5 billion, of which $30.6 billion consisted of direct net costs and $11.9 billion of indirect net costs.

Fix and Passel sharply attacked Huddle's estimates on various grounds.[31] They asserted that he had made three major errors in estimating taxes received from immigrants. First, he had estimated the income of legal immigrants who had entered since 1970 on the basis of income of immigrants to Los Angeles County since 1980 rather than the income of all immigrants to the United States since 1970. This substantially biased downward the estimate compared to the true figure. Second, his underestimate of the income of immigrants led to an understatement of the rate at which immigrants were taxed. Finally, Huddle failed to figure in many taxes at all, including the social security tax, unemployment insurance tax, and gasoline tax. Fix and Passel concluded that the three immigrant groups Huddle examined actually paid $50 billion more in taxes than Huddle had estimated. Fix and Passel also contended that Huddle had overestimated the benefits received by the three immigrant populations by $10 billion. These errors implied that instead of a direct net cost of $30.6 billion, there was a direct net benefit of $29.4 billion. Fix and Passel further disputed Huddle's estimate of $11.9 billion for the costs to displaced natives; they maintained that the actual costs of displacement were substantially less than Huddle presumed and that an accurate estimate of indirect effects must include positive impacts as well. Fix and Passel argued that, overall, immigration had positive net fiscal consequences for the United States when both the direct and indirect impacts were aggregated.

The work of Fix and Passel thus casts considerable doubt on the validity of Huddle's estimate of the direct and indirect net fiscal cost of immigration to the United States. Nevertheless, we should recognize that there is as yet no consensus among experts on the total (both direct and indirect) net fiscal impact of immigration to the United States. But it should soon be possible to reach consensus on the direct net fiscal impact of immigration to the United States, as future studies are likely to point to clearer answers. Moreover, there does seem to be agreement that the total net fiscal impact for the federal government appears to be more positive than the impact for state and local governments.

Equity

As I pointed out in Chapter 2, there are two contrasting views concerning how equity should be defined: a libertarian view and an egalitarian view. Libertarians, on the one hand, believe equity is achieved when each individual is rewarded in proportion to her or his economic contribution to society within a free market. Accordingly, any governmental regulations that restrict free immigration to the United States introduce labor monopolies that destroy equity. When laws restrict free immigration, some of the people who should be allowed to compete for desirable jobs are not allowed to do so. Certain natives then receive economic rewards larger than what they would be entitled to under free market conditions. What is more, laws restricting immigration also create inequity for employers and owners of land and capital by prohibiting employers from hiring undocumented immigrants and thus preventing them from maximizing returns on their land, capital, and entrepreneurial skills.

Egalitarians, on the other hand, believe equity is best achieved when the gap in economic rewards separating the rich from the poor is small. Egalitarians therefore favor a policy of substantial income transfer from the rich to the poor by means of progressive taxation and means-tested entitlement programs. But the egalitarian notion of equity creates a dilemma regarding the desirable level of immigration: Equity might best be achieved by a policy that restores the status of the native-born poor at the expense of denying an opportunity to a much poorer person who would like to be a legal immigrant to the United States, or it might come about by a policy that does just the opposite.

Let me illustrate this dilemma by presenting hypothetical arguments by spokespersons for each of these two positions. The first might come from an African American who believes the government should reduce the level of immigration, legal and illegal, into the United States. The second might be that of an undocumented Mexican immigrant, a mestizo (of mixed indigenous and European ancestry) who believes he has a moral right freely to enter the United States to live and work. If you believe in the egalitarian notion of equity, you will have to judge for yourself the merit of these two contrasting arguments.

Argument of the African American

The white men forcibly brought my ancestors here from Africa on slave ships. Those who survived the voyage were sold into slavery. My ancestors were in slavery for more than 200 years. When they were finally emancipated at the time of the Civil War, each was promised 40 acres and a mule. But the white men running the government reneged on that promise. As a result of slavery, we African Americans cannot enjoy the same socioeconomic status whites do. Despite our efforts, because we start at the bottom it is harder for us to rise as far as do groups who start higher up. Right now a lot of Mexican immigrants are slipping into this country illegally and making things even harder for us. Where we have finally succeeded in getting a few decent jobs, the Mexicans come onto the scene and are willing to work for less. The whites who run our government promised to do something about this. Back in 1986 they passed a law that was supposed to stop those Mexicans from coming in illegally. The law made it illegal for employers knowingly to hire illegal aliens. But what happened? Illegal aliens presented fake certificates to the employers. Then many of those employers said, "If no one can accuse me of knowingly hiring illegal aliens, why not go ahead and hire them?" If we African Americans are to have the chances in life that we ought to have, the government has got to do more to keep out illegal aliens.

Argument of the Undocumented Mexican Immigrant

Some people say I have no right to be in this country. They say I am an illegal alien. But who was the first illegal alien in America? Christopher Columbus. He sailed to our continent from Europe. Following Columbus, Spaniards came to Mexico and conquered the indigenous Mexican peoples. They forced them to work in the silver mines. Because the Mexican peoples were not immune to the diseases the Spaniards brought with them, many of the Mexicans died. It was truly a holocaust. Finally, early in the nineteenth century, Mexico fought for and won its independence from Spain. But shortly afterward, you Yankees began to take advantage of us. My government invited your people to come to the northeast part of my country, to Texas, and to settle—but to obey the laws of Mexico. But your settlers wanted to run things by themselves, and they declared their independence from us. When my government objected to their declaration of independence in Texas, your country declared war on my country. Your troops marched all the way to Mexico City. You were too powerful for us. We had to give you half our territory. Not only did you take Texas but also California, Arizona, New Mexico, Utah, and parts of Colorado, Wyoming, and Oklahoma. So now here I am in California. You took this place from my people. So I have just as much right to be here as you do. Maybe more.

Preservation or Modification of Existing American Culture

Currently, a major concern over the volume of immigration, particularly immigration from Mexico and other Spanish-speaking countries, is that it may imperil the role of English as the dominant language in the United States. Morris Janowitz, a well-known sociologist from the University of Chicago, writes:

Mexicans, together with other Spanish-speaking populations, are creating a bifurcation in the social-political structure of the United States that approximates nationality division. . . . The presence of Mexico at the border of the United States, plus the strength of Mexican cultural patterns, means that the "natural history" of Mexican immigrants has been and will be at variance with that of other immigrant groups. For sections of the Southwest, it is not premature to speak of a cultural and social irredenta—sectors of the United States which have in effect become Mexicanized and, therefore, under political dispute.[32]

Is it likely that the American Southwest could become an area where Spanish was the official language? Recent social science findings shed light on this question. Let me first cite some findings from my own study of parents of Mexican origin in Los Angeles County.[33] My findings concerning native tongues and the ability to speak English by nativity and legal status are shown in Table 8.1. Almost all immigrants gave Spanish as their native language; less than half the native-born citizens of Mexican descent considered English their native tongue. A high proportion of immigrants, particularly undocumented immigrants, did not speak English well. Among the native-born of Mexican descent, however, almost all were fluent in English.

Further important data come from the Latino National Political Survey. Conducted in 1989–1990, this survey queried individuals eighteen years old and over who declared themselves to be of Mexican, Cuban, or Puerto Rican descent in forty areas of the nation where the number of people of such descent was relatively large. In addition the survey queried a small sample of non-Hispanic whites in the same set of areas.[34] We may concentrate our attention on the results for persons of

TABLE 8.1   Percentage Distributions by Mother Tongue and Ability to Speak English for Mothers and Fathers of Mexican Origin, Los Angeles County, 1980–1981

	Mothers			*Fathers*		
	Undocumented	*Legal Immigrant*	*Native-born Citizen*	*Undocumented*	*Legal Immigrant*	*Native-born Citizen*
Mother tongue						
Total	100.0	100.0	100.0	100.0	100.0	100.0
English	0.2	0.2	47.3	0.0	0.7	38.8
Spanish	99.6	98.0	32.9	99.6	98.4	42.7
Other language	0.0	0.0	0.0	0.4	0.9	0.0
Both English and Spanish	0.2	1.8	19.8	0.0	0.0	18.5
Ability to speak English						
Total	100.0	100.0	100.0	100.0	100.0	100.0
Fluent	1.3	18.7	94.4	3.4	22.1	91.8
Moderate	9.6	16.2	4.3	18.1	36.8	4.4
With difficulty	23.4	38.1	0.8	51.4	33.4	3.8
None	66.0	27.0	0.5	27.0	7.7	0.0
Weighted number of cases	3,298	1,711	1,831	2,752	1,655	1,320

SOURCE: David M. Heer, *Undocumented Mexicans in the United States* (New York: Cambridge University Press, 1990), p. 124.

Mexican descent, by far the largest of the three Hispanic groups from which responses were obtained (although results for persons of Cuban or Puerto Rican origin are quite similar). Survey findings are shown in Tables 8.2 through 8.6.

From Table 8.2 we see that Spanish is the dominant language spoken at home among persons of Mexican descent born outside the United States. In contrast, less than 12 percent of persons of Mexican descent born in the United States spoke only Spanish or more Spanish than English at home. Table 8.3 presents data on whether U.S. citizens and residents should learn English. It is obvious that almost everyone of Mexican origin in the United States, regardless of birthplace, believes that U.S. citizens and residents should learn English.

Table 8.4 presents data on whether English should be the official language of the United States. Before discussing these data, however, we need to take a look at a social movement that rapidly acquired political clout in the 1980s as immigration into the United States swelled. The movement was spearheaded by an organization called U.S. English, whose honorary chair was S. I. Hayakawa, a Japanese American who was a former Republican senator from California, a former president of the California State University at San Francisco, and a semanticist. The group's major effort was in behalf of a proposed referendum to amend California's constitution to make English the official language of the state. California Proposition 63 was placed on the ballot on November 4, 1986. It was opposed by most of the Democractic political leaders of the state and by California's Republican governor, George Deukmejian. Despite the opposition of so many political leaders, voters passed it by an overwhelming 73.2 percent. As a result, California became the seventh state

TABLE 8.2   Percentage Distribution by Language Spoken at Home for Persons of Mexican Origin, 1989–1990

	Foreign-born (n 5 = 781)	Born in the United States (n 5 = 765)
Total	100.0	100.0
Only Spanish	52.3	2.8
More Spanish than English	26.2	8.8
Both languages equally	12.6	25.6
More English than Spanish	6.1	32.7
Only English	2.9	30.1

SOURCE: Rodolfo O. de la Garza, Louis DeSipio, F. Chris Garcia, John Garcia, and Angelo Falcon, eds., *Latino Voices: Mexican, Puerto-Rican, and Cuban Perspectives on American Politics* (Boulder: Westview Press, 1992), p. 42.

TABLE 8.3   Percentage Distribution of Responses to Question Whether U.S. Citizens and Residents Should Learn English for Persons of Mexican Origin, 1989–1990

	U.S. Citizen (n = 862)	Not a U.S. Citizen (n = 657)
Total	100.0	100.0
Strongly agree	29.1	23.6
Agree	62.3	69.9
Disagree	7.2	5.3
Strongly disagree	1.4	1.2

SOURCE: Rodolfo O. de la Garza, Louis DeSipio, F. Chris Garcia, John Garcia, and Angelo Falcon, eds., *Latino Voices: Mexican, Puerto-Rican, and Cuban Perspectives on American Politics* (Boulder: Westview Press, 1992), pp. 98, 177.

in the nation to adopt English as its official language.[35] As of July 1992, nineteen states had made English their official language, either by legislation or as part of the state constitution. Besides California, these included such large states as Florida, Georgia, Illinois, North Carolina, and Virginia.[36] According to Table 8.4, among non-Hispanic whites, 79.3 percent agreed or strongly agreed that English ought to be the official language of the United States—a result congruent with the vote in California in favor of Proposition 63. Even among persons of Mexican origin, a substantial proportion agreed that English ought to be the official language

TABLE 8.4   Percentage Distribution of Responses to Question Whether English Should Be the Official Language of the United States for Persons of Mexican Origin and Non-Hispanic Whites, 1989–1990

	Persons of Mexican Origin		Non-Hispanic Whites (n = 435)
	U.S. Citizen (n = 852)	Not a U.S. Citizen (n = 624)	
Total	100.0	100.0	100.0
Strongly agree	13.7	8.4	45.6
Agree	30.7	33.7	33.7
Disagree	39.2	47.4	17.3
Strongly disagree	16.4	10.5	3.4

SOURCE: Rodolfo O. de la Garza, Louis DeSipio, F. Chris Garcia, John Garcia, and Angelo Falcon, eds., *Latino Voices: Mexican, Puerto-Rican, and Cuban Perspectives on American Politics* (Boulder: Westview Press, 1992), pp. 97, 176.

of the United States. Among those who were U.S. citizens, 44.3 percent agreed; among those who were not, 42.1 percent agreed.

Tables 8.5 and 8.6 present data on attitudes toward bilingual education among persons of Mexican origin in the United States. Before we look at these tables, it would be helpful to review the history of bilingual education in the United States. Federal funding for bilingual education began under the auspices of the Bilingual Education Amendments of the Elementary and Secondary Education Act of 1968.[37] In 1974 the U.S. Supreme Court delivered a key decision with respect to bilingual education in *Lau v. Nichols.* Kinney Lau, a student of Chinese origin in San Francisco, was attending a school that offered no special help to non-English-speaking students. In deciding the case, the Supreme Court declared that non-English-speaking children had a constitutionally protected right to special language programs. The Court did not, however, specify the nature of the bilingual education programs that were mandatory.[38] The nature of bilingual education programs proved to be a point of major conflict. On the one hand, organizations such as U.S. English believed that the sole purpose of bilingual programs should be to ensure that non-English-speaking students learn English as rapidly as possible.[39] On the other hand, many Hispanic leaders believed bilingual education should prepare students to use both English and Spanish. Democratic senator Joseph Montoya of New Mexico summarized this latter viewpoint when he wrote, "It is wrong to assume that all bicultural children speak English poorly or that they do not need the assistance of this act if they already speak English well or fairly well. . . . However, the sense of the bill is that bilingual ability is an advantage and that the ability to speak, *read and write,* in both languages is needed to fully educate these children."[40] Opponents of Montoya's view argued that the attempt

TABLE 8.5   Percentage Distribution of Responses to Question on Attitude Toward Bilingual Education for Persons of Mexican Origin Who Are U.S. Citizens, 1989–1990 (n = 866)

Total	100.0
Strongly support	37.1
Support	42.5
Feel uncertain	13.0
Oppose	5.3
Strongly oppose	2.1

SOURCE: Rodolfo O. de la Garza, Louis DeSipio, F. Chris Garcia, John Garcia, and Angelo Falcon, eds., *Latino Voices: Mexican, Puerto-Rican, and Cuban Perspectives on American Politics* (Boulder: Westview Press, 1992), p. 99.

TABLE 8.6   Percentage Distribution of Responses to Question on Objectives of Bilingual Education for Persons of Mexican Origin Who Are U.S. Citizens, 1989–1990 (n = 809)

Total	100.0
To learn English	14.7
To learn two languages	70.3
To maintain Spanish	9.1
Other	5.9

SOURCE: Rodolfo O. de la Garza, Louis DeSipio, F. Chris Garcia, John Garcia, and Angelo Falcon, eds., *Latino Voices: Mexican, Puerto-Rican, and Cuban Perspectives on American Politics* (Boulder: Westview Press, 1992), p. 99.

to maintain student ability to speak Spanish as well as English would only retard their aquisition of English.

Table 8.5 shows that persons of Mexican origin in the United States who were U.S. citizens strongly supported the concept of bilingual education. What is more to the point, 70.3 percent of them endorsed the idea that the purpose of bilingual education is to teach both English and Spanish, and only 14.7 percent endorsed the idea that the purpose of bilingual education is to teach only English. The empirical question that has not yet been answered is whether the attempt to have students of Hispanic origin proficient in both English and Spanish will slow their acquisition of English.

In my opinion it is unlikely that increased immigration of Hispanics will endanger the dominance of English in the United States. But if the heavy flow of Hispanic immigration continues and there is some prospect that such immigration will lead to increased proportions of the population who cannot speak English, American voters have shown that they are willing to take political action to see that English remains the dominant language in the United States.

Ethnic and Class Conflict

In Chapter 2 I pointed out that an increased flow of immigrants was likely to lead to greater ethnic conflict. I also pointed out that a large influx of unskilled immigrants, by heightening the degree of income inequality in the nation, might increase class conflict. In Chapter 4 I gave ample illustrations from U.S. history of how immigrant flows induced ethnic conflict. To demonstrate that immigration today is still related to ethnic conflict, we might look at an incident that occurred at the University of Southern California (USC). USC has more than 3,000 international students. In addition, many students who are residents of the

United States are recent immigrants from abroad. On the night of April 22, 1994, Turkish students on campus were celebrating Turkish Cultural Night. Following the celebration, a group of Turkish students were attacked by five Armenian students in front of a USC dormitory, one Armenian punching two of the Turkish students in the face. The Armenian students had been protesting Turkish Cultural Night because it took place only two days prior to the anniversary of the Turkish massacre of Armenians on April 24, 1915, and thus "demeaned the symbolism of this day. . . . Many Armenians felt it as a slap in the face to the Armenian cause."[41]

Historian Arthur M. Schlesinger Jr. has reflected on the impact of immigration on ethnic conflict and has come to the conclusion that we must desist from a policy of ethnic separatism and favor a policy of educating our residents to recognize the values they hold in common. He summarizes his argument as follows:

> America has so long seen itself as the asylum for the oppressed and persecuted—and has done itself and the world so much good thereby—that any curtailment of immigration offends something in the American soul. No wants wants to be a Know-Nothing. Yet uncontrolled immigration is an impossibility; so the criteria of control are questions the American democracy must confront. We have shifted the basis of admission three times this century—from national origins in 1924 to family reunification in 1965 to needed skills in 1990. The future of immigration policy depends on the capacity of the assimilation process to continue to do what it has done so well in the past: to lead newcomers to an acceptance of the language, the institutions, and the political ideals that hold the nation together.[42]

The Power of the United States in International Affairs

The Maintenance of Friendly Relations with Other Nations

During the cold war between the United States and its allies versus the Soviet Union and its allies, from 1945 through 1991, the power of the United States in international affairs was a salient consideration in policy concerning immigration. In this period U.S. refugee policy was in large part determined by the desire to show the world that the United States would not desert its anti-Communist supporters even though their nations had fallen under Communist rule. Moreover, it is likely that a principal motivation in 1965 for doing away with immigration quotas based on national origins was the desire to court nations outside of northwest Europe. The United States wanted them to stay on its side rather than switch over to the side of the Communists.

With the end of the cold war, is the position of the United States in international affairs so strong that it no longer needs allies? If so, U.S. immigration policies could be enacted without taking into account the reactions of other nations. Alternatively, will the United States once again become one of several nations in an alliance against a second set of nations opposed to U.S. interests? If we look at the matter historically, we can easily see that the United States has in the past often found itself part of such an alliance. The thirteen colonies succeeded in obtaining independence from Great Britain under circumstances in which France, Britain's most formidable rival, sided with the American revolutionaries. Again, in the War of 1812, between the United States and Britain, France was a U.S. ally. During World War I the United States allied itself with Great Britain, France, Russia, Italy, and Japan to defeat Germany, Austro-Hungary, and Turkey. During World War II the United States was allied with Great Britain, the Soviet Union, and China to defeat Germany, Japan, and Italy. So it is not unreasonable to presume that in the future the United States may again find itself as part of a coalition in a bipolar power conflict. If so, it will be important whether the two nations that share a land boundary with the United States, Mexico and Canada, are allies rather than enemies.

There are disagreements between Canada and the United States, and we should not disregard them. But they pale in magnitude compared to the disagreements between Mexico and the United States. Historically, the most important cause of enmity dates from the war the two countries waged from 1846 to 1848, at the end of which Mexico was forced to cede half its territory to the United States. The salience of this war to the Mexican public is made manifest in the gigantic memorial to the "boy-heroes" erected in Chapúltepec Park in Mexico City to commemorate the teenage cadets who lost their lives in the struggle to defend Mexico City against the U.S. invaders in 1847.

Enmity between the two nations also arose when the United States interfered in the Mexican revolution. In April 1914 President Woodrow Wilson landed U.S. Marines in Veracruz following an incident a month earlier in which Mexican authorities had arrested U.S. sailors in Tampico. In 1916 General John Pershing invaded Mexico in pursuit of the Mexican revolutionary leader Pancho Villa, following an incident in which Pancho Villa had invaded Columbus, New Mexico. Meanwhile, in Europe, World War I was in full swing. In early 1917 the German government sent a secret telegram to Mexico proposing that the Mexican government attack the United States; in return Germany promised to restore to Mexico its former territory that had been annexed to the United States. The German telegram was decoded by the British government and publicized before the Mexican government had a chance to reply. The public release of the telegram was instrumental in mobilizing the American public in favor of the declaration of war against Germany that took place in April of that year. Mexico did not become a German ally during World War I.[43] Nevertheless, it is significant that the German government believed that Mexican animosity against the United States was sufficient to make it worthwhile to attempt to recruit Mexico to attack the United States.

More recently, as I noted in Chapter 4, the Mexican government has become very much concerned with U.S. immigration policy with respect to Mexican citizens. The current position of the Mexican government is perhaps best exemplified in the following quotation by Andrés Rozental, deputy secretary for foreign affairs of Mexico, in the opening address at a 1993 conference on Mexican labor migration to the United States:

> Mexico recognizes every nation's right to set the laws and regulations that, in use of its sovereign faculties, it considers appropriate to regulate the entry of foreigners into its territory. . . . However, Mexico considers that repressive measures cannot adequately regulate migratory labor fluxes between the two nations, as these only propitiate a rise in border violence. Furthermore, our country holds that given we are neighbors, and that there is a growing interrelationship and marked asymmetry between the two societies, generation of migratory fluxes in both directions is inevitable. These fluxes provide benefits, although they also imply costs that can be mitigated if we work in a spirit of cooperation and recognition both of reality and of shared interests.
>
> As a result of this, the Mexican government has sought dialogue instead of confrontation in treating issues associated with Mexican labor migration, under a framework that gives priority to protection of its citzens' human rights in the United States, to applying programs that seek to reduce the level of border violence, and to promoting a multilateral agreement that would define the rights of international labor migrants.[44]

Optimum Population Sizes

In his book *General Theory of Population*, the prominent French economist-demographer Alfred Sauvy presented a deductive argument in which he contended that the population size that will maximize the military power of a nation is always larger than the population size that will maximize its standard of living (see Chapter 2).[45]

Sauvy's argument is illustrated in Figure 8.1. In this graph both the standard of living (i.e., output per capita) and marginal output (the additional output provided by an extra unit of population) for a nation are plotted against national population size. Also shown in the graph is a horizontal line indicating the minimum output per person required for minimum subsistence. On this graph P_e represents the population size that maximizes the standard of living, that is, the population size where

FIGURE 8.1   Relationships Among Population Size, Standard of Living, and Military Power

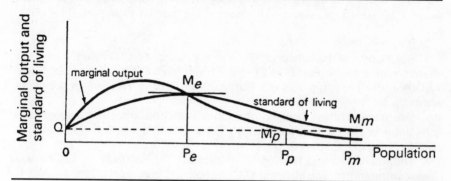

SOURCE: Alfred Sauvy, *General Theory of Population* (New York: Basic Books, 1969), p. 52.

the standard of living line is highest. P_e is also the point at which the marginal output line intersects with the line for the standard of living. To the right of P_e, the marginal output is less than the output per capita, that is, the standard of living. A point to the right of P_e,P_p, represents the population size that will maximize military power. P_p occurs at the point where the marginal output intersects the horizontal line of minimum subsistence. P_m is the maximum possible population. It lies even further to the right than P_p. P_m occurs at the point where the standard of living line descends to the horizontal line of minimum subsistence.

Sauvy does not try to estimate where the current population of any given nation falls on his graph. One might speculate that the population of China is currently at a point somewhere to the right of P_p and to the left of P_m. If so, this might explain the strict antinatalist policy of the Chinese government despite its apparent desire to increase its power in international affairs. One might also speculate that the current U.S. population lies somewhere between P_e and P_p. If so, an increased number of immigrants might simultaneously increase the power of the United States in international affairs while decreasing the average standard of living. Nevertheless, even if immigration would reduce the average standard of living, it is by no means certain that the standard of living of the native population would suffer because of immigration. It is quite possible that the overall average standard of living would decline solely because the immigrants received relatively little output compared to natives. For its part, the native population, many of whom would be complements in the production process to immigrants, might see a rise in average standard of living.

Notes

1. U.S. Bureau of the Census, *The Foreign Born Population in the United States: 1990*, CPH-L-98, prepared by Susan J. Lapham (Washington, D.C., 1993), pp. 5–6.

2. Ibid., pp. 19–21.

3. U.S. Bureau of the Census, *1990 Census of Population, Social and Economic Characteristics, California*, 1990 CP-2-6 (Washington, D.C.: Government Printing Office, 1993), sec. 1, p. 302; U.S. Bureau of the Census, *The Foreign Born Population*, p. 20.

4. U.S. Bureau of the Census, *1990 Census of Population, the Foreign-born Population in the United States*, 1990 CP-3-1 (Washington, D.C.: Government Printing Office, 1993), p. 166.

5. Thomas Muller and Thomas J. Espenshade, *The Fourth Wave: California's Newest Immigrants* (Washington, D.C.: Urban Institute Press, 1985); Kevin F. McCarthy and R. Burciaga Valdez, *Current and Future Effects of Mexican Immigration in California* (Santa Monica: RAND Corporation, 1985).

6. Muller and Espenshade, *The Fourth Wave*, pp. 95–101.

7. Southern California Association of Governments, *Southern California: A Region in Transition*, Vol. 3 (Los Angeles: SCAG, 1984), p. 8.

8. David M. Heer, *Undocumented Mexicans in the United States* (New York: Cambridge University Press, 1990), p. 66.

9. William H. Frey, *Interstate Migration and Immigration for Whites and Minorities, 1985–90: The Emergence of Multi-ethnic States*, Research Reports No. 93-297 (Ann Arbor: Population Studies Center, University of Michigan, 1993), table 5.

10. Muller and Espenshade, *The Fourth Wave*, pp. 111–112.

11. McCarthy and Burciaga Valdez, *Current and Future Effects*, pp. 44–45.

12. D. M. Heer, V. Agadjanian, F. Hammad, Y. Qiu, and S. Ramasundaram, "A Comparative Analysis of the Position of Undocumented Mexicans in the Los Angeles County Workforce in 1980," *International Migration*, Vol. 30, No. 2 (June 1992), pp. 101–126.

13. Richard Mines and Jeffrey Avina, "Immigrants and Labor Standards: The Case of California Janitors," in Jorge A. Bustamante, Clark W. Reynolds, and Raúl A. Hinojosa Ojeda, eds., *U.S.-Mexico Relations: Labor Market Interdependence* (Stanford: Stanford University Press, 1992), pp. 429–448.

14. Roger Waldinger, "Who Makes the Beds? Who Washes the Dishes? Black/Immigrant Competition Reassessed," Department of Sociology, UCLA, February 1992.

15. Muller and Espenshade, *The Fourth Wave*, pp. 148–151.

16. McCarthy and Burciaga Valdez, *Current and Future Effects*, p. 45.

17. Muller and Espenshade, *The Fourth Wave*, pp. 151–153.

18. Ibid., pp. 142–144.

19. McCarthy and Burciaga Valdez, *Current and Future Effects*, pp. 51–52.

20. See Julian L. Simon, *The Economic Consequences of Immigration* (Cambridge, Mass.: Basil Blackwell, 1989), pp. 225–252; George J. Borjas, *Friends or Strangers: The Impact of Immigrants on the U.S. Economy* (New York: Basic

Books, 1990), pp. 79–96; Staughton Y. Lewis, "Impacts of U.S. Natives' Employ-ment and Earnings: A Summary of the Evidence," in Thomas J. Espenshade, ed., *A Stone's Throw from Ellis Island: Economic Implications of Immigration to New Jersey* (Lanham, Md.: University Press of America, 1994), pp. 169–215; Michael Fix and Jeffrey S. Passel, *Immigration and Immigrants: Setting the Record Straight* (Washington, D.C.: Urban Institute, 1994), pp. 77–83.

21. Thomas J. Espenshade and Tracy Ann Goodis, *Recent Immigrants to Los Angeles: Characteristics and Labor Market Impacts*, Policy Discussion Paper, Program for Research on Immigration Policy, PRIP-UI-3. Washington, D.C.: Urban Institute, 1985, pp. 26–27.

22. Frank D. Bean, B. Lindsay Lowell, and Lowell J. Taylor, "Undocumented Mexican Immigrants and the Earnings of Other Workers in the United States," *Demography*, Vol. 25, No. 1 (February 1988), pp. 35–52; Frank D. Bean, Edward E. Telles, and B. Lindsay Lowell, "Undocumented Migration to the United States: Perceptions and Evidence," *Population and Development Review*, Vol. 13, No. 4 (December 1987), pp. 671–690.

23. Michael J. White and Lori M. Hunter, "The Migratory Response of Native-born Workers to the Presence of Immigrants in the Labor Market," paper deliv-ered at the annual meeting of the Population Association of America, Cincin-nati, March 1993.

24. Borjas, *Friends or Strangers*, p. 85.

25. Ray Marshall, "Immigration in the Golden State: The Tarnished Dream," in David Simcox, ed., *U.S. Immigration in the 1980s: Reappraisal and Reform* (Boulder: Westview Press, 1988), p. 191.

26. For a summary of many of the studies on this topic, see Eric S. Rothman and Thomas J. Espenshade, "Fiscal Impacts of Immigration to the United States," *Population Index*, Vol. 58, No. 3 (Fall 1992), pp. 381–415.

27. Fix and Passel, *Immigration and Immigrants,* pp. 63–67.

28. U.S. Bureau of the Census, *Statistical Abstract of the United States, 1993* (Washington, D.C.: Government Printing Office, 1993), p. 331.

29. Simon, *The Economic Consequences of Immigration*, pp. 125–127.

30. Donald Huddle, *The Costs of Immigration* (Washington, D.C.: Carrying Capacity Network, 1993).

31. Fix and Passel, *Immigration and Immigrants,* pp. 60–62.

32. Morris Janowitz, *The Reconstruction of Patriotism: Education for Civic Consciousness* (Chicago: University of Chicago Press, 1983), pp. 129, 137.

33. Heer, *Undocumented Mexicans,* p. 124.

34. Rodolfo O. de la Garza, Louis DeSipio, F. Chris Garcia, John Garcia, and Angelo Falcon, eds., *Latino Voices: Mexican, Puerto-Rican, and Cuban Perspec-tives on American Politics* (Boulder: Westview Press, 1992).

35. "California Becomes Seventh State to Declare English Its Official Language in Landslide Election Victory," *Update*, Vol. 4, No. 6 (November-December 1986), pp. 1–3.

36. David W. Stewart, *Immigration and Education: The Crisis and the Oppor-tunities* (New York: Lexington Books, 1993), p. 162.

37. Linda Chavez, *Out of the Barrio: Towards a New Politics of Hispanic As-similation* (New York: Basic Books, 1991), p. 12.

38. Stewart, *Immigration and Education,* pp. 40–43.

39. Ibid., pp. 161–162.

40. Chavez, *Out of the Barrio,* pp. 17–18.

41. Tracie Tso, "Ethnic Tensions Flare on Campus," *Daily Trojan* (University of Southern California), April 25, 1994, p. 1.

42. Arthur M. Schlesinger Jr., *The Disuniting of America: Reflections on a Multicultural Society* (New York: Norton, 1992), p. 121.

43. Alan Riding, *Distant Neighbors: A Portrait of the Mexicans* (New York: Vintage Books, 1985), pp. 44–48.

44. Andrés Rozental, "Introduction by Honorable Andrés Rozental, Deputy Foreign Affairs Minister of Mexico," in Secretaría de Relaciones Exteriores, *La migración laboral mexicana a Estados Unidos de América: Una perspectiva bilateral desde México* (Mexico City: Secretaría de Relaciones Exteriores, 1994), pp. 18–19.

45. Alfred Sauvy, *General Theory of Population* (New York: Basic Books, 1969), pp. 51–59.

9 Proposals for Change in U.S. Immigration Law

In the first section of this chapter, I provide data on the attitude of the American population toward immigration as revealed by recent public opinion polls. I believe this is a necessary preliminary to a critique of current immigration law. Following that introductory section, is a nutshell summary of my own proposals for change in immigration law. In the final sections of this chapter I discuss in more detail my own and alternative proposals concerning (1) the proper volume of immigration; (2) a new status I suggest be created; (3) ways for dealing with undocumented immigrants, refugees, and asylees; and (4) the criteria by which nonrefugee immigrants and legal entrants should be admitted.

Current Public Opinion Concerning Immigration

To be very brief, the American public believes that current levels of immigration are too high and that illegal immigration is a serious problem. Consider the results of a Roper poll taken in March 1990. Commissioned by the Federation for American Immigration Reform (FAIR), the poll contained a large number of questions concerning public attitudes to immigration. It is significant that this survey was taken just prior to the passage of the Immigration Act of 1990, which substantially raised the limits of legal immigration to the United States. It was also taken just prior to a severe economic downturn that left the economy in a depressed state until 1994. The March 1990 poll was based on interviews with a nationally representative cross-section of 1,144 adults aged eighteen and older. Among respondents with an opinion, 55.8 percent believed that the number of immigrants allowed into the United States each year was too many. Only 33.7 percent thought the actual number was about right, and a small 10.5 percent thought the actual number was too few. Fully 86 percent of all respondents expressed an opinion on this question, an indication that the issue was salient to the great majority of respondents. The poll revealed some differences in attitude by age. Respondents under thirty were more favorable to a larger volume of immigration than were older respondents. Among respondents under age thirty with an opinion on the issue, only 46.2 percent believed there were too many immigrants.

The 1990 Roper poll also asked questions concerning illegal immigration. Among respondents with an opinion, 80.2 percent considered the problem of illegal immigration serious enough to require government action, and 84.0 percent felt the federal government was doing a fair or poor job of controlling illegal immigration. Finally, 75.5 percent favored a law forbidding the hiring of illegal aliens.[1]

Before concluding this section, let me briefly cite the results of two additional surveys. In Chapter 8 I mentioned a 1989–1990 survey of persons of Mexican, Cuban, and Puerto Rican origin in forty areas of the United States. As you may remember, the survey also queried a small sample of non-Hispanic whites living in areas where Hispanics were concentrated. In this survey adult U.S. citizens were asked to respond to a question concerning their attitude to the current volume of immigration to the United States. Among non-Hispanic whites 73.8 percent agreed or strongly agreed that the current volume of immigration was too high. This figure is considerably higher than the corresponding figure from the Roper poll for the total population of the United States. A plausible reason for the difference is that non-Hispanic whites living in areas of relatively heavy Hispanic concentration also live in areas where there is a heavy immigrant concentration. Furthermore, attitudes of non-Hispanic whites toward immigrants may be more negative in such areas than elsewhere. In an additional important finding, the National Latino Political Survey revealed that a majority of U.S. citizens of Mexican, Puerto Rican, or Cuban descent also thought there were too many immigrants. Among citizens of Mexican descent, 75.2 percent agreed or strongly agreed; among those of Puerto Rican descent, 79.4 percent; and among those of Cuban descent, 65.5 percent.[2]

Finally, a second Roper poll, commissioned by FAIR and conducted in 1992 during the height of the severe economic downturn, revealed that 69 percent of the American public wanted Congress to repeal the 1990 Immigration Act, which had substantially increased legal immigration over the previous level. Moreover, 55 percent were in favor of a freeze on immigration while a revamping of the nation's immigration policies took place.[3]

Suggestions for Revisions to Immigration Policy

Given the negative stance toward current immigration levels manifested in recent American public opinion polls, anyone who defends the current level of immigration must present persuasive reasons for such an unpopular view. The following is a summary of my proposals for immigration legislation. These are based on my premise that the current level of U.S. immigration is about right.

1. Nevertheless, existing law unduly restricts the supply of immigration slots from nations where the demand for immigration to the United States is high. This situation causes illegal immigration, particularly from Mexico. As a solution to this problem, the United States should expand the future possibilities for Mexican and Canadians to live and work in the United States in the newly created status of legal entrant, a status that would allow an individual to live and work in the United States without access to means-tested entitlement programs. Furthermore, as a strictly onetime measure, the United States should also allow all undocumented immigrants who currently have been in the United States for at least one year the opportunity to become legal entrants.

2. There should be a major revamping of U.S. laws with respect to curbing illegal immigration such that the harmful side effects of these laws are minimized while effective procedures with minimal side effects are maximized.

3. The United States needs little change in the law with respect to refugees and should retain provisions in current law that give major power to the president in deciding refugee quotas. The United States does, however, need to reform our procedures with respect to asylees to reduce the current lengthy waiting period before asylum claims can be adjudicated.

4. The United States must drastically reform laws concerning who should be admitted to the country. The United States should set an annual worldwide quota for the number of nonrefugee, nonasylee legal immigrant and legal entrant admissions and then auction off the slots so that each immigrant or entrant pays the going market price. Furthermore, the U.S. government needs to make these permits marketable so that if immigrants or entrants decide to leave the United States, in the general case, they may sell their permits to others who wish to come to the United States.

So that you may relate my policy preferences to my own values and interests, let me be frank in admitting that these preferences reflect my own position as a native-born, white, upper-middle-class professional of northwestern European origin who has a libertarian bent.[4]

The Proper Volume of Immigration

I propose policy that would allow an annual net legal immigration of noncitizens into the United States of approximately 700,000 persons. This is slightly higher than the estimated current net legal immigration of noncitizens, which the U.S. Bureau of the Census estimates to be

640,000. But the Bureau of the Census also assumes that net illegal immigration is 200,000 per year.[5] If my proposals reduce net illegal immigration by at least 60,000 persons per year, they will result in a lower level of total noncitizen net immigration into the United States than currently obtains. Specifically, I propose the following: (1) the admission of 150,000 legal entrants from either Canada or Mexico each year through purchase of permits at the market price, (2) the admission of 350,000 permanent legal residents each year through purchase of permits at the market price, and (3) the admission of up to 200,000 refugees and asylees per year with any slots not taken up by refugees or asylees allocated to permanent legal residents through purchase of permits at the market price. Since permits for legal entrance or legal residence would in general be marketable, it would follow that immigrants who later decided to leave the United States would sell their permits. Hence the increase in total number of permits actually sold would be almost exactly proportionate to the number of noncitizen emigrants, and the total number of permits the U.S. government issued per year would equal the net legal immigration of noncitizens.

Although the majority of American people would like to see the current volume of immigration reduced, the *Wall Street Journal* has called for open borders, with the implication that the current volume of immigration should be substantially increased.[6] Because of several factors I consider important, I favor approximately the same volume of net immigration as the United States has now.

First, I would agree that the standard of living of at least some Americans has been adversely affected by the current volume of immigrant flow. Nevertheless, I believe that a very large proportion of Americans, including myself, have clearly benefited economically from this influx. In coming to this belief, I have been impressed with the argument that an influx of hardworking, well-motivated manual workers enhances the competitiveness of U.S. industry and thus provides additional jobs for Americans who are either managers or professionals or who in any other way serve as complements to new immigrants. Simply put, if we compare the U.S. labor force relative to that of the rest of the world, the United States is oversupplied with managers and professionals and undersupplied with persons capable of performing manual labor competently and responsibly.

Second, I am concerned about the future of our social security system when the baby-boom cohort reaches retirement age. A substantial volume of immigrants, particularly if they immigrate as young adults, will help obviate the future crisis in our social security system.

Nevertheless, I fear that too high an immigrant flow will exacerbate ethnic and class conflict in the United States. So even if a higher immigration flow would prove helpful in raising the standard of living of a sizable segment of the American native-born population, it might not be worth the added class and ethnic conflict.

The New Status of Legal Entrant

I propose that all persons who currently have continuously resided in the United States illegally for at least one year should—on a onetime basis only—be allowed the privilege of changing their status to that of legal entrant for a fee of $225.[7] I also propose that henceforth the U.S. government auction off each year 150,000 permits to citizens of Canada and Mexico allowing them to become legal entrants to the United States.

Legal entrants would have the right to reside and work in the United States for the rest of their lifetimes. They would not have the right to means-tested entitlement programs or the benefits of the Medicare program of the social security system. Their right to become a permanent legal resident would rest on the same grounds as that of any other alien. They would, however, have rights to the old-age, survivors, and disability insurance programs of the social security system; unemployment benefits; a public education through high school; and emergency and pregnancy-related health care. Their native-born children would continue to have all the rights of U.S. citizens. With respect to responsibilities, legal entrants would be expected to pay all U.S. taxes but would not be required to register for military service.

Moreover, I would allow any Canadian or Mexican who had paid the market price for a legal entry permit to sell that permit back to the U.S. government. This sale might take place upon the occasion of departure from the United States or becoming a permanent legal resident of the United States. Individuals who sold permits back to the U.S. government would be allowed to assume that the original permits were valid for fifty years from date of issue. For example, if someone sold it five years after issue, it would be good for forty-five additional years and the seller would be given a refund equal to 90 percent of the current market price. A marketable system would be of great importance since many Mexicans and Canadians might decide they no longer wanted to live in the United States or, alternatively, might decide they wanted to become permanent legal residents of the United States. I would add a stipulation that the entry permit could be sold back to the U.S. government by a Mexican only at a U.S. consulate in Mexico and by a Canadian only at a U.S. consulate in Canada. In this way it would not be possible for individuals to sell their permits and then remain in the United States surreptitiously. The U.S. government would piece together remaining years from the permits sold back to it and would issue one new permit for each fifty years of nonuse from previously issued permits. In order to prevent persons with expired permits from staying in the United States after their permits had expired, the government would not sell permits for less than a lifetime.

Given the size of the quota and the marketability of the permit, I believe that purchase of the permit would represent a good bargain. Accordingly, in my opinion, relatively few persons from either Mexico or Canada would enter the United States as undocumented persons.

Why should the new status of legal entrant be created? And why should undocumented persons who have been in the United States for a year or more receive the temporary opportunity to become legal entrants for the small fee of $225? The most important value served is the assurance that Canada and Mexico remain friendly to the United States in the case of any future bipolar conflicts. Moreover, as I noted in Chapter 8, the past relationship between the United States and Mexico has often been distinctly frigid. At the same time, the friendship of Mexico is of strategic importance to the United States. As of 1981 Mexico's proven oil reserves of 72 billion barrels were the fourth largest in the world, and its production of petroleum was also the fourth largest (smaller only than that of the Soviet Union, Saudi Arabia, and the United States).[8]

Moreover, I believe that political stability in Mexico will be endangered if the net flow of immigration to the United States is sharply reduced.[9] The Mexican labor force is slated to grow rapidly during the next decade. Consider the results of a recent projection that assumes a net international out-migration from Mexico of 100,000 persons per year and what the researchers consider to be reasonable assumptions concerning other components of Mexican labor-force growth (i.e., declining fertility, declining mortality, rising female labor-force participation rates but declining male labor-force participation rates). Under such a scenario the size of the Mexican labor force would increase from 22 million persons in 1980 to almost 47 million in the year 2005. This implies an average annual absolute increase of almost 1 million persons per year and an annual percentage increase of about 3 percent.[10] In this context of rapid labor-force growth, emigration to the United States provides the safety valve necessary for political stability in Mexico.

Beyond that, I believe that the status of undocumented immigrant is the cause of many worries and unhappy events. Not only that, but the U.S. taxpayer will benefit if deportations and the fear of deportation cease, as both reduce the productivity of undocumented workers. My own survey of Los Angeles County parents provided evidence that fear of deportation decreased the probability that undocumented married women would work.[11] If this phenomenon currently exists, fewer taxes can be collected from undocumented persons than would be the case if their status were legalized.

Should we provide additional amnesties in the future? No. My reasoning is that with a system of legal immigration that provides a better chance for immigration to those who most want to become U.S. residents—namely, a system in which slots are auctioned off—there is no justification for further amnesties.

Finally, why do I favor creating the new status of legal entrant rather than (1) expanding the opportunity of Mexicans and Canadians to become permanent legal residents or (2) instituting a guest-worker program on the pattern of the former *bracero* program in the United States, or the many programs formerly prevalent in European nations? I do not advocate simply expanding the number of permanent immigrant slots for Canadians and Mexicans because I believe there are large numbers of Canadians and Mexicans who would like to work in the United States and who will never need means-tested entitlement programs. My plan allows these individuals a chance to purchase the right to live and work in the United States at a cheaper price than the right to live, work, *and* enjoy access to means-tested entitlement programs in the United States. Moreover, having legal entrants rather than permanent legal residents improves the net tax consequences. Not only are expenditures on entitlement programs reduced, but also labor-force participation will be greater so that more taxes will be collected. I do not favor the type of program exemplified by the *bracero* program or by guest-worker programs in Europe because they place too many governmental restrictions on the rights of employers; I believe that employers should decide who is to have which job rather than have governments decide this question.

The Proper Enforcement of Immigration Law

The United States should try to enforce its immigration laws with the fewest possible undesirable side effects and at minimum cost. To my mind, this implies that it should concentrate on enforcing immigration law at the border and official points of entry and should deemphasize immigration-law enforcement elsewhere.

I favor the abolition of employer sanctions. My views on this issue are in accordance with those of Republican senator Orrin Hatch of Utah and Democratic senator Edward Kennedy of Massachusetts, who have introduced legislation for repeal of such sanctions.[12] I believe employer sanctions have probably had some effect in reducing the net flow of undocumented immigration into the nation. Nevertheless, I also believe there is evidence that they may have resulted in additional discrimination against Hispanics who are legally present. Moreover, employer sanctions require that certain records be kept, which is costly to the employers and is eventually paid for by the American consumer. Finally, the enforcement of employer sanctions requires time and effort on the part of INS personnel that might better be spent on other activities.

In contrast to my viewpoint, others have argued that employer sanctions need to be strengthened, saying that a more secure identification system is needed. David North, who has written extensively on this subject, notes that three threats must be avoided: counterfeiting, alteration, and impersonation.[13] As a measure to avoid counterfeiting, FAIR has advocated a call-in system by which employers could verify a job applicant's social security number by telephone. The government agency responsible for such a system would then give the employer written confirmation that the number had been checked and had been found to be genuine, releasing the employer from any charge of violating the immigration law.[14]

FAIR's proposal would no doubt reduce the problem of counterfeit documents but would probably aggravate the problem of impersonation, which I regard as the most intractable difficulty. Impersonation can occur when an individual uses someone else's birth certificate to apply for a driver's license or social security card. A foolproof system, then, must begin with a foolproof birth certificate: The birth certificate should include a thumbprint that can be matched to that of the individual who presents the birth certificate to obtain another document such as a social security card or driver's license. The social security card, if used as evidence of right for employment, must also have that same thumbprint, as well as a photograph and, as North suggests, some encrypted data (such as mother's maiden name). It is obvious, of course, that such a foolproof system would take many decades to put fully into effect.

The development of a fraudproof social security card (or other worker identification card) is often perceived as a grave violation of civil liberties. Annelise Anderson has argued that once such a card had been created the government would inevitably use it for purposes other than merely preventing the employment of undocumented workers. In her words, "No totalitarian government operates without one."[15]

In advocating the end of employer sanctions, I also urge that additional steps be taken to reduce both illegal entries without inspection and legal entries at official points of inspection by people who intend to abuse their visas.

Let us consider first the problem of visa abusers at official points of inspection. The director of the Statistics Division of the INS observed that "in 1992 roughly half of the unauthorized immigrant population had originally entered with valid temporary visas; the other half entered without inspection."[16] North has suggested (and I concur) that all non-immigrants entering the United States by air be required to have a non-refundable return airline ticket. Visa abusers would thus at least lose the cost of their return ticket.[17]

How can we reduce entries without inspection at the border? During summer 1984 I had occasion to observe the means used to secure the Olympic Village set up on the University of Southern California campus for the athletes participating in the various events. I noticed that the athletes were protected by two parallel lines of high, barbed-wire fences. Anyone attempting to penetrate into the village would not only have to climb up and down fences but would also be subject to guards patrolling the territory between the fences. It seems to me such a system of double fences would be ideal for selected portions of the U.S.-Mexican border. The single fence precisely at the border, now existing across from Tijuana, Mexicali, and other Mexican border cities, can easily be scaled with the help of refrigerators or earthen mounds on the Mexican side. Once immigrants have scaled the fence, it is often easy for them to escape further into the United States. North has already said that the single fence should be removed from its present location, right on the border, to a distance somewhat north of the border, allowing the U.S. Border Patrol to watch both sides of the fence rather than only the one north of the border.[18] I agree with North that the first fence should be a few feet north of the border. With the two parallel fences I advocate and the first fence north of the border, the border patrol could exert a constant presence not only in the corridor between the two fences but on the side of the fence closest to Mexico.

Dealing with Refugees and Asylees

In Chapter 4 I described the provisions of the Refugee Act of 1980, which still governs current U.S. policy. That law defined a refugee as "any person who is outside any country of such person's nationality . . . and who is unable or unwilling to avail himself or herself of the protection of that country because of persecution or a well-founded fear of persecution due to race, religion, nationality, membership in a particular group, or political opinion." Under this law the president of the United States is given substantial power: He is required to state in advance the ceiling on the total number of refugees and the number from each region of the world. Congress must then hold a hearing concerning these numbers. The 1980 law recognized that there would be a much larger pool of potential refugees than the limited number who would be admitted under the president's ceiling. Accordingly, the law provided further instructions as to priorities. These were, however, somewhat contradictory. On the one hand, the law declared that refugees should be admitted if they were "of special humanitarian concern to the United States." This phrase apparently justified giving preference to refugees from states overrun by Communist forces. On the other hand, it stated "that the plight of the refugees themselves as opposed to national origins or political considerations should be paramount."[19] This statement apparently called for a lack of preference to refugees from Communist governments as opposed to other types of authoritarian regimes. Nevertheless, the power given to the president under the law guaranteed that it would be the president who would be responsible for deciding which refugees should be admitted to the United States and which should not.

The 1980 act stipulated that the "normal" number of refugee and asylee admissions be 50,000 per year. The president would have to justify in advance any number above that. In fact, refugee and asylee admissions under the act have averaged almost 100,000 per year since the law became effective. Moreover, the 1980 act did not supersede the Cuban Refugee Act of 1966. Accordingly, in fiscal 1992, of the total 117,037 refugees and asylees who became permanent legal residents of the United States, over 5,000 were admitted under the Cuban Refugee Act.[20]

Lawrence Fuchs, the former executive director of President Carter's Select Commission on Immigration and Refugee Policy, criticized President Reagan's policy of favoring asylees from Communist-dominated governments over those from authoritarian non-Communist governments. In particular, he cited disapprovingly the far higher admission rates for asylees from Nicaragua than from El Salvador or Guatemala and from Cuba as compared to Haiti.[21] Nevertheless, giving principal authority to the president to determine who should be admitted as a refugee or asylee seems to me to be the only practical course. Those who dislike the existing presidential policy on refugees should make sure that in the next election they vote for a president with different criteria for admission. Aristide Zolberg, another prominent expert on refugee policy, observes that such policy is unavoidably political because it involves making choices that can be made only by political criteria. He points out that such criteria have been used in the United States since the very beginning. For example, the Alien and Sedition Acts of 1798 were enacted by the ruling Federalist Party to allow the U.S. government to expel aliens sympathetic to the radical ideas of the French Revolution.[22]

The one change I would propose in the Refugee Act of 1980 is to place a ceiling of 200,000 per year on refugee and asylee admissions to the United States. This would in turn modify the Immigration Act of 1990, which sets an annual ceiling of 10,000 asylees per year who can be admitted as permanent legal residents. My proposal for a maximum of

200,000 refugees and asylees is substantially higher than the 141,000 persons admitted to the United States as permanent legal residents in fiscal 1992 as refugee and asylee adjustments or as parolees.[23]

Because refugees are admitted to the United States from outside the country, the U.S. government has complete control over their entry. Asylees, in contrast, ask for asylum when already in the United States. As I pointed out in Chapter 4, many applicants for asylum do so not because they fear persecution but only because applicants for asylum are entitled to secure a U.S. work permit. Because of the advantages conferred upon those who seek asylum, the number who request asylum is large relative to the number who are granted asylum. This situation results in a massive backlog of asylum applicants: As of February 1994 there were around 364,000 asylum cases pending. At that time Attorney General Janet Reno announced that she favored a $130 application fee for asylum claimants; this fee could be waived for claimants who could not pay. An INS spokesperson claimed that the actual cost of processing each application for political asylum was $616. The waivable $130 fee, however, would enable the INS to process asylum claims more rapidly.[24]

Warren Leiden, executive director of the American Immigration Lawyers Association, opposed the proposed fee, saying that 70 to 80 percent of all asylum applicants would apply for the fee waiver and deciding whether to waive the fee would take up a considerable amount of immigration judges' time that might otherwise be spent in adjudicating asylum claims.[25] INS commissioner Doris Meissner announced on March 29, 1994, that the INS would expand its staff handling asylum claims from 150 to 334 and that the number of immigration judges would be increased from eighty-five to 135; the Clinton administration planned to ask Congress for $64 million for fiscal 1995 to fund these personnel increases. According to Jeanne Butterfield of the American Immigration Lawyers Association, the added judges would not be sufficient to handle the total caseload of asylum applicants.[26]

Indeed, in my opinion a doubling of personnel devoted to asylum claims will hardly be enough to reduce the current backlog. In fiscal 1992 almost 104,000 asylum claims were received but only about 10,000 claims were adjudicated and an additional 12,000 cases were otherwise closed. Thus the number of pending asylum claims rose from 137,000 at the beginning of the fiscal year to 219,000 at the end of the year.[27]

I believe that it is not sensible to institute new proceedings to determine whether a claimant should have to pay an asylum fee. But it is necessary for the U.S. government to increase its funding of asylum adjudications manyfold, and increased fees are the only way to accomplish this. I would charge all asylum claimants a fee of $225, the same amount I would charge currently undocumented residents who wish to become legal entrants. Of course many asylum claimants would be unable to pay this fee on their own; I would expect that charitable organizations would arise to provide legitimate asylum claimants with the funds to pay the application fee. Donations to such charitable organizations would of course be tax-deductible, so the federal government would still be subsidizing much of the required fee for applicants who could not pay. With the increased funding from the $225 fee, it should be possible for the U.S. government to provide the staffing necessary to eliminate the tremendous backlog of asylum cases.

The Criteria for Immigrant Admissions

In my opinion the most inequitable aspect of the current law for immigrant admissions is the equal quota for all nations regardless of their population size and the demand of their citizens to immigrate to the United States. Four leading immigration scholars, Pastora San Juan Cafferty, Barry R. Chiswick, Andrew M. Greeley, and Teresa A. Sullivan, have advocated that the United States rid itself of these quotas.[28] Under current law the annual per country limit for independent nations, set at 7 percent of the total family and employment limits for all nations, is 25,620.[29] This limit is the same for China, with a population in 1994 of almost 1.2 billion, and for Grenada, with a population of approximately 100,000.[30] I believe the United States should imitate its northern neighbor, Canada, and admit immigrants only on the basis of their personal characteristics and without regard to their nation of origin.[31]

My proposal to admit immigrants by auctioning off permits is much more controversial than my proposal to admit immigrants without respect to nation of origin. Nevertheless, I am not alone in advocating this change; several leading economists have favored the idea for some time. The auction proposal was first advanced by Chiswick in 1982.[32] Gary S. Becker, later the winner of the Nobel Prize in economics, wrote a paper supporting the idea in 1987.[33] Julian Simon, another strong proponent of such a permit auction, counts among fellow backers of the idea Milton Friedman, also a winner of the Nobel Prize in economics, and Mark Rosenzweig, formerly the codirector of research for the Select Commission on Immigration and Refugee Policy.[34]

In terms of equity, the proposal to auction off permits to the highest bidder has a major advantage. As economist Jagdish Bhagwati has pointed out, under the current system of preferences for immigration to the United States, the limited number of immigrants who meet the requirements for admission enjoy a sizable economic windfall. This windfall is particularly large if they come from one of the less-developed nations, where their earnings would be much less than in the United States.[35] It seems only fair, therefore, to have immigrants pay for the privilege of becoming permanent legal residents of or legal entrants to the United States.

Before I present other advantages of the proposal, let me be more explicit about details. All applicants to become permanent legal residents or legal entrants would have to submit a winning bid in a daily auction for such permits. Each day in which an auction was held, a daily quota would be announced. Assume the daily quota was 1,600 permits to become a legal permanent resident. Then the highest 1,600 bids submitted that day would receive permits. These persons would be obliged to pay the price they had bid, but since the minimum accepted bid at the previous day's auction would be known beforehand, no one would bid much higher than the minimum bid accepted at the previous auction.

I also propose that persons becoming permanent legal residents who are spouses or minor children of U.S. citizens be given a 50 percent rebate upon presenting proof of such a relationship to a U.S. citizen. I would allow permanent legal residents who had paid a market fee for admittance the right to sell the permits unless they had lived in the United States for five years or more. Such a sale could occur only in a U.S. consulate in the seller's own country of origin. An individual who had received a 50 percent rebate in the original purchase would have to pay back to the U.S. government half the price the individual received in the sale. The marketability of the permits to be a permanent legal resident would ensure that the net flow of legal immigrants would be almost as large as the quota (the difference being immigrants of five or more years' duration of residence who later emigrated). It would further mean that the total number of permits on the market would always be considerably larger than the number of new permits the U.S. government sold each year (i.e., 550,000 minus the number of refugees and asylees admitted the previous year).

The auction system would not supersede provisions of the immigration law designed to screen out undesirable persons. In other words, I advocate that no one be allowed to submit a bid to become a permanent legal resident or a legal entrant without first being screened to determine that the individual did not have a criminal record, was not likely to become a public charge, did not favor the violent overthrow of the U.S. government, and did not have a communicable disease or the AIDS virus. I would also charge each individual a fee for this screening equal to the cost to the U.S. government.

Current U.S. immigration law greatly favors family reunification and, to some extent, the admission of persons with high-level occupational skills. My proposal would still favor family reunification but would reduce its relative weight as a criterion for admission. I would grant a 50 percent rebate to new permanent legal residents who were the spouses or minor children of U.S. citizens. Under current law not only spouses and minor children of U.S. citizens but also the parents of U.S. citizens age twenty-one and older enter without quota. I would give no rebate to the parents of U.S. citizens aged twenty-one and older. Under my proposal, though, a high proportion of the immigrants selected would likely have family already in the United States, as these immigrants would find it much easier to pay the required fee.

I believe my proposal would lead to an increase in the average skill level of permanent legal residents. Persons willing to pay a market-set fee would likely have considerable confidence in their ability to earn a high income in the United States. My proposal would thus have favorable tax consequences in two ways: The U.S. government would receive money for granting permits for permanent legal residence, and those selected for permanent legal residence would also pay more money in taxes than is the case under current criteria for immigrant selection.

My proposal should also serve to reduce the ratio of elderly immigrants to immigrants of working age. This would come about in part because I suggest that no special consideration be given to parents of U.S. citizens and in part because a young adult has more motivation to pay a set fee to become a permanent legal resident of the United States than does an older person. Such a change in the age composition of newly admitted permanent legal residents should lessen the future crisis for our social security system.

Reaching Your Own Policy Conclusions

Now you know which policies I favor. But the purpose of this book is not to force on you my own policy preferences. Instead, it is to help you intelligently reach your own conclusions. Yours will differ from mine to the extent that you have other values and evaluate the validity of social science findings differently. I hope each of you will devote some thought to immigration policy. Without effort from all citizens, the democratic form of government cannot succeed.

Notes

1. Roper Organization, "American Attitudes Toward Immigration, June 1990," *FAIR/Information Exchange,* September 11, 1990.

2. Rodolfo O. de la Garza, Louis DeSipio, F. Chris Garcia, John Garcia, and Angelo Falcon, eds., *Latino Voices: Mexican, Puerto-Rican, and Cuban Perspectives on American Politics* (Boulder: Westview Press, 1992), p. 101.

3. Federation for American Immigration Reform, "New Roper Poll Finds Growing Public Demand for Reduced Immigration," *Federation for American Immigration Reform Immigration Report,* Vol. 21, No. 4 (June 1992), p. 1.

4. Let me also say that the proposals I present in the current volume are very similar to those I presented in my earlier book, *Undocumented Mexicans in the United States* (New York: Cambridge University Press, 1990), pp. 206–211. They differ mostly in that in the earlier book I did not present policy proposals with respect to refugees and asylees, though in that book I did present a more comprehensive discussion about proposals concerning the proper enforcement of immigration law that other experts have advocated.

5. U.S. Bureau of the Census, "Population Projections of the United States by Age, Sex, Race, and Hispanic Origin: 1993 to 2050," prepared by Jennifer Cheeseman Day, *Current Population Reports*, Ser. P-25, No. 1104 (November 1993), p. xxxviii.

6. "Review and Outlook: Simpson-Volstead-Mazzoli," *Wall Street Journal*, July 3, 1987, p. 10.

7. This fee, after adjustment for inflation, is roughly congruent with the $185 fee that applicants for legalization of status paid under the Immigration Reform and Control Act of 1986.

8. Manuel R. Millor, *Mexico's Oil: Catalyst for a New Relationship with the U.S.?* (Boulder: Westview Press, 1982), pp. 61–62.

9. David M. Heer, "Values at Stake for Both Mexico and the United States," in Secretaría de Relaciones Exteriores, *La migración laboral mexicana a Estados Unidos de América: Una perspectiva bilateral desde México* (Mexico City: Secretaría de Relaciones Exteriores, 1994), pp. 275–278.

10. James B. Pick, Edgar W. Butler, and Raul Gonzalez Ramirez, "Projection of the Mexican National Labor Force, 1980–2005," *Social Biology*, Vol. 40, No. 304 (Fall-Winter 1993), pp. 161–190.

11. Heer, *Undocumented Mexicans*, pp. 166, 200.

12. Federation for American Immigration Reform, "Employer Sanctions Repeal Bill Introduced," *Federation for American Immigration Reform Immigration Report*, Vol. 11, No. 11 (November 1991), p. 1.

13. David S. North, *Enforcing the Immigration Law: A Review of the Options* (Washington, D.C.: New Transcentury Foundation, 1980), pp. 55–75.

14. Federation for American Immigration Reform, *Ten Steps to Securing America's Borders* (Washington, D.C.: Federation for American Immigration Reform, 1989), pp. 7–9.

15. Annelise Anderson, *Illegal Aliens and Employer Sanctions: Solving the Wrong Problem* (Stanford, Calif.: Hoover Institution Press, 1986).

16. Robert Warren, "Estimates of the Unauthorized Immigrant Population Residing in the United States, by Country of Origin and State of Residence: October 1992," paper presented at the conference "California Immigration 1994," Sacramento, April 29, 1994.

17. North, *Enforcing the Immigration Law*, pp. 35–39 and appendix pp. 1–6.

18. Ibid., p. 43

19. Aristide Zolberg, "The Roots of U.S. Refugee Policy," in Robert W. Tucker, Charles B. Keely, and Linda Wrigley, eds., *Immigration and U.S. Foreign Policy* (Boulder: Westview Press, 1990), p. 114.

20. U.S. Department of Justice, Immigration and Naturalization Service, *Statistical Yearbook of the Immigration and Naturalization Service, 1992* (Washington, D.C.: Government Printing Office, 1993), p. 37.

21. Lawrence Fuchs, "Principles vs. Expediency in U.S. Immigration Policy," in David Simcox, ed., *U.S. Immigration in the 1980s* (Boulder: Westview Press, 1988), pp. 250–253.

22. Zolberg, "The Roots of U.S. Refugee Policy," pp. 99–100.

23. U.S. Department of Justice, *Statistical Yearbook, 1992*, pp. 37–38.

24. Reuter / Deborah Zabarenko, "U.S. Plans to Charge Political Asylum-Seekers $130," ClariNet Electronic News Service, February 18, 1994.

25. Associated Press, "$130 Asylum Fee Planned," ClariNet Electronic News Service, February 18, 1994.

26. Associated Press, "U.S. to Speed Asylum Decisions," ClariNet Electronic News Service, March 29, 1994.

27. U.S. Department of Justice, *Statistical Yearbook, 1992*, p. 85.

28. Pastora San Juan Cafferty, Barry R. Chiswick, Andrew M. Greeley, and Teresa A. Sullivan, *The Dilemma of American Immigration: Beyond the Golden Door* (New Brunswick, N.J.: Transaction Books, 1983), p. 182.

29. U.S. Department of Justice, *Statistical Yearbook, 1992*, p. A.2-2.

30. Population Reference Bureau, *1994 World Population Data Sheet* (Washington, D.C.: Population Reference Bureau, 1994).

31. For a summary of the main provisions of Canadian immigration law, see U.S. Bureau of the Census, "Migration Between the United States and Canada," *Current Population Reports,* Ser. P-23, No. 161 (February 1990), pp. B.4 –B.9.

32. Barry R. Chiswick, "The Impact of Immigration on the Level and Distribution of Economic Well-being," in Barry R. Chiswick, ed., *The Gateway: U.S. Immigration Issues and Policies* (Washington, D.C.: American Enterprise Institute for Public Policy Research, 1982), pp. 308–310.

33. Gary S. Becker, "A Radical Proposal to Improve Immigration Policy," Department of Economics, University of Chicago, 1987.

34. Julian L. Simon, *The Economic Consequences of Immigration* (Cambridge, Mass.: Basil Blackwell, 1989), pp. 329–336.

35. Jagdish M. Bhagwati, "Taxation and International Migration: Recent Policy Issues," in Chiswick, *The Gateway,* pp. 86–103.

Bibliography

Alegría, Tito. "Ciudad y transmigración en la frontera de México con Estados Unidos." *La frontera norte,* Vol. 2, No. 4 (1990), pp. 7–38.

Anderson, Annelise. *Illegal Aliens and Employer Sanctions: Solving the Wrong Problem.* Stanford, Calif.: Hoover Institution Press, 1986.

Aponte, David. "Creará tensiones tratar a migrantes con medidas policiacas, dice Solana." *La Jornada* (Mexico City), October 10, 1993, p. 3.

———. "Levantará EU frente a Tecate otra barda metálica en apoyo a la que construye junto a Tijuana." *La Jornada* (Mexico City), October 20, 1993, p. 1.

———. "Propone la SRE crear un documento migratario para residentes fronterizos." *La Jornada* (Mexico City), October 27, 1993, p. 3.

Associated Press. "$130 Asylum Fee Planned." ClariNet Electronic News Service, February 18, 1994.

———. "U.S. to Speed Asylum Decisions," ClariNet Electronic News Service, March 29, 1994.

Bean, Frank D.; Roland Chanove; Robert G. Cushing; Rodolfo de la Garza; Gary P. Freeman; Charles W. Haynes; and David Spener. *Illegal Mexican Migration and the United States/Mexico Border: The Effects of Operation Hold the Line on El Paso/Juarez.* Washington, D.C.: U.S. Commission on Immigration Reform, 1994.

Bean, Frank D.; Thomas J. Espenshade; Michael J. White; and Robert F. Dymowski. "Post-IRCA Changes in the Volume and Composition of Undocumented Migration to the United States: An Assessment Based on Apprehensions Data." In Frank D. Bean, Barry Edmonston, and Jeffrey S. Passel, eds., *Undocumented Migration to the United States: IRCA and the Experience of the 1980s.* Washington, D.C.: Urban Institute Press, 1990, pp. 111–158.

Bean, Frank D.; B. Lindsay Lowell; and Lowell J. Taylor. "Undocumented Mexican Immigrants and the Earnings of Other Workers in the United States." *Demography,* Vol. 25, No. 1 (February 1988), pp. 35–52.

Bean, Frank D.; Edward E. Telles; and B. Lindsay Lowell. "Undocumented Migration to the United States: Perceptions and Evidence." *Population and Development Review,* Vol. 13, No. 4 (December 1987), pp. 671–690.

Becker, Gary S. "A Radical Proposal to Improve Immigration Policy." Department of Economics, University of Chicago, 1987.

Bernard, William S. "Immigration: History of U.S. Policy." In Stephan Thernstrom, ed., *Harvard Encyclopedia of American Ethnic Groups.* Cambridge: Harvard University Press, 1980, pp. 486–495.

Bhagwati, Jagdish M. "Taxation and International Migration: Recent Policy Issues." In Barry R. Chiswick, ed., *The Gateway: U.S. Immigration Issues and Policies.* Washington, D.C.: American Enterprise Institute for Public Policy Research, 1982, pp. 86–103.

Blacker, C. P. "Stages in Population Growth." *Eugenics Review*, Vol. 39, No. 3 (October 1947), pp. 88–102.

Blessing, Patrick J. "Irish." In Stephan Thernstrom, ed., *Harvard Encyclopedia of American Ethnic Groups*. Cambridge: Harvard University Press, 1980, pp. 524–545.

Borjas, George J. *Friends or Strangers: The Impact of Immigrants on the U.S. Economy*. New York: Basic Books, 1990.

Briggs, Vernon M. Jr. *Immigration Policy and the American Labor Force*. Baltimore: Johns Hopkins University Press, 1984.

———. *Mass Immigration and the National Interest*. Armonk, N.Y.: M. E. Sharpe, 1992.

Buel, Stephen. "Clinton Revises Haitian Policy." UPI Newswire, ClariNet Electronic News Service, January 15, 1993.

Bustamante, Jorge A. "Immigration from Mexico: The Silent Invasion Issue." In Roy Bryce-Laporte, ed., *Sourcebook on the New Immigration: Implications for the United States and the International Community*. New Brunswick, N.J.: Transaction Books, 1980, pp. 139–144.

Cafferty, Pastora San Juan; Barry R. Chiswick; Andrew M. Greeley; and Teresa A. Sullivan. *The Dilemma of American Immigration: Beyond the Golden Door*. New Brunswick, N.J.: Transaction Books, 1983.

"California Becomes Seventh State to Declare English Its Official Language in Landslide Election Victory." *Update*, Vol. 4, No. 6 (November-December 1986), pp. 1–3.

"California Laws '94." *Los Angeles Times*, December 31, 1993, p. A3.

Centro Nacional de Información y Estadísticas del Trabajo (CENIET). *Los trabajadores mexicanos en Estados Unidos: Resultados de la Encuesta Nacional de Emigracíon a la frontera norte del país y a los Estados Unidos*. Mexico City: CENIET, 1982.

Chavez, Linda. *Out of the Barrio: Towards a New Politics of Hispanic Assimilation*. New York: Basic Books, 1991.

Chavez, Stephanie, and James Quinn. "Substandard Housing: Garages: Immigrants In, Cars Out." *Los Angeles Times*, May 24, 1987, p. 1.

Chiswick, Barry R. "The Impact of Immigration on the Level and Distribution of Economic Well-being." In Barry R. Chiswick, ed., *The Gateway: U.S. Immigration Issues and Policies*. Washington, D.C.: American Enterprise Institute for Public Policy Research, 1982, pp. 289–313.

Clark, Rebeccah L.; Jeffrey S. Passel; Wendy N. Zimmerman; and Michael E. Fix. *Fiscal Impacts of Undocumented Aliens: Selected Estimates for Seven States*. Washington, D.C.: Urban Institute Press, 1994.

Cole, Jeff. "INS Arrests, Deports over 200 Employees of California Firm." *Wall Street Journal*, January 18, 1993, p. A7B.

Commission on Population Growth and the American Future. *Population and the American Future*. Washington, D.C.: Government Printing Office, 1972.

Cornelius, Wayne A. "From Sojourners to Settlers: The Changing Profile of Mexican Immigration to the United States." In Jorge A. Bustamante, Clark W. Reynolds, and Raúl A. Hinojosa Ojeda, eds., *U.S.-Mexico Relations: Labor Market Interdependence*. Stanford: Stanford University Press, 1992, pp. 155–195.

————. *The Future of Mexican Immigrants in California: A New Perspective for Public Policy.* Working Papers in U.S.-Mexican Studies, No. 6. La Jolla: Program in United States–Mexican Studies, University of California, San Diego, 1981.

Corwin, Arthur F. "The Numbers Game: Estimates of Illegal Aliens in the United States, 1970–80." *Law and Contemporary Problems,* Vol. 45, No. 2 (1982), pp. 274–276.

————. "A Story of Ad Hoc Exemptions: American Immigration Policy Toward Mexico." In Arthur F. Corwin, ed., *Immigrants—and Immigrants: Perspectives on Mexican Labor Migration to the United States.* Westport, Conn.: Greenwood Press, 1978, pp. 136–175.

Corwin, Arthur F., and Johnny M. McCain. "Wetbackism Since 1964: A Catalogue of Factors." In Arthur F. Corwin, ed., *Immigrants—and Immigrants: Perspectives on Mexican Labor Migration to the United States.* Westport, Conn.: Greenwood Press, 1978, pp. 67–107.

Crane, Keith; Beth J. Asch; Joanna Zorn Heilbrunn; and Danielle C. Cullinane. *The Effect of Employer Sanctions on the Flow of Undocumented Immigrants to the United States.* Washington, D.C.: RAND Corporation and Urban Institute Press, 1990.

Crewdson, John. *The Tarnished Door: The New Immigrants and the Transformation of America.* New York: Times Books, 1983.

Davidson, Joe. "Baird Says She Regrets Hiring Illegal Aliens." *Wall Street Journal,* January 20, 1993, p. A14.

Davis, Kingsley. *Human Society.* New York: Macmillan, 1949.

de la Garza, Rodolfo O.; Louis DeSipio; F. Chris Garcia; John Garcia; and Angelo Falcon, eds. *Latino Voices: Mexican, Puerto-Rican, and Cuban Perspectives on American Politics.* Boulder: Westview Press, 1992.

de la Madrid H., Miguel. "Mexico: The New Challenges." *Foreign Affairs,* Vol. 63, No. 1 (1984), pp. 62–76.

"Desplomo comercial en El Paso por el bloqueo del SIN." *Diario 29, El Nacional* (Tijuana, Mexico), October 14, 1993, p. 30.

Divine, Robert A. *American Immigration Policy, 1924–1952.* New York: Da Capo Press, 1972.

Duncan, Otis Dudley, and Beverly Duncan. "A Methodological Analysis of Segregation Indexes." *American Sociological Review,* Vol. 20 (1955), pp. 210–217.

Easterlin, Richard A. "Immigration: Economic and Social Characteristics." In Stephan Thernstrom, ed., *Harvard Encyclopedia of American Ethnic Groups.* Cambridge: Harvard University Press, 1980, pp. 476–486.

Espenshade, Thomas J. *A Short History of U.S. Policy Towards Illegal Migration.* Policy Discussion Paper, Program for Research on Immigration Policy, PRIP-UI-8. Washington, D.C.: Urban Institute, 1990.

————. "Undocumented Migration to the United States: Evidence from a Repeated Trials Model." In Frank D. Bean, Barry Edmonston, and Jeffrey S. Passel, eds., *Undocumented Migration to the United States.* Washington, D.C.: Urban Institute Press, 1990, pp. 159–181.

Espenshade, Thomas J., and Tracy Ann Goodis. *Recent Immigrants to Los Angeles: Characteristics and Labor Market Impacts.* Policy Discussion Paper, Program for Research on Immigration Policy, PRIP-UI-3. Washington, D.C.: Urban Institute, 1985.

Federation for American Immigration Reform. "Employer Sanctions Repeal Bill Introduced." *Federation for American Immigration Reform Immigration Report*, Vol. 11, No. 11 (November 1991), p. 1.

———."The Immigration Reform and Control Act of 1986." *FAIR Legislative Bulletin* (1986), pp. 7–8.

———. "New Roper Poll Finds Growing Public Demand for Reduced Immigration," *Federation for American Immigration Reform Immigration Report*, Vol. 21, No. 4 (June 1992), p. 1.

Ten Steps to Securing America's Borders. Washington, D.C.: Federation for American Immigration Reform, 1989.

Feldman, Paul, and Patrick J. McDonnell. "U.S. Judge Blocks Most Sections of Prop. 187." *Los Angeles Times*, December 15, 1994, p. A1.

Fix, Michael, and Jeffrey S. Passel. *Immigration and Immigrants: Setting the Record Straight.* Washington, D.C.: Urban Institute, 1994.

Frey, William H. *Interstate Migration and Immigration for Whites and Minorities, 1985–90: The Emergence of Multi-ethnic States."* Research Reports No. 93-297. Ann Arbor: Population Studies Center, University of Michigan, 1993.

Frisbie, Parker. "Illegal Migration from Mexico to the United States: A Longitudinal Analysis." *International Migration Review*, Vol. 9, No. 1 (1975), pp. 3–13.

Fuchs, Lawrence. "Principles vs. Expediency in U.S. Immigration Policy." In David Simcox, ed., *U.S. Immigration in the 1980s: Reappraisal and Reform.* Boulder: Westview Press, 1988, pp. 245–257.

Goren, Arthur A. "Jews." In Stephan Thernstrom, ed., *Harvard Encyclopedia of American Ethnic Groups.* Cambridge: Harvard University Press, 1980: pp. 571–598.

Gouldner, Alvin W. "Anti-Minotaur: The Myth of a Value-free Sociology." In William Feigelman, ed., *Sociology Full Circle: Contemporary Readings on Society.* New York: Praeger, 1976, pp. 14–22.

Grant, Madison. *The Passing of the Great Race, or the Racial Basis of European History.* New York: Scribner, 1916.

Greenwood, Michael J., and John M. McDowell. "The Supply of Immigrants to the United States." In Barry R. Chiswick, ed., *The Gateway: U.S. Immigration Issues and Policies.* Washington, D.C.: American Enterprise Institute for Public Policy Research, 1982, pp. 54–85.

Gregory, Peter. "The Determinants of International Migration and Policy Options for Influencing the Size of Population Flows." In Sergio Díaz-Briquets and Sidney Weintraub, eds., *Determinants of Emigration from Mexico, Central America, and the Caribbean.* Boulder: Westview Press, 1991, pp. 49–73.

Hansen, Marcus Lee. *The Atlantic Migration, 1607–1860.* Cambridge: Harvard University Press, 1941.

Harwood, Edwin. *In Liberty's Shadow: Illegal Aliens and Immigration Law Enforcement.* Stanford, Calif.: Hoover Institution Press, 1986.

Heer, D. M.; V. Agadjanian; F. Hammad; Y. Qiu; and S. Ramasundaram. "A Comparative Analysis of the Position of Undocumented Mexicans in the Los Angeles County Workforce in 1980." *International Migration*, Vol. 30, No. 2 (June 1992), pp. 101–126.

Heer, David M. *Society and Population,* 2d ed. Englewood Cliffs, N.J.: Prentice-Hall, 1975.

———. *Undocumented Mexicans in the United States.* New York: Cambridge University Press, 1990.

———. "Values at Stake for Both Mexico and the United States." In Secretaría de Relaciones Exteriores, *La migración laboral mexicana a Estados Unidos de América: Una perspectiva bilateral desde México.* Mexico City: Secretaría de Relaciones Exteriores, 1994, pp. 275–278.

Heer, David M., and Pini Herman. *A Human Mosaic: An Atlas of Ethnicity in Los Angeles County, 1980–1986.* Panorama City, Calif.: Western Economic Research Company, 1990.

Heer, David M., and Jeffrey S. Passel. "Comparison of Two Methods for Estimating the Number of Undocumented Mexican Adults in Los Angeles County." *International Migration Review,* Vol. 21, No. 4 (Winter 1987), pp. 1446–1473.

Herman, Pini; David M. Heer; Hsinmu Chen; Fayez Hammad; Yilan Qiu; and Maurice D. Van Arsdol Jr. "Redistribution and Assimilation of New Ethnic Populations in Los Angeles: 1980–1986." Paper presented at the Twelfth World Congress of Sociology, Madrid, July 1990.

Hernandez, Marita. "INS Reports 'Dramatic' Rise in Fake Work Papers." *Los Angeles Times,* November 17, 1988, p. 1.

Higham, John. *Send These to Me: Immigrants in Urban America,* rev. ed. Baltimore: Johns Hopkins University Press, 1984.

———. *Strangers in the Land: Patterns of American Nativism, 1860–1925.* New York: Atheneum, 1973.

Hirschman, Charles. "Prior U.S. Residence Among Mexican Immigrants." *Social Forces,* Vol. 56, No. 4 (1978), pp. 1179–1201.

Hoefer, Michael D. "Background of U.S. Immigration Policy Reform." In Francisco L. Ribera-Batiz, Selig L. Sechzer, and Ira N. Gang, eds., *U.S. Immigration Policy Reform in the 1980s.* New York: Praeger, 1991, pp. 17–44.

Hoffman, Abraham. "Mexican Repatriation During the Great Depression: A Reappraisal." In Arthur F. Corwin, ed., *Immigrants—and Immigrants: Perspectives on Mexican Labor Migration to the United States.* Westport, Conn.: Greenwood Press, 1978, pp. 225–247.

Huddle, Donald. *The Costs of Immigration.* Washington, D.C.: Carrying Capacity Network, 1993.

Huntington, Ellsworth. *The Character of Races as Influenced by Physical Environment, Natural Selection and Historical Development.* New York: Scribner, 1924.

"The Immigration Reform and Control Act of 1986." *FAIR Legislative Bulletin* (1986), pp. 7–8.

Hutchinson, E. P. *Legislative History of American Immigration Policy, 1798–1965.* Philadelphia: University of Pennsylvania Press, 1981.

Independent Federation of Chinese Students and Scholars. "IFCSS Keeps Track of CSPA Implementation." News Release No. 5082 of the Independent Federation of Chinese Students and Scholars, November 30, 1993.

Janowitz, Morris. *The Reconstruction of Patriotism: Education for Civic Consciousness.* Chicago: University of Chicago Press, 1983.

Jasso, Guillermina, and Mark R. Rosenzweig. *The New Chosen People: Immigrants in the United States.* New York: Russell Sage Foundation, 1990.

Jefferson, Thomas. "Thomas Jefferson on Population."*Population and Development Review,* Vol. 19, No. 1 (March 1993), pp. 175–181.

Jones, Maldwyn Allen. *American Immigration,* 2d ed. Chicago: University of Chicago Press, 1992.

Juffras, Jason. *Impact of the Immigration Reform and Control Act on the Immigration and Naturalization Service.* Washington, D.C.: RAND Corporation and Urban Institute Press, 1991.

Kitano, Harry H. L. "Japanese." In Stephan Thernstrom, ed., *Harvard Encyclopedia of American Ethnic Groups.* Cambridge: Harvard University Press, 1980, pp. 561–571.

Klein, Dianne. "A Hit or Miss Approach to Curbing Deportable Felons." *Los Angeles Times,* November 27, 1993, p. A1.

Kraly, Ellen Percy. "U.S. Refugee Policies and Refugee Migration Since World War II." In Robert W. Tucker, Charles B. Keely, and Linda Wrigley, eds., *Immigration and U.S. Foreign Policy.* Boulder: Westview Press, 1990, pp. 78–98.

Kubiske, Lisa. "A Survey of Immigrant Visa Applicants Handled by the Mexico City Consular District." *FAIR/Information Exchange,* October 15, 1985.

Lai, H. M. "Chinese." In Stephan Thernstrom, ed., *Harvard Encyclopedia of American Ethnic Groups.* Cambridge: Harvard University Press, 1980, pp. 217–234.

Lamm, Richard D., and Gary Imhoff. *The Immigration Time Bomb.* New York: Truman Talley Books / E. P. Dutton, 1985.

Lauter, David. "Clinton Asks New Rules on Asylum." *Los Angeles Times,* July 28, 1993, p. A1.

Lauter, David, and Ronald J. Ostrow. "Under Fire, Baird Withdraws Bid for Attorney General." *Los Angeles Times,* January 22, 1993, p. A1.

Lee, Everett S. "A Theory of Migration." *Demography,* Vol. 3, No. 1 (1966), pp. 47–57.

Lesko Associates. "Final Report: Basic Data and Guidance Required to Implement a Major Illegal Alien Study." Prepared for the U.S. Immigration and Naturalization Service, Washington, D.C., October 1975.

Levine, Daniel B.; Kenneth Hill; and Robert Warren, eds. *Immigration Statistics: A Story of Neglect.* Washington, D.C.: National Academy Press, 1985.

Lewis, Staughton Y. "Impacts of U.S. Natives' Employment and Earnings: A Summary of the Evidence." In Thomas J. Espenshade, ed., *A Stone's Throw from Ellis Island: Economic Implications of Immigration to New Jersey, Md.:* Lanham, University Press of America, 1994, pp. 169–215.

MacDonald, John S., and Leatrice D. MacDonald. "Chain Migration, Ethnic Neighborhood Formation, and Social Networks." *Milbank Memorial Fund Quarterly,* Vol. 52, No. 1 (January 1964), pp. 82–97.

Mahony, Archbishop Roger. "Statement on Those Who Will Not Qualify for Legalization Under the New Immigration Reform and Control Act of 1986." Archdiocese of Los Angeles, April 13, 1987.

Marshall, Ray. "Immigration in the Golden State: The Tarnished Dream." In David Simcox, ed., *U.S. Immigration in the 1980s: Reappraisal and Reform.* Boulder: Westview Press, 1988, pp. 181–198.

Martin, Philip L., and J. Edward Taylor. *Harvest of Confusion: SAWs, RAWs, and Farmworkers.* Policy Discussion Paper, Program for Research on Immigration Policy, PRIP-UI-4. Washington, D.C.: Urban Institute, 1988.

Massey, Douglas S.; Rafael Alarcón; Jorge Durand; and Humberto González. *Return to Aztlan: The Social Process of International Migration from Western Mexico.* Berkeley: University of California Press, 1987.

McCarthy, Kevin F., and R. Burciaga Valdez. *Current and Future Effects of Mexican Immigration in California.* Santa Monica: RAND Corporation, 1985.

Melendy, H. Brett. "Filipinos." In Stephan Thernstrom, ed., *Harvard Encyclopedia of American Ethnic Groups.* Cambridge: Harvard University Press, 1980, pp. 354–362.

Meyer, Josh. "Fake Green Card Ring Was Largest in U.S." *Los Angeles Times,* September 29, 1991, p. B1.

Millor, Manuel R. *Mexico's Oil: Catalyst for a New Relationship with the U.S.?* Boulder: Westview Press, 1982.

Mines, Richard, and Jeffrey Avina. "Immigrants and Labor Standards: The Case of California Janitors." In Jorge A. Bustamante, Clark W. Reynolds, and Raúl A. Hinojosa Ojeda, eds., *U.S.-Mexico Relations: Labor Market Interdependence.* Stanford: Stanford University Press, 1992, pp. 429–448.

Miranda, Martina M. "Comerciantes de Tijuana y de San Diego se openen activamente a la Operación dignidad." *Diario 29, El Nacional* (Tijuana, Mexico), October 26, 1993, p. 5.

Morris, Milton D. *Immigration—The Beleaguered Bureaucracy.* Washington, D.C.: Brookings Institution, 1985.

Muller, Thomas. *Immigrants and the American City.* New York: New York University Press, 1993.

Muller, Thomas, and Thomas J. Espenshade. *The Fourth Wave: California's Newest Immigrants.* Washington, D.C.: Urban Institute Press, 1985.

Mydans, Seth. "For Winners in Visa Lottery, Round 2." *New York Times,* November 29, 1991, p. A-22.

Myrdal, Gunnar. *An American Dilemma: The Negro Problem and Modern Democracy.* New York: Harper & Brothers, 1944.

North, David S. *Enforcing the Immigration Law: A Review of the Options.* Washington, D.C.: New Transcentury Foundation, 1980.

Notestein, Frank W. "The Economics of Population and Food Supplies." In *Proceedings of the Eighth International Conference of Agricultural Economists.* London: Oxford University Press, 1953, pp. 15–31.

Notimex. "Refrendó Solana la defensa de indocumentados ante Janet Reno." *Diario 29, El Nacional* (Tijuana, Mexico), October 12, 1993, p. 3.

"187 Approved in California." *Migration News,* Vol. 1, No. 11 (December 1994), pp. 1–5.

"187—Enforcement Stayed." *Migration News,* Vol. 2, No. 1 (January 1995), pp. 3–4.

Passel, Jeffrey S., and Karen A. Woodrow. "Geographic Distribution of Undocumented Immigrants: Estimates of Undocumented Aliens Counted in the 1980 Census by State." *International Migration Review,* Vol. 18, No. 3 (Fall 1984), pp. 642–671.

Pear, Robert. "Bush Rejects Bill on Chinese Students." *New York Times,* December 1, 1989, p. A-9.

Peterson, Linda S., and Robert Warren. "Determinants of Unauthorized Migration to the United States." Center for International Research, U.S. Bureau of the Census, 1989.

Pick, James B.; Edgar W. Butler; and Raul Gonzalez Ramirez. "Projection of the Mexican National Labor Force, 1980–2005." *Social Biology,* Vol. 40, No. 304 (Fall-Winter 1993), pp. 161–190.

Piore, Michael. *Birds of Passage: Migrant Labor and Industrial Societies.* Cambridge: Cambridge University Press, 1979.

Pogatchnik, Shawn. "Congress Urged to Adopt Better ID for Legal Workers." *Los Angeles Times,* March 31, 1990, p. A18.

Pollard, A. H.; Farhat Yusuf; and G. N. Pollard. *Demographic Techniques,* 3d ed. Sydney: Pergamon Press, 1990.

Population Reference Bureau. *1994 World Population Data Sheet.* Washington, D.C.: Population Reference Bureau, 1994.

————. *1992 World Population Data Sheet.* Washington, D.C.: Population Reference Bureau, 1992.

Portes, Alejandro. "Unauthorized Immigration and Immigration Reform: Present Trends and Prospects." In Sergio Díaz-Briquets and Sidney Weintraub, eds., *Determinants of Emigration from Mexico, Central America, and the Caribbean.* Boulder: Westview Press, 1991, pp. 75–97.

Reimers, David M. "Recent Immigration Policy: An Analysis." In Barry R. Chiswick, ed., *The Gateway: U.S. Immigration Issues and Policies.* Washington, D.C.: American Enterprise Institute for Public Policy Research, 1982, pp. 13–53.

Renteria, Horacio. "Se redujo en más del 60% el cruce de Mexicanos a EU durante dos dias." *Diario 29, El Nacional* (Tijuana, Mexico), November 22, 1993, p. 3.

"Review and Outlook: Simpson-Volstead-Mazzoli." *Wall Street Journal,* July 3, 1987, p. 10.

Riding, Alan. *Distant Neighbors: A Portrait of the Mexicans.* New York: Vintage Books, 1985.

Rolph, Elizabeth S. *Immigration Policies: Legacy from the 1980s and Issues for the 1990s.* Santa Monica: RAND Corporation, 1992.

Roper Organization. "American Attitudes Toward Immigration, June 1990." *FAIR/Information Exchange,* September 11, 1990.

Rotella, Sebastian. "Costs, Risks of Halting Illegal Immigrants Debated." *Los Angeles Times,* November 20, 1993, p. 1.

————. "Texas Border Crackdown Stems Tide, Raises Tensions." *Los Angeles Times,* October 2, 1993, p. A1.

Rothman, Eric S., and Thomas J. Espenshade. "Fiscal Impacts of Immigration to the United States." *Population Index,* Vol. 58, No. 3 (Fall 1992), pp. 381–415.

Rozental, Andrés. "Introduction by Honorable Andrés Rozental, Deputy Foreign Affairs Minister of Mexico." In Secretaría de Relaciones Exteriores, *La migración laboral mexicana a Estados Unidos de América: Una perspectiva bilateral desde México.* Mexico City: Secretaría de Relaciones Exteriores, 1994, pp. 18–19.

Rubin, Ernest. "Immigration and the Economic Growth of the U.S.: 1790–1914." *RGEMP [Research Group for European Migration Problems] Bulletin,* Vol. 7 (October-December 1959), pp. 87–95.

"Salvadorans' TPS to Expire." *Migration News,* Vol. 2, No. 1 (January 1995), pp. 1–2.

Sanchez, Leonel. "Protest Rally at Border Fence Caps Boycott by Mexicans." *San Diego Union-Tribune,* November 22, 1993, p. B1.

Sauvy, Alfred. *General Theory of Population.* New York: Basic Books, 1969.

Schlesinger, Arthur M. Jr. *The Disuniting of America: Reflections on a Multicultural Society.* New York: Norton, 1992.

Select Commission on Immigration and Refugee Policy. *U.S. Immigration Policy and the National Interest: The Final Report and Recommendations of the Select Commission on Immigration and Refugee Policy to the Congress and the President of the United States.* Washington, D.C.: Government Printing Office, 1981.

"Será permanente Operación Bloqueo aún sin fondos: Patrulla fronteriza." *Diario 29, El Nacional* (Tijuana, Mexico), October 20, 1993, p. 30.

Simcox, David. "Overview—A Time of Reform and Reappraisal." In David Simcox, ed., *U.S. Immigration in the 1980s: Reappraisal and Reform.* Boulder: Westview Press, 1988, pp. 1–63.

Simon, Julian L. *The Economic Consequences of Immigration.* Cambridge, Mass.: Basil Blackwell, 1989.

————. *The Ultimate Resource.* Princeton, N.J.: Princeton University Press, 1981.

Southern California Association of Governments. *Southern California: A Region in Transition,* Vol. 3. Los Angeles: SCAG, 1984.

Spengler, Joseph J. "Values and Fertility Analysis." *Demography,* Vol. 3, No. 1 (1966), pp. 109–130.

Stark, Oded, and D. Levhari. "On Migration and Risk in LDCs."*Economic Development and Cultural Change,* Vol. 31, No. 1 (1982), pp. 191–196.

Stark, Oded, and J. Edward Taylor. "Relative Deprivation and Migration: Theory, Evidence, and Policy Implications." In Sergio Díaz-Briquets and Sidney Weintraub, eds., *Determinants of Emigration from Mexico, Central America, and the Caribbean.* Boulder: Westview Press, 1991, pp. 121–144.

Stewart, David W. *Immigration and Education: The Crisis and the Opportunities.* New York: Lexington Books, 1993.

Stoddard, Lothrop. *The Rising Tide of Color Against White World Supremacy.* New York: Scribner, 1920.

Thompson, Warren S. *Population and Peace in the Pacific.* Chicago: University of Chicago Press, 1946.

Tomsho, Robert. "Matter of Principle: High School in El Paso Gives the Border Patrol a Civil-Rights Lesson." *Wall Street Journal,* February 23, 1993, p. A1.

Tso, Tracie. "Ethnic Tensions Flare on Campus." *Daily Trojan* (University of Southern California), April 25, 1994, p. 1.

United Nations. Department for Economic and Social Information and Policy Analysis. *World Population Prospects, the 1992 Revision.* ST/ESA/Ser.A/135. New York: United Nations, 1993.

UPI. "Supreme Court Allows Forcible Return of Haitian Boat People." UPI Newswire, ClariNet Electronic News Service, June 21, 1993.

U.S. Bureau of the Census. *The Foreign Born Population in the United States: 1990.* CPH-L-98. Prepared by Susan J. Lapham. Washington, D.C., 1993.

————. "German, Irish, English, Afro-American Top '90 Ancestry Lists." *Census and You,* Vol. 28, No. 2 (February 1993), p. 6.

———. "Migration Between the United States and Canada." *Current Population Reports,* Ser. P-23, No. 161 (February 1990).

———. *1980 Census of Population, Detailed Population Characteristics: California.* PC80-1-D6. Washington, D.C.: Government Printing Office, 1982.

———. *1990 Census of Population, Social and Economic Characteristics, California.* 1990 CP-2-6. Washington, D.C.: Government Printing Office, 1993.

———. *1990 Census of Population, The Foreign-born Population in the United States.* 1990 CP-3-1. Washington, D.C.: Government Printing Office, 1993.

———. "One in Four of Nation's Foreign Born Arrived Since 1985." *Census and You,* Vol. 28, No. 2 (February 1993), p. 1.

———. "Population Projections of the United States by Age, Sex, Race, and Hispanic Origin: 1993 to 2050." Prepared by Jennifer Cheeseman Day. *Current Population Reports,* Ser. P-25, No. 1104 (November 1993).

———. "Population Projections of the United States by Age, Sex, Race, and Hispanic Origin: 1992 to 2050." Prepared by Jennifer Cheeseman Day. *Current Population Reports,* Ser. P-25, No. 1092 (November 1992).

———. "State Population Estimates by Age and Sex: 1980 to 1992." Prepared by Edwin R. Byerly. *Current Population Reports,* Ser. P-25, No. 1106 (November 1993).

———. *Statistical Abstract of the United States, 1993.* Washington, D.C.: Government Printing Office, 1993.

———. *Statistical Abstract of the United States, 1992.* Washington, D.C.: Government Printing Office, 1992.

U.S. Commission on Civil Rights. *Counting the Forgotten: The 1970 Census Count of Persons of Spanish Speaking Background in the United States.* Washington, D.C.: U.S. Commission on Civil Rights, 1974.

U.S. Commission on Immigration Reform. *U.S. Immigration Policy: Restoring Credibility.* Washington, D.C.: U.S. Commission on Immigration Reform, 1994.

U.S. Department of Justice. Immigration and Naturalization Service. "Adjustment of Status: Certain Nationals of the People's Republic of China." *Federal Register,* July 1, 1993, p. 35832.

———. *Advanced Report, Immigration Statistics: Fiscal Year 1992.* Washington, D.C.: Government Printing Office, 1993.

———. *An Immigrant Nation: United States Regulation of Immigration, 1798–1991.* Washington, D.C.: Government Printing Office, 1991.

———. *Immigration Reform and Control Act: Report on the Legalized Alien Population.* Washington, D.C.: Government Printing Office, 1992.

———. *1974 Annual Report.* Washington, D.C.: Government Printing Office, 1974.

———. *Statistical Yearbook of the Immigration and Naturalization Service, 1989.* Washington, D.C.: Government Printing Office, 1990.

———. *Statistical Yearbook of the Immigration and Naturalization Service, 1990.* Washington, D.C.: Government Printing Office, 1991.

———. *Statistical Yearbook of the Immigration and Naturalization Service, 1991.* Washington, D.C.: Government Printing Office, 1992.

————. *Statistical Yearbook of the Immigration and Naturalization Service, 1992.* Washington, D.C.: Government Printing Office, 1993.

————. Office of Strategic Planning. Statistics Division. *Estimates of the Resident Illegal Alien Population: October 1992.* Washington, D.C., 1993.

————. *Provisional Legalization Application Statistics, December 1, 1991.* Washington, D.C., n.d.

U.S. General Accounting Office. *Immigration Reform: Employer Sanctions and the Question of Discrimination.* Washington, D.C.: Government Printing Office, 1990.

————. *Trauma Care Reimbursement: Poor Understanding of Losses and Coverage for Undocumented Aliens.* GAO/PEMD-93-1. Washington, D.C.: Government Printing Office, 1992.

"US Changes Asylum Regulations." *Migration News,* Vol. 2, No. 1 (January 1995), pp. 2–3.

"US Sets Quota for Cuban Immigrants." *Migration News,* Vol. 1, No. 9 (October 1994), pp. 2–3.

Vigil, James Diego. *El Jardin: An Ethnographic Enumeration of a Barrio in Greater East Los Angeles.* Washington, D.C.: U.S. Bureau of the Census, 1987.

Villalpando, Rubén; Angel Amador Sánchez; and Rodrigo Ibarra. "Estrangulan el puente libre Juárez–El Paso." *La Jornada* (Mexico, City), October 10, 1993, p. 1.

Waldinger, Roger. "Who Makes the Beds? Who Washes the Dishes? Black/Immigrant Competition Reassessed." Department of Sociology, UCLA, February 1992.

Ward, David. "Immigration: Settlement Patterns and Spatial Distribution." In Stephan Thernstrom, ed., *Harvard Encyclopedia of American Ethnic Groups.* Cambridge: Harvard University Press, 1980, pp. 496–508.

Warren, Robert. "Estimates of the Unauthorized Immigrant Population Residing in the United States, by Country of Origin and State of Residence: October 1992." Paper delivered at the conference "California Immigration 1994," Sacramento, April 29, 1994.

Warren, Robert, and Ellen Percy Kraly. *The Elusive Exodus: Emigration from the United States.* Washington, D.C.: Population Reference Bureau, 1985.

Warren, Robert, and Jeffrey S. Passel. "A Count of the Uncountable: Estimates of Undocumented Aliens Counted in the 1980 United Sates Census." *Demography,* Vol. 24, No. 3 (August 1987), pp. 375–393.

Weaver, Glen. "Benjamin Franklin and the Pennsylvania Germans." *William and Mary Quarterly,* Vol. 14 (1957), pp. 536–559.

Weber, Max. "Value-judgments in Social Science." In W. G. Runciman, ed., *Max Weber: Selections in Translation.* Cambridge: Cambridge University Press, 1978, pp. 69–78.

White, Michael J., and Lori M. Hunter. "The Migratory Response of Native-born Workers to the Presence of Immigrants in the Labor Market." Paper delivered at the annual meeting of the Population Association of America, Cincinnati, March 1993.

Whittemore, L. H. "Can We Stop the Invasion of Illegal Aliens?" *South Bend Tribune,* February 29, 1976.

Wilkinson, Tracy. "Salvadorans Gird for Losses as Special Status in U.S. Ends."
    Los Angeles Times, December 1, 1994, p. A1.
Woodrow, Karen A. "Emigration from the United States: Multiplicity Survey Evi-
    dence." U.S. Bureau of the Census, August 28, 1991.
Woodrow-Lafield, Karen A. "Undocumented Residents in the United States in
    1989–90: Issues of Uncertainty in Quantification." Paper delivered at the an-
    nual meeting of the American Sociological Association, Miami Beach, August
    13–17, 1993.
World Bank. *World Development Report 1993*. New York: Oxford University
    Press, 1993.
Zall, Barnaby. "The U.S. Refugee Industry: Doing Well by Doing Good." In David
    Simcox, ed., *U.S. Immigration in the 1980s: Reappraisal and Reform*. Boulder:
    Westview Press, 1988, pp. 258–268.
Zazueta, Carlos H., and César Zazueta. *En las puertas de paraíso*. Mexico City:
    CENIET, 1980.
Zolberg, Aristide. "The Roots of U.S. Refugee Policy." In Robert W. Tucker,
    Charles B. Keely, and Linda Wrigley, eds., *Immigration and U.S. Foreign Pol-
    icy*. Boulder: Westview Press, 1990, pp. 99–120.

About the Book and Author

Immigration policy is one of the most contentious issues facing the United States today. The bitter national debate over California's Proposition 187, the influx of Cuban refugees into Miami, and the continuous, often illegal, crossings over the Mexican border into Texas and California are just a few of the episodes that have created a furor on local, state, and federal levels.

In this timely and informative book, David Heer invites readers to examine the data and the trends of immigration to the United States and, ultimately, make up their own minds about what our national immigration policy ought to be. He demonstrates how social science findings, together with a conscious recognition of our individual values, are necessary for the formation of a balanced policy for immigration.

Some of the the nation's collective values that may be affected by U.S. immigration policy are the standard of living in this country, the preservation of existing American culture, ethnic and class conflict, and the power of the United States in international affairs. Heer examines the impact of these values on immigration policy and traces the history of U.S. immigration and immigration law and patterns of immigration to the United States. Finally, he offers proposals for change to existing immigration policy.

David M. Heer is professor of sociology and director of the Population Research Laboratory at the University of Southern California.

Index

ACLS. *See* American Council of Learned Societies
Adams, John, 33
Adams, John Quincy, 34
Adoptions, 84
AFDC. *See* Aid to Families with Dependent Children
Afghans, 42
AFL. *See* American Federation of Labor
Africans, 28–29, 37, 86(table), 114(table), 141(table), 143–144(tables), 145, 154, 157. *See also* Blacks
Age, in study data, 87, 88(table), 96, 97, 99, 104(table), 119(table) 120, 125, 131(fig.), 137, 138, 140, 149, 155, 157, 173, 222
Agricultural workers, 50, 56, 60–61. *See also* Special agricultural worker legalizations
Aid to Families with Dependent Children (AFDC), 9, 98–99(table), 102(table), 123–124
Alexander I (czar of Russia), 33
Alien and Sedition Acts (1798), 33, 218
Alien entries. *See* Apprehensions; Deportation; Undocumented persons
Alien registration, 49, 89, 90, 96, 97, 110–111
Amerasians, 81, 84, 85(table)
"America for Americans" (slogan), 36
American Council of Learned Societies (ACLS), 46
American Dilemma, An: The Negro Problem and Modern Democracy (Myrdal), 19–20
American Federation of Labor (AFL), 41, 43, 45, 56
American Immigrant Lawyers Association, 219
American Legion, 45, 54
American Party, 36
American Protective Association, 40
Amnesty, 48, 59, 179, 215
Anderson, Annelise, 13, 216
Apprehensions, 57, 61, 67, 101, 102(table), 121, 165, 167–169, 170, 172, 173, 174, 177
Arabs, 42
Armenians, 55
Artisans, 32, 34
Asch, Beth, 173
Asians, 1, 3, 30(table), 39, 52, 54, 86(table), 113, 114(table), 141(table), 143–144(tables), 152(table), 157
Asiatic barred zone, 42, 44, 49
Assimilation, 12, 129, 202
Asylees, 7, 56, 61–63, 65, 66, 70, 81(table), 84, 85(table), 91, 121, 211, 212, 218–220
Austrians, 51
Austro-Hungarians, 39
Avina, Jeffrey, 187

Badillo, Herman, 57–58
Baird, Zoe, 66
Baltimore, Lord (founder of Maryland Colony), 31

Bangladeshis, 141(table), 143–144(tables), 154
Barabba, Vincent, 57–58
Bean, Frank, 173, 190
Becker, Gary S., 220
Bhagwati, Jagdish, 220
Bilingual education, 200–201
Bilingual Education Amendments (Elementary and Secondary Education Act (1968)), 200
Birds of Passage: Migrant Labor and Industrial Societies (Piore), 109
Blacker, C. P., 138
Blackmun, Harry, 66
Blacks, 31, 52, 130, 132(table), 185, 187–188, 190, 191, 195–196. *See also* Africans
Boas, Franz, 42
Bolshevik Revolution, 43
Border crossings, 66–67, 163, 164–165, 166, 167, 169, 170, 173
    fences, 169–170, 217
    See also Apprehensions; Border Patrol, U.S.; Entry
Border Patrol, U.S., 4, 47–48, 60, 66–67, 164, 167–170, 172, 173, 174–175, 177
Borjas, George J., 149–150, 191
Bowsher, Charles, 176
Boycott, 68
Boyd, Doris, 188
Bracero program, 50, 215. *See also* Mexican Labor Program
Brazilians, 34, 141(table), 143–144(tables), 154
Brechtel, John, 174
Brigham, Carl, 44
British, 29–31, 32, 33, 34, 37, 39, 46–47, 86(table), 87, 95(table), 103, 104(table), 105(table), 106, 107(table), 108(table), 125, 126(table), 127(table), 129, 141(table), 143–144(tables), 152(table)
Brown, Kathleen, 69
Bunton, Lucius, 175
Bush, George, 63, 65, 70, 91
Bustamante, Jorge, 58
Butterfield, Jeanne, 219

Cafferty, Pastora San Juan, 220
Calderón Sol, Armando, 70
California, 37, 38, 39, 45, 68–69, 95, 189. *See also* Los Angeles; San Diego
California Joint Immigration Committee, 45
Canadians, 2, 29(table), 30(table), 34, 47, 48, 49, 86(table), 94, 95(table), 104(table), 105(table), 107(table), 108(table), 113, 114(table), 125, 126(table), 127(table), 138, 152(table), 163, 212, 213, 214, 215
Capital ownership, 8, 9, 183, 185, 189, 193
Caribbean nations, 52, 86(table), 154
Carter, Jimmy, 57, 58, 62
Castro, Fidel, 62, 151

Castro, Frank Paul, 166
Census (1970, 1980), 94, 95, 96, 97, 114, 115, 116, 128, 186
Census (1990), 4, 89, 90, 91, 92, 93, 127, 128, 153, 184, 186
Census, Bureau of the, 101–102, 111, 116–117, 129, 140, 211–212
Central Americans, 86(table), 101, 132
Chain migration, 147
Chapman, Leonard, 57, 167
Character of Races as Influenced by Physical Environment, Natural Selection and Historical Development, The (Huntington), 44
Chiang Kai-shek, Madame, 50
Children, 46, 64, 81(table), 82–83(table), 84, 91, 111, 113, 119(table), 120–121, 124, 129, 130, 178, 213, 221–222
China, U.S. treaties with, 38–39
Chinese, 37, 48, 50, 85(table), 86(table), 87, 91, 95(table), 104(table), 105(table), 107(table), 108(table), 126(table), 127(table), 132–133(table), 141(table), 143–144(tables), 152(table)
Chinese Exclusion Acts (1882, 1892, 1902), 38–39
Chinese Student Protection Act (1992), 65
Chiswick, Barry R., 220
Citizens' Committee to Repeal Chinese Exclusion, 50
Civil Rights, U.S. Commission on, 115
Cleveland, Grover, 40
Clinton, Bill, 65–66, 67, 69, 70, 121, 219
Cohort, 110
Cold War, 15, 50–52, 202
Colombians, 86(table), 95(table), 104(table), 105(table), 107(table), 108(table), 126(table), 127(table), 152(table)
Communists, 15, 43, 51, 52, 62
Congress, 32, 38, 44, 47, 55, 122, 176, 219
Consular Affairs, Bureau of (Dept. of State), 4, 161–164
Convicts, 37, 38
Coolidge, Calvin, 45, 46
Corruption, 162, 166–167, 177
Corwin, Arthur, 90, 93, 96
Cost of living, 189. *See also* Standard of living
Coyotes, 149, 170
Crane, Keith, 173
Crewdson, John, 93, 161, 162, 166, 174
Criminals, 36
Cuban Refugees Act (1966), 54, 62, 218
Cubans, 53–54, 70, 86(table), 95(table), 104(table), 105(table), 107(table), 108(table), 126(table), 127(table), 151, 152(table), 197, 198, 210
boat-lift, 61–62
Cullinane, Danielle, 173
Cultural diversity, 12–13
Cultural preservation, 11–13. *See also* English language

Daughters of the American Revolution, 54
Davis, Kingsley, 138
de la Madrid, Miguel, 59
Demographic transition, theory of, 137–140
Dependency. *See* Public charges
Dependency ratios, in population studies, 119(table), 120
Dependent legalization. *See* Immigration and Reform Control Act legalizations, dependents; Legalizations, dependents
Deportation, 32, 43, 48–49, 64, 91, 92, 120, 121, 122, 167, 168(table), 214. *See also* Temporary protected status
Deukmejian, George, 198

Developed nations, 7–8, 113, 138–139, 140, 141(table), 143–144(tables), 157
Discrimination, 176–177, 215–216
Displaced Persons Act (1948), 51, 53
Dissimilarity, index of, 129, 130, 132–133(table)
Distance, as determinant in immigration, 150, 152(table), 153, 154, 155, 156, 157. *See also* Transportation
Diversity immigrants, 64, 81, 83(table), 85(table), 153
Documentation, 13, 58, 59, 163, 165–166, 176
entry permit system, 67, 211, 212, 213–214, 219, 220–222
fraud, 61, 68, 70, 165–166, 170, 174, 216
Doe, Plyler v., 69, 121–122
Dominicans, 85(table), 86(table), 87, 104(table), 105(table), 106, 107(table), 108, 126(table), 127(table), 152(table)
Dutch, 29, 31
Dymowski, Robert, 173

Economic production, 7–9, 43
complements/substitutes, 8–9, 183, 185, 186, 187, 189, 190, 205, 212
impact of immigration on, 8–11, 14, 183–194, 204–205, 212
Ecuadorans, 126(table)
Education, 5, 53, 54, 64, 98–99(table), 100, 101, 102(table), 105(table), 106, 155, 158, 186. *See also* Schools
Egalitarianism, 11, 194, 195
Egyptians, 141(table), 143–144(tables)
Elderly, 119(table), 120, 222
Eisenhower, Dwight, 53
El Jardin (Los Angeles neighborhood), 92
El Paso (Tex.), 66–67, 169, 175
El Salvadorans, 62, 64, 65, 70, 84, 85(table), 86(table), 87, 91, 94, 95(table), 104(table), 105(table), 106, 107(table), 108(table), 121, 127(table), 128, 132, 152(table), 187
Emerson, Ralph Waldo, 12
Emigration, 4, 34, 77, 79, 109, 142, 151, 152(table), 153–155
estimates of U.S., 110–116
Employer sanctions, 57, 58, 59, 60, 61, 68, 170–171, 174, 175–177, 215–216
Employment, 53, 43, 98–99(table), 102(table), 106, 107(table), 146, 187–189. *See also* Labor force
Employment-based immigration, 55, 63, 80, 81(table), 82–83(table), 85(table)
English language, 12, 60, 98–99(table), 100, 101, 102(table), 105(table), 106, 124, 147, 156, 196–198, 199(table)
as official language, 198–200
Entitlements, 9–10, 60, 68, 98(table), 100, 101, 102(table), 122, 123–124, 191, 192, 211, 213, 215
Entry, 47–48, 66, 102(table), 162, 163, 164–165, 212. *See also* Border crossings
Entry permit system. *See under* Documentation
Equity, 10–11, 194–196
Espenshade, Thomas, 167–169, 173, 185, 189, 190
Ethnic conflict, 13, 201–202, 212–213
Ethnic enclaves, 4, 147. *See also* Residential segregation
Ethnic desireability, 40, 41, 42, 43, 44. *See also* Quotas, national origins
Europeans, 1, 28, 48, 86(table), 114(table), 141(table), 143–144(tables), 152(table)

northern/western, 3, 29, 30(table), 44, 45, 46
southern/eastern, 3, 30(table), 37, 39, 40, 42, 43, 44, 45, 46
Exclusions, 15, 45
Expulsions, 33. *See also* Deportation

FAIR. *See* Federation for American Immigration Reform
Families, 39, 54, 55, 63, 81(table), 82–83(table), 84, 85(table), 123, 146, 156, 178, 221–222. *See also* Children; Parents; Spouses
Family-planning, 140
Famine, 36
Fascists, 15, 51
Federalist Party, 33
Federation for American Immigration Reform (FAIR), 209, 210, 216 Fertility, 41–42, 103, 104(table), 140, 192
Filipinos, 29(table), 39, 49, 51, 85(table), 86(table), 87, 94, 95(table), 104(table), 105(table), 106, 107(table), 108, 125, 126(table), 127(table), 132–133(table), 141(table), 143–144(tables), 151, 152(table)
Fillmore, Millard, 36
Fiscal impact, of immigration, 189–190, 193, 194
Fix, Michael, 191, 193–194
Ford, Gerald, 57
Ford Foundation, 172
Foreign Affairs, 59
Foreign-born, 1, 4, 28(table), 37, 77, 79, 101, 102, 103–109, 116–117, 127, 130, 131(table), 132–133, 184–185. *See also* National origins
Fortune, 49
Franklin, Benjamin, 12
French, 31, 32, 33, 141(table), 143–144(tables)
French Revolution, 33
Friedman, Milton, 220
Fuchs, Lawrence, 58, 218
Fürstenwater, Baron von, 34

GAO. *See* General Accounting Office
General Accounting Office (GAO), 175, 176
General Theory of Population (Sauvy), 204–205
Gentlemen's agreement (Japan-U.S.), 39, 45
Germans, 12, 29, 31, 32, 33, 34, 35, 36, 39, 46–47, 49, 51, 85(table), 103, 104(table), 105(table), 107(table), 108(table), 125, 126(table), 127(table), 129, 141(table), 143–144(tables), 203–204
GNP. *See* Gross national product
Gold Rush, 37
Goodis, Tracy Ann, 190
Gouldner, Alvin, 2, 18–19
Grant, Madison, 43
Great Depression, 48
Greeks, 54, 126(table)
Greeley, Andrew M., 220
Greenwood, Michael J., 155
Gross national product (GNP), 10, 14, 152(table), 153, 154, 156
Guatemalans, 62, 94, 95(table), 104(table), 105(table), 107(table), 108(table), 127(table), 128, 132, 187
Guest-workers, 60, 215
Guyana, 126(table), 154

Haitians, 62, 65, 66, 84, 85(table), 86(table), 94, 95(table), 104(table), 105(table), 107(table), 108(table), 126(table), 127(table), 152(table)

Hamilton, Alexander, 32
Hansen, Marcus, 46
Harding, Warren, 44
Hatch, Orrin, 215
Hawaiian Sugar Planters Association, 49
Hayakawa, S. I., 198
Hayes, Rutherford B., 38
Headright system, 30
Head tax, 38, 48
Health care, 68, 69, 122, 179, 189, 213
Heer, David M., 97, 98–99(table), 100–101, 130, 145, 146, 185, 187, 193, 197, 214
Heilbrunn, Joanna, 173
Herman, Pini, 92, 130
Hesburgh, Theodore M., 58
Hill, Joseph, 46
Hirschman, Charles, 178
Hispanics, 59, 132, 133(table), 186, 187, 190
Hoover, Herbert, 47, 48
Housing, 92–93. *See also* Residential segregation
Huddle, Donald, 193, 194
Hughes, Charles E., 45
Human Mosaic, A: An Atlas of Ethnicity in Los Angeles County, 1980–1986 (Heer and Herman), 130
Humphrey, Hubert, 52
Hungarians, 53
Huntington, Ellsworth, 44

Identification. *See* Documentation
Illegal alien, 37, 53, 56, 93. *See also* Undocumented persons
Illegal immigration, 3, 57–58, 156–157, 167–169, 210, 211, 212
Immigrant flow, 77, 79, 149
Immigrant stock, 77, 79, 89, 101–102, 112, 150, 152(table), 153, 154, 158
Immigration, 2, 8, 24, 33–34, 115–116, 150
economic impact of, 8–11, 14, 183–194, 204–205, 212
propensity for, 4, 145–158
proposed policy revisions, 210–222
ratio to emigration, 113, 114(table)
restrictions, 14, 15, 27–28, 33, 36, 37, 38, 39, 40, 41–42, 43, 45, 47–48, 159, 211. *See also* Quotas
volume, 5, 29(table), 32, 35, 77, 118–120, 137, 142, 149, 158, 211–212
See also Documentation; Entry; Legal entrants; Legalizations; National origins; Net immigration; Permanent legal residents; Population; Quotas; Undocumented persons
Immigration Act (1990), 3, 63–65, 80, 91, 120–121, 164, 178
Immigration Acts (1907, 1917, 1921, 1924), 42, 44–46, 47, 110
Immigration Acts (1952, 1965, 1976), 53, 54–55, 56–57
Immigration and Naturalization Service (INS), 4, 57, 61, 80, 89, 124–126, 219
law enforcement, 60, 101, 102(table), 115–116, 164–171
Statistics Division, 93, 216–217
Immigration and Refugee Policy, Select Commission on, 58–59
Immigration-law enforcement, 4, 5, 171–177, 215–217. *See also* Consular Affairs, Bureau of; Immigration and Naturalization Service
Immigration Reform, U.S. Commission on, 58, 65

Immigration Reform and Control Act (IRCA) (1986)
legalizations, 1, 2, 3, 60, 61, 62, 66, 80, 81(table), 84,
85(table), 90, 94, 95(table), 100–101, 123, 157, 164,
173, 174, 193
dependents, 64, 81, 83(table), 84, 85(table), 87, 91, 100,
120–121
See also Employer sanctions; Special agricultural
worker legalizations
Immigration Restriction League, 40
Immigration Review, Executive Office for (Dept. of
Justice), 164
Income, 7, 14, 98–99(table), 106–109, 148, 149, 150, 191,
192, 193–194, 222
Indentured servants, 30, 32
Indians (American), 28, 100, 130, 132(table)
Indians (Asian), 42, 51, 86(table), 87, 95(table), 104(table),
105(table), 106, 107(table), 108, 126(table),
127(table), 141(table), 143–144(tables), 152(table)
Individual fitness, 47
Indochinese, 15, 42, 81(table)
Indonesians, 141(table), 143–144(tables), 154
Information network, 149, 150, 153, 154, 158
INS. *See* Immigration and Naturalization Service
Inspections, 164–167, 216, 217
Interest groups, 2, 3, 14–15, 40–41, 59
Internal Security Act (1950), 15, 51–52, 89
International relations, 14–15, 151, 156, 202–205, 214
IQ test, 44
Iranians, 86(table), 94, 95(table), 103, 104(table),
105(table), 107(table), 108(table), 127(table),
141(table), 143–144(tables), 152(table)
IRCA. *See* Immigration Reform and Control Act
legalizations
Irish, 13, 29, 31, 32, 33, 34, 35, 36, 37, 39, 46–47, 64, 65,
85(table), 86(table), 152(table), 153
Ulster, 31, 35
Italians, 39, 46, 52, 54, 103, 104(table), 105(table),
107(table), 108(table), 125, 126(table), 127(table),
129, 141(table), 143–144(tables)

Jamaicans, 86(table), 95(table), 104(table), 105(table),
107(table), 108(table), 126(table), 127(table),
152(table)
Janowitz, Morris, 196
Japanese, 14, 39, 45, 50, 86(table), 104(table), 105(table),
106, 107(table), 108(table), 127(table),
132–133(table), 141(table), 143–144(tables),
152(table)
Jasso, Guillermina, 114, 115–116, 155, 156, 157
Jefferson, Thomas, 13, 33
Jews, 31, 40, 43, 49, 51, 52, 55
Jobs, 43, 146, 176–177. *See also* Employment
Johnson, Albert, 46
Johnson, Lyndon B., 53, 54, 166, 178
Judd, Walter, 50

Kampucheans, 15, 55, 84
Kennedy, Edward, 176, 215
Kennedy, John F., 54, 56
Kennedy, Robert, 54
Kleindienst, Richard, 166
Know-Nothing movement, 3, 36
Koreans, 86(table), 104(table), 105(table), 106, 107(table),
108(table), 126(table), 127(table), 132–133(table),
141(table), 143–144(tables), 152(table)

Kraly, Ellen Percy, 112
Kubiske, Lisa, 178

Labor certification, 55, 56, 178. *See also* Work
authorization
Labor force, 9, 40, 102(table), 106, 107(table), 109, 155,
157–158, 183–191, 212
skilled/unskilled, 8, 9, 13, 32, 34, 54, 63, 65, 83(table),
183, 184, 187, 191, 193
Labor migration, 9, 183–184, 186, 190, 204, 214
Labor unions, 40, 41, 43, 45, 56, 187–188
Landownership, 8, 9, 183, 185, 189, 193
Laotians, 15, 55, 85(table)
Latino National Political Survey, 197
Lau v. Nichols, 200
Lee, Everett, 145–146
Legal aid, 178–179
Legal entrants, 5, 211, 212, 213–215
Legal immigrants, 1, 3, 5, 27, 29(table), 30(table), 49, 53,
80–88, 197(table). *See also* Permanent legal residents
Legalizations, 56, 62, 83, 122, 178, 222
dependents, 64, 81(table), 85(table), 87
See also Families; Immigration Reform and Control Act
legalizations; Special agricultural worker
legalizations; *under* Undocumented persons
Lehman, Herbert, 52
Leiden, Warren, 219
Lesko Associates, 57–58
Less-developed nations, 8–9, 113, 138–139, 140,
141(table), 143–144(tables), 153, 157, 163–164
Levhari, D., 148
Libertarianism, 10–11, 194–195
Literacy test, 40–41, 42, 43, 47–48
Lodge, Henry Cabot, 40, 45
Lorenz curve, 129
Los Angeles area (Calif.), 92–93, 95, 96, 103, 130, 131(fig.),
132–133
Los Angeles County Parents Survey, 98–99(table), 100,
193, 213, 214
Lottery, 64
Lowell, B. Lindsay, 190

Mahony, Roger, 100
Manufacturing, 186, 189
Marriage, 146, 170. *See also* Spouses
Marshall, Ray, 191
Mazzoli, Romano, 59
McCarran, Pat, 52–53
McCarthy, Kevin, 185, 187, 189
McDowell, John M., 155
McKinley, William, 41
Medicaid/Medicare, 9, 102(table), 122, 179, 213
Meissner, Doris, 66, 70, 219
"Methodological Note on Facts and Valuations in Social
Science, A" (Myrdal), 19
Mexican Labor Program, 50, 56. *See also Bracero* program
Mexicans, 2, 3, 29(table), 30(table), 47–48, 50, 56–57, 64,
65, 85, 86(table), 90, 101, 102(table), 103, 104(table),
105(table), 106, 107(table), 108(table), 109, 115,
127(table), 151, 163, 167, 172, 197, 198, 210
legal entrant status, 212, 213, 214, 215
legalized, 61, 84, 85(table), 86(table), 87, 94, 101, 178
in Los Angeles, 98–99(table), 100, 131(fig.), 132–133,
184–190, 193, 197, 214

naturalized, 125, 126(table), 127(table), 128
undocumented, 22–23, 90, 93, 94, 95(table), 178, 187
Mexico, 114(table), 141(table), 143–144(table), 152(table), 153, 214
crossing barriers, 169–170
and U.S. relations, 59–60, 66–68, 69, 203–204, 214
Middle East, 55
Migration, 4, 128–129, 137, 140, 156–157, 183–184, 186, 190
propensity for, 145–150. *See also under* Immigration
Military, 14, 146, 151, 156, 204–205, 213
Mind of Primitive Man (Boas), 42
Mines, Richard, 187
Montoya, Joseph, 200
Muller, Thomas, 185, 186, 189
Multiplicity survey, 111, 112
Murray, Al, 167
Myrdal, Gunnar, 2, 19–20, 116

National Association of Manufacturers, 40
National Grange, 45
National Latino Political Survey, 210
National origins, 1–2, 28–29, 30(table), 31(table), 84–86, 95(table), 113, 114(table), 126(table). *See also under* Quotas
Nation of Immigrants, A (Kennedy), 54
Native-born, 4, 41–42, 79, 100, 104, 105(table), 106, 107(table), 108(table), 130, 132–133(table), 187
impact of immigration on, 183–184, 188, 190, 192, 193, 194, 205
of Mexican origin, 98–99(table), 100, 187, 197, 198
Naturalization, 4, 31, 32–33, 36, 37, 45, 124–126, 127–128
Naturalization Act (1790), 32
Net contribution of immigration, 79, 116–117
Net immigration, 77, 79, 110, 112, 113, 171–172, 211–212
in population studies, 77, 79, 116–120, 140, 142, 158–159
Networks. *See* Information networks
Network sampling, 111
Nicaraguans, 62
Nichols, Lau v., 200
Nigeria, 141(table), 143–144(tables)
Nixon, Richard, 10, 166–167
North, David, 216, 217
North Americans, 114(table), 141(table), 143–144(tables), 152(table)
Notestein, Frank, 138

Occupational preferences. *See* Employment-based immigration
Oceania, 86(table), 114(table), 141(table), 143–144(tables)
Omnibus Budget Reconciliation Act (1986), 122
Open borders, 212
Operation Blockade, 66–67
Operation Clean Sweep (Dept. of Justice), 166–167
Operation Dignity, 68
Operation Hold the Line, 67
Opinion, 5, 41, 43, 49, 209–210
Order of the Star-Spangled Banner, 36
Osborn, Henry Fairfield, 44

Pakistanis, 95(table), 141(table), 143–144(tables)
Palmer, A. Mitchell, 43
Parents, 56, 83, 98–99(table), 100, 122, 178, 197, 214, 222

Parole, 53–54, 55, 56, 81(table), 84
Passel, Jeffrey, 21–24, 89, 93, 94, 96, 97, 128, 191, 193–194
Passing of the Great Race, The (Grant), 43
Paupers, 27, 36, 37
Pearl Harbor attack (1941), 45, 50
Permanent legal residents, 53, 54, 56, 60, 65, 92, 126, 212, 213, 218–219, 221
families of, 60, 61, 64, 122, 146, 170
1992 admissions, 80–88
and prior undocumented status, 177–179
residence, 90, 96, 113, 114(table), 123, 148
rights of, 90, 122–123
See also Legal immigrants; Mexicans
Persecution, 11
Pershing, John, 203
Peruvians, 95(table)
Peterson, Linda, 156, 158
Pfaelzer, Mariana, 69
Philippines, immigrants from. *See* Filipinos
Philippines Independence Act (1934), 49
Piore, Michael, 109
Plyler v. Doe, 121–122
Poles, 33, 85(table), 94, 103, 104(table), 105(table), 107(table), 108(table), 127(table), 152(table)
Policy, and values, 2, 8, 24, 202
Political participation, 36
Population, 4, 7, 10, 12, 14, 27, 41–42, 44, 77, 150–151, 152(table), 153, 154, 156, 204–205
and natural increase, 79, 138, 152(table), 153, 154
and net contribution of immigration, 79, 116–117
and net immigration, 77, 79, 116–120, 140, 142, 158–159
projections/forecasts, 116–117, 118(table), 119–120, 137, 138–140, 141(table), 143–144(tables), 144
See also Immigrant flow; Immigrant stock
Population Growth and the American Future, Commission on, 10
Portes, Alejandro, 151, 156
Portuguese, 54, 104(table), 105(table), 107(table), 108(table), 126(table), 127(table)
Poverty, 106, 107, 108
Power, in international affairs. *See* International relations
Program for Research on Immigration Policy (RAND Corporation and Urban Institute), 172
Proposition 63 (Calif.), 198
Proposition 187 (Calif.), 68–70, 122
Protestants, 11, 13, 31, 35, 36, 40
Public assistance income, 191–192. *See also* Entitlements
Public charges, 38, 48, 49, 122, 123
Puerto Ricans, 197, 198, 210

Quota Board, 46–47
Quotas, 43, 46, 50, 151, 211, 220
eastern/western hemisphere, 45–46, 47, 48, 54, 55, 56, 101, 114, 115
exemptions, 52, 81–84, 123
national origins, 44, 46–47, 52, 54
preference system, 53, 55, 56, 63, 64, 80, 81(table), 82–83(table), 220–221
refugee, 49, 51, 211
uniform, 54–55, 64, 151
unused, 51, 52

"Race suicide," 42
Racial superiority, 43, 44

Raids, 60, 115–116, 170
RAND Corporation, 172, 185, 187, 189, 191
Rayburn, Sam, 53
Reagan, Ronald, 59, 60, 62, 89, 218
Refugee Act (1980), 55, 61, 62, 217–218
Refugee Parolees Act (1978), 55
Refugee Relief Act (1953), 53
Refugees, 3, 4, 7, 15, 33, 49, 51, 53, 55–56, 62, 70, 81(table), 84, 85(table), 121, 191, 193, 211, 212, 217–219
    resettlement, 4, 123–124
    See also Asylees; Parole
Relative deprivation, 147–148, 157. *See also* Residential segregation
Religious practice, 147
Reno, Janet, 67, 219
Report on Manufactures (Hamilton), 32
Republican Party, 33, 41
Residence, 77, 87, 90, 91, 92, 96, 97, 101, 103, 112, 113, 123, 148
Residential segregation, 129–130, 131(fig.), 132–133, 148
Reyes, Silvestre, 66–67
Rights, 4, 90, 120–123, 174–175, 179
Rising Tide of Color, The (Stoddard), 44
Risk aversion, 148–149
Rodino, Peter, 57, 166
Roman Catholics, 13, 31, 35, 36, 40, 100
Roosevelt, Franklin Delano, 48, 49, 50
Roosevelt, Theodore, 39, 41
Roper polls (1990), 209, 210
Rosenzweig, Mark, 114, 115–116, 155, 156, 157, 220
Ross, Edward, 42
Rozental, Andrés, 204
Russians, 33, 39, 43. *See also* Soviet Union, immigrants from

Salinas, Carlos, 69
Sanctions. *See* Employer sanctions
San Diego (Calif.), 169–170, 174–175
Santamaria, Oscar, 70
Sargent, Aaron, 38
Sauvy, Alfred, 14, 204
SAW. *See* Special agricultural worker legalizations
Scandinavians, 39, 46–47
Schlesinger, Arthur M., Jr., 202
Schools, 39, 68, 69, 121, 190, 193, 213. *See also* Education
Scots, 29, 31(table)
Seasonal agricultural workers. *See* Special agricultural worker legalizations
Segregation, 39. *See also* Residential segregation
Senate Immigration Committee, 47
Settlers, 4, 109
Sex, in study data, 87, 88(table), 96, 97(table), 98–99(table), 104(table), 114–115, 137, 138, 140, 155, 173
Simon, Julian, 10, 192, 220
Simpson, Alan, 59
Simpson-Mazzoli bill, 59–60
Slavery, 27, 29, 36
Social science, 2–3, 17–24, 41–42, 43
Social security, 192, 212, 213
Social welfare, 9–10. *See also* Entitlements
Sojourners, 4, 109, 114, 148
Solana, Fernando, 67
SOS "Save our state" initiative, 68, 69

South Africans, 85(table)
South Americans, 86(table), 114(table), 141(table), 143–144(tables), 152(table)
Soviet Union, immigrants from, 55, 81(table), 86(table), 104, 105(table), 107(table), 108(table), 114(table), 125, 126(table), 127(table), 152(table)
    former, 85(table), 87, 141(table), 143–144(tables)
    See also Russians
Spanish language, 197–198
Special agricultural worker (SAW) legalizations, 60, 61, 81(table), 90–91, 93, 94, 95(table), 96, 97, 99, 101, 173
Spengler, Joseph J., 47, 145
Spouses, 46, 52, 64, 81(table), 82–83(table), 84, 91, 97, 120–121, 124, 146, 155–156, 170, 178, 221–222
Standard of living, 8–11, 14, 183–194, 204–205, 212
Stark, Oded, 147–148
State, Department of, 48, 49
Stoddard, Lothrop, 44
Students, 65, 68
Study of American Intelligence (Brigham), 44
Subsidies, 33
Sullivan, Teresa A., 220
Supreme Court, U.S., 37, 65, 66, 69, 90, 121, 122, 200
Swedish, 31(table), 46–47
Swiss, 34

Taft, William, 41
Taiwanese, 86(table), 95(table), 104(table), 105(table), 106, 107(table), 108(table), 127(table), 152(table)
Tarnished Door, The (Crewdson), 161, 166
Taxation, 9–10, 98–99(table), 193, 194, 213, 215, 222
Taylor, J. Edward, 147–148
Taylor, Lowell, 190
Temporary protected status, 64–65, 70, 91, 93, 121
Temporary resident alien, 60
Texas, 68, 95, 96. *See also* El Paso
Texas proviso, 53
Thais, 141(table), 143–144(tables)
Thompson, Warren S., 138
Tijuana (Mexico), 68
Tobago, 126(table)
Tourist industry, 163, 164
Transportation, 7, 32, 34–35, 37, 149, 150. *See also* Distance
Trinidad, 126(table)
Truman, Harry, 51, 52, 53
Turks, 15, 141(table), 143–144(tables)

U.S. English, 198
Undocumented persons, 13, 62, 65, 91, 98, 99, 122, 158, 177, 187, 193, 214, 216–217
    blockade of, 66–67
    characteristics by sex, 98–99(table), 100, 193, 213, 214
    estimates of, 20–24, 57–58, 88–89, 90, 91–97
    language, 100, 197
    legalization, 4, 57, 58, 59, 60, 61, 177–179
    naturalization, 128
    residence, 92, 95, 96, 97
    rights of, 4, 120–122, 179
    See also Apprehensions; Deportation; Employer sanctions; Mexicans
"Undocumented Residents in the United States in

1989–90: Issues of Uncertainty in Quantification"
(Woodrow-Lafield), 91
Unemployment, 9, 98–99(table), 100, 102(table), 106,
107(table), 173, 183, 185–186, 190, 213
Unions, 40, 41, 43, 45, 56, 187–188
United Kingdom immigrants. *See* British
United Nations, population projections, 137, 138–140,
141(table), 142–143(tables), 144
United Nations Protocol on the Status of Refugees,
55
United States, 140, 141(table), 142, 143–144(tables), 145.
See also International relations
United States Legal Services Corporation, 178–179
Urban Institute, 68, 172, 176, 185, 189, 191

Valdez, R. B., 185, 187, 189
Values, and policy, 2, 8, 17–20, 24, 202
Vietnamese, 15, 55, 86(table), 87, 104(table), 105(table),
107(table), 108(table), 127(table), 132(table),
141(table), 143–144(tables), 152(table)
Vigil, James Diego, 92
Villa, Francisco (Pancho), 203
Virginia Colony, 30, 31
Visas, 4, 47, 48, 49, 51, 53, 92, 156, 157
abuse, 101, 102(table), 142, 161, 162, 163–164, 172,
216–217
Voluntary departure, 121

Wages, 9, 13, 40, 56, 98–99(table), 102(table), 109, 150,
155, 173, 183, 184, 186–187, 189, 190, 191
Waldinger, Roger, 188
Walker, Francis, 41
Wall Street Journal, 212
Warren, Robert, 21–24, 89, 93, 94, 96, 112, 128, 156, 158
Washington, George, 32
Weber, Max, 2, 17–18, 24
Welsh, 29, 31
Westat survey, 100–101
Western expansion, 32, 34
White, Michael, 173
Whites, non-Hispanic, 186, 188, 190, 197, 199
Wilson, Pete, 69
Wilson, Woodrow, 42, 203
Women, 52, 98–99(table), 114, 115, 116, 146. *See also* Sex,
in study data
Woodrow-Lafield, Karen, 91, 92, 93, 94, 112, 128
Work authorization, 63, 64, 65, 67, 70, 121, 175, 219. *See
also* Labor certification
Workplace investigations, 170
World immigration market, 33–34, 150
World War I, 42
World War II, 49, 51

Yerkes, Robert, 44

Zolberg, Aristide, 218